"World War II was horrific, and we must never forget. *Surviving Hitler, Evading Stalin* is a must-read that sheds light on the pain the Nazis and then the Russians inflicted on the German Jews and the German people. Mildred Schindler Janzen's story, of how she and her mother and brother survived the war and of the special document that allowed Mildred to come to America, is compelling. Mildred's faith sustained her during the war's horrors and being away from her family, as her faith still sustains her today. *Surviving Hitler, Evading Stalin* is a book worth buying for your library, so we never forget."

—CYNTHIA AKAGI, PH.D., NORTHCENTRAL UNIVERSITY

"*Surviving Hitler, Evading Stalin* is a compelling and from-the-heart account of God's providence and the resiliency of the human spirit, as demonstrated in the life of a teenage girl. In the face of nearly insurmountable life challenges in Germany during and following World War II, Mildred Schindler Janzen found herself transplanted in rural Kansas. Guided by her strong faith in God and aided by the generosity of strangers and family, Mildred is not only a survivor but also an inspiration to her family, church, and community."

—REV. DR. RANDALL C. TSCHETTER, DIRECTOR
NORTH AMERICAN BAPTIST HERITAGE COMMISSION

"The memoir of Mildred Schindler Janzen will inform and inspire all who read it. This is a work that pays tribute to the power and resiliency of the human spirit to endure, survive, and overcome in pursuit of the freedom and liberty that all too many take for granted."

—KIRK FORD, JR., PROFESSOR EMERITUS, HISTORY, MISSISSIPPI COLLEGE,
AUTHOR OF *OSS AND THE YUGOSLAV RESISTANCE, 1943–1945*

"A compelling first-person account of life in Germany during the rise of Adolph Hitler and the Nazi Party. A well written, true story of a young woman overcoming the odds and rising above the tragedies of loss of family and friends during a savage and brutal war, culminating in her triumph in life through sheer determination and will. A life lesson for us all."

—COL. FRANK JANOTTA (RETIRED), MISSISSIPPI ARMY NATIONAL GUARD

"I wish all in the world could read Mildred's story about this loving steel magnolia of a woman who survived life under Hitler's reign. Mildred never gave up, but with each suffering grew stronger in God's strength and eternal hope. Beautifully written, this life story will captivate, encourage, and empower its readers to stretch themselves in life, in love, and with God, regardless of their circumstances. I will certainly recommend this book."

—RENAE BRAME, AUTHOR OF *DAILY DEVOTIONS WITH OUR BELOVED, GOD'S PEACEFUL WATERS FLOW,* AND *SNOW AND THE ETERNAL HOPE*

"Pack your bags and get ready to embark on a journey with Mildred Schindler Janzen as she takes you from adventure to adventure while growing up on the family farm in Nazi Germany under Hitler's regime."

—DEBORAH MALONE, AUTHOR OF THE *TRIXIE MONTGOMERY COZY MYSTERY SERIES, SKYE SOUTHERLAND COZY MYSTERY SERIES,* AND AWARD-WINNING *BLOOMING IN BROKEN PLACES*

"How utterly inspiring to read the life story of a woman whose every season reflects God's safe protection and unfailing love. When young Mildred Schindler escaped Nazi Germany, only to have her father taken by the Russians and her mother and brother hidden behind Eastern Europe's Iron Curtain, she courageously found a new life in America. *Surviving Hitler, Evading Stalin* is Mildred's personal witness to God's guidance and provision at every step of that perilous journey. How refreshing to view a full life from beginning to remarkable end—always validating that nothing is impossible with God. Read this book, and you will discover the author's secret to life: "*My story is a declaration that choosing joy and thankfulness over bitterness and anger, even amid difficult circumstances, leads to a happy, healthier life.*" May we all learn from such history."

—LUCINDA SECREST MCDOWELL, AUTHOR OF *SOUL STRONG* AND *LIFE-GIVING CHOICES*

SURVIVING HITLER, EVADING STALIN

One Woman's Remarkable Escape from Nazi Germany

Mildred Schindler Janzen

with

Sherye S. Green

May the story of my life bring you
joy, hope, and peace

Mildred Schindler Janzen

SUNBURY PRESS
Mechanicsburg, PA USA

Published by Sunbury Press, Inc.
Mechanicsburg, Pennsylvania

www.sunburypress.com

For information about special discounts for bulk purchases, please contact Sunbury Press Orders Dept. at (855) 338-8359 or orders@sunburypress.com.

To request one of our authors for speaking engagements or book signings, please contact Sunbury Press Publicity Dept. at publicity@sunburypress.com.

FIRST SUNBURY PRESS EDITION: November 2020

Set in Adobe Garamond | Interior design by Crystal Devine | Cover by Terry Kennedy | Edited by Abigail Henson.

Publisher's Cataloging-in-Publication Data
Names: Janzen, Mildred Schindler, author | Green, Sherye S., author.
Title: Surviving Hitler, evading Stalin : one woman's remarkable escape from Nazi Germany / Mildred Schindler Janzen with Sherye S. Green.
Description: First trade paperback edition. | Mechanicsburg, PA : Sunbury Press, 2020.
Summary: A true story of a teenage farm girl from Germany who is captured by Soviet troops in the waning days of World War II.
Identifiers: ISBN 978-1-620064-04-7 (softcover).
Subjects: BIOGRAPHY AND AUTOBIOGRAPHY / Personal Memoirs | RELIGION / Christian Living/Personal Memoirs | HISTORY / Military / World War II.

Product of the United States of America
0 1 1 2 3 5 8 13 21 34 55

Continue the Enlightenment!

Dedication

This book is dedicated to my Mutti and Pappa, whose Christian example and steadfast guidance gave me the courage to face the many twists and turns of my life's journey. These amazing parents laid the groundwork in me that provided inspiration and motivation to carry on—at a tender young age—embracing the incredible path of my life that God prepared for me. May the story of my life—challenges I faced and triumphs I celebrated—be a testimony of God's guidance and hope to my family, to my friends, and to all who need encouragement.

Contents

Foreword

Sheltered from the gathering storm that would rain destruction upon the world, Mildred Schindler Janzen and her family lived within the secure rhythms of seedtime and harvest on their family farm in the serenity of rural Germany.

Then, when she was ten, that storm burst across the borders of Germany into Poland, and suddenly the world was at war. The years that followed chronicle the harrowing experiences of her family's struggle to survive the authoritarian boot of Nazism and the onslaught of Soviet soldiers after the war ended.

A part war drama, part coming-of-age story, part spiritual pilgrimage, this is the story of a young woman who experienced more hardships before graduating high school than most people do in a lifetime. Yet her heartaches are only half the story; the other half is a story of resilience, of leaving her lifelong home in Germany to find a new home, a new life, and a new love in America.

Her story is a journey of faith—at times, frightening; at other times, inspiring; at all times, under the providential care of God, whom she came to know intimately along the way.

In a few short years, all witnesses to World War II will be gone, the stories they have lived dying with them. The loss is incalculable, not only to history but to the future of humanity.

At 91, Mildred Schindler Janzen has given us a time capsule of that war and the years following it, filled with pristinely preserved memories of a bygone era. That time capsule was entrusted to Sherye Green, who unpacked each memory with white-gloved reverence. She examined each photograph, each letter, each bit of memorabilia, corroborating them with historical accounts and the testimonies of others. She has painstakingly pieced together those remnants of Mildred's life to form a compelling memoir.

I commend both for the legacy they have left us.

And I recommend it to you, the reader, to inspire the legacy you will one day leave to those you love.

Ken Gire
NYT bestselling author of *All the Gallant Men*

Preface

Have you ever wondered what it must have been like growing up as a girl in Nazi Germany? Have you ever wondered how it must have been to witness the rise and fall of the Third Reich? What if, at the war's end, you were able to escape Russian-occupied Germany because you had been born in the United States of America? And what if, when you arrived in this new land, the people living there welcomed you with open arms? What would be your response if given a new lease on life?

One month before my sixteenth birthday, my parents, younger brother, and I faced an unexpected horror on the morning of February 1, 1945, when Russian soldiers invaded our family farm in Radach, Germany. Having survived life in Nazi Germany during the reign of the deranged Adolph Hitler, we now faced a new enemy—Stalin's Red Army. The capture of my family took us on an odyssey that would eventually lead to the disappearance of my father, Fritz, to my internment in a Russian laundry camp, and to the discovery of a hidden document that would forever change the course of my life. A tattered, water-stained piece of paper, which had been saved by my parents and miraculously survived the war, became my ticket to escape communist domination, eventually bringing my mother, Mutti, and my brother, Horst, to freedom as well.

Although I speak with a definite German accent, I am as American as apple pie. You would be hard-pressed to find a more ardent patriot and supporter of this country. Watching Old Glory wave in the breeze fills my heart with pride and joy. I take my citizenship very seriously. It is a treasure I hold dear.

I can never repay the debt of gratitude I owe to my parents, Fritz and Anna Schindler. I cannot comprehend the lengths they went to ensure my welfare.

Since coming to the United States in 1947, I have tried my best to say "thank you" by working hard and passing along the ideals of faith, honesty, and integrity to my four children—Karen, Kenton, Susan, and Galen—that Pappa and Mutti modeled for Horst and me. I worked hard to live a life of selfless service to others, following the example my country's founders set forth when they established the United States of America.

When learning that my maiden name is Schindler and that I also grew up in Germany, many assume I am related to the industrialist Oskar Schindler, who saved the lives of some twelve-hundred Jewish workers. Even though Schindler's resistance to the sick ideologies and inhumane practices of the Nazi Reich was more visible than ways in which my family refused to fall for the schemes of the madman, our two families' stories bear witness to the lives of good, honest, hard-working Germans who did what they could to stand up against evil. We are kindred spirits but not kin.

I am now ninety-one years old, and despite many trials and tribulations, I have had a good life. The Lord protected me during agonizing wartime experiences, especially those of the brutal and terrifying Russian occupation. He still guides and protects me. I had a loving, caring husband for over sixty-five years. I have loving and caring children to help me.

My memories of those wartime incidents are crisp and sharp as if I were looking at a postcard. My World War II history lessons were probably learned in a much different manner than were yours. My survival in that period has taught me many valuable lessons. Life is hard, but God is good.

In the first few years after I traveled far across an ocean I had never seen to begin a new life among people I did not know, many interviews and speaking engagements came my way. Because German immigrants settled this central Kansas area, I quickly became somewhat of a well-known local personality. Due to the welcoming spirit of the people of Kansas and my status as a fellow American citizen, people were genuinely interested to hear the story of how I survived a time of war in the land of America's arch-nemesis at the time— Germany. Numerous newspaper articles were written about my experiences. Reading back through this historical record of my life has helped me piece together many details which have faded through the years.

Four years ago, I began the process of writing down the details of my life story. This book is the completion of that endeavor. My children must have a chronological record of the stories of specific events of which they had heard while growing up. I also have six grandchildren and two great-grandchildren.

Their shared German ancestry is rich and noble and one of which they should be incredibly proud.

My children and grandchildren were privileged to have my mother, their Mutti, with them growing up. Her joyful spirit, strength, and good humor blessed all our lives tremendously. Without Mutti's encouragement, guidance, and protection, I would have surely perished or suffered indescribable horrors at the hands of Russian soldiers. Although she passed away over twenty years ago, I feel her with me every day. Mutti continues to guide me still.

I also wish to leave a testimony for the younger American generation that is coming of age at this present time. Do not ever take the legacy of your birthright for granted. Oppose evil at every opportunity. Speak out against injustice. Most importantly, pay attention in your history class. History can repeat itself; many of my generation bear witness to that fact.

My story is one of God's deliverance, His providence, and the many ways He intervenes in the lives of His people. It is my prayer that, through my story, you might gain new insight into this dark and troubled chapter of world history. If you, like me, are a survivor of World War II or some other military conflict, I pray that you find peace. If you are enduring an internment of the mind, facing a dark night of the soul, or confronting some life-threatening illness, I pray this story will give you courage and hope.

May yours be a life filled with joy.

Mildred Schindler Janzen
Ellsworth, Kansas
November 2020

MAP OF POST-WAR GERMANY

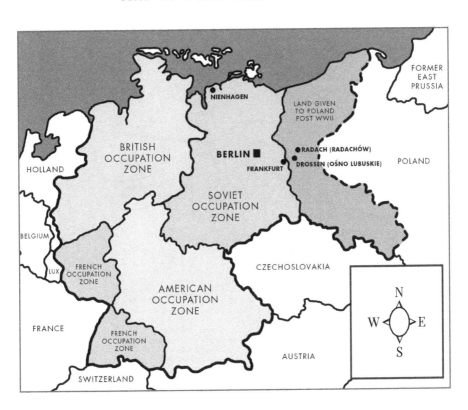

RADACH FARM FAMILIES MAP

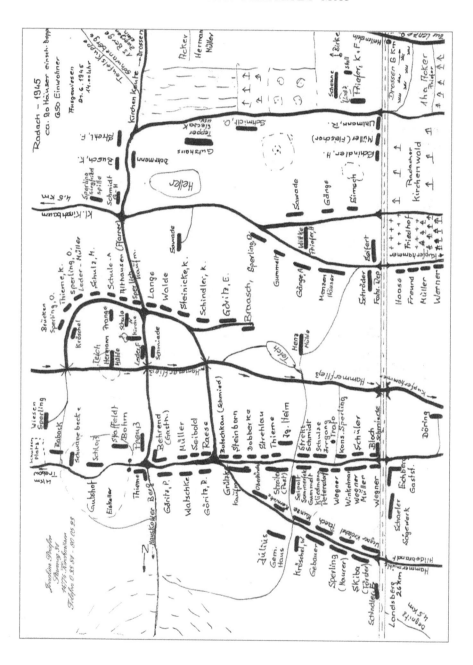

DIAGRAM OF SCHINDLER FARM

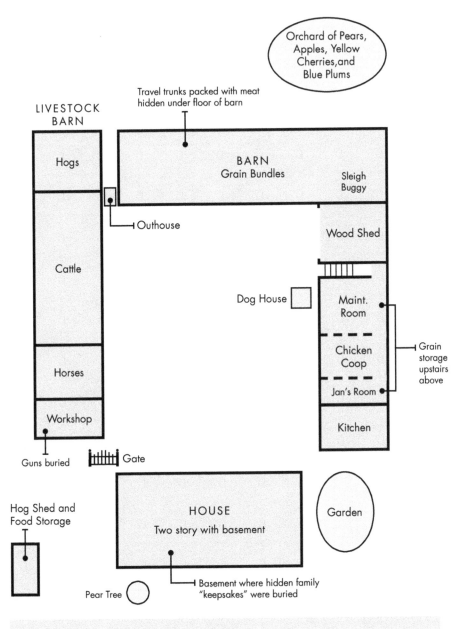

Orchard of Pears, Apples, Yellow Cherries, and Blue Plums

Travel trunks packed with meat hidden under floor of barn

LIVESTOCK BARN

Hogs

BARN
Grain Bundles

Sleigh Buggy

Outhouse

Wood Shed

Cattle

Dog House

Maint. Room

Grain storage upstairs above

Chicken Coop

Horses

Jan's Room

Workshop

Kitchen

Guns buried

Gate

Hog Shed and Food Storage

HOUSE
Two story with basement

Garden

Basement where hidden family "keepsakes" were buried

Pear Tree

ROAD

PART I

Surviving Hitler: My Life in Nazi Germany

". . . I would like to tell the young historians,
the German as well as the foreign ones,
that they must try . . . to imagine life under a dictatorship.
Sometimes even the small things in everyday life
brought great dangers with them."

—Reinhard Goerdeler, from *Voices from The Third Reich* [1]

CHAPTER ONE

An Idyllic Life

T he years of my childhood were some of the happiest of my life. Our family of four—my parents, younger brother, Horst, and myself—lived on a farm near the little town of Radach, Germany, situated in the German state of Brandenburg, about one hundred twenty kilometers (seventy-five miles) northeast of Berlin. The farm spread across some one hundred twenty-one hectares (three-hundred acres) and had been in my father's family for generations. This farm had also been my Pappa's childhood home. One of five children, he grew up tending these same fields and running through these very fruit orchards with his oldest sister, Anna, his younger sisters Marie and Ida, and his younger brother, Hermann. Now it was our home and what a wonderful one it was.

Although the name given to me on my birth certificate is Mildred, my parents and brother Horst called me Mickchen (pronounced MIH-kheeyn), a term of endearment also used by my friends. Pappa was the name by which I called my father, Fritz Schindler, as it was what my mother called him. Mutti was the name by which I called my mother, Anna. *Mutter* is the German word for mother, but *Mutti*, a more personal form of that word, is the nickname that would stay with her for the remainder of her life. Pappa called Mutti by the name Annchen (pronounced AHN-kheeyn), the German version of Anna. My parents provided a loving, safe, and secure environment in which Horst and I thrived.

As I grew older, I learned that Pappa had not always lived on the farm that was now ours. Perhaps because of dire economic conditions in Germany, he had struck out in 1922 to find adventure and work in America as a *thrasher*, one

Anna Gerlach Schindler as a young girl

Early portrait of my Pappa, Fritz Robert
Schindler

My Pappa was such a distinguished fellow.

Mutti, Horst (left – age 4), and Mildred (right – age 6)

skilled in the practice of separating wheat. My mother traveled to America to marry him and begin their life together. He and Mutti had been married several years when the letter from my Grandpa arrived, telling Pappa that his mother, Marie, had died and that Grandpa needed him to return to Germany to help run the farm. In Germany, tradition holds that the son always takes over the family business. There was already a son, Pappa's younger brother, Hermann, who lived in Radach and could have helped.

Grandpa said, "No, he's not a farmer."

As an obedient son, Pappa obligingly returned home.

* * *

My earliest memories in Germany are of our large slate-covered, two-story stone house. Various types of fruit trees and fragrant lilac bushes growing to one side of the house, a large vegetable garden on the other, which provided an abundant supply of raspberries, gooseberries, cabbage, and other green vegetables. The first floor of our home contained a parlor and a dining room, Pappa's and Mutti's bedroom, and a bedroom shared by Horst and me. Tucked underneath the dormer windows that spread out across the rooftop were the rooms of the second floor, which included an extra bedroom used occasionally by visiting family members and a smoke room for curing various types of meat. Underneath our house was a brick-floored basement.

Three barns were built around our home to form a square. The first barn, out our back door to the left, was for the livestock and held stalls for the hogs, cattle, and horses. This barn also housed Pappa's workshop. The second barn, out our back door to the right, contained our kitchen, chicken coop, maintenance work-room, an open wood-shed area, and a store-room. The second story of this building was where we stored the grain. The third barn, out our back door and across an extensive yard area, was where we placed the grain bundles after the rye harvest. Our sleigh and buggy belonged in this building. The outhouse stood between the barn to the left and the one farthest away from the house.

As the farmer's wife, Mutti maintained careful inventory records of our farm.[1] This is a partial record I found, years after my mother's death, written in her careful, precise hand:

House	1 machine to sift and clean rye
2 livestock barns	2 machines to chop hay for livestock
1 shed for wood and coal and machinery	1 machine to grind rye and oats
1 barn for hogs	1 manure spreader
1 barn for rye and oats	1 grain drill
60 morgen* farm ground	1 mowing machine
14 morgen pasture (to make hay)	1 straw cutter
25 morgen forest	1 grass cutter
2 horses	1 potato planter
7 milk cows	1 potato sorter
4 calves	1 potato digger machine
2 sheep	2 hay machines
8 hogs	6 different plows
45 chickens	3 harrows
2 geese	3 farm wagons with harnesses
12 turkeys	2 harnesses for carriage
3 motors	1 cultivator
1 thrashing machine	6 bicycles

*A *morgen* was a term describing a unit of measurement of land in Germany at this time. Derived from the German word meaning "morning," the term

First steps

Mickchen and Horst, ages 3 and 1

The only surviving picture of our family

initially described how much land one oxen could plow in one workday. Although comparisons vary, one morgen generally was equivalent to "about 0.25 to 1.3 hectares," an area between .6 and 3.2 acres.[2]

* * *

While growing up, we had a German Shepherd. His name was Rife, and he was mainly a watchdog. We would tie him up during the day by his dog-house, with a chain long enough to allow him to walk around a pretty good distance out into the yard. Each day when the chickens were released from their coop, they seemed to know just how close they could get to Rife without being caught. At night, he freely roamed the compound formed by the four main buildings of our farm and the gates between them. Later, after he died, we got another German Shepherd and named him Lux.

As little children, my brother and I toddled around after Pappa and Mutti, even as they were out in the fields. By the time we each reached the ages of four or five, we were given simple, yet meaningful chores to complete. Horst and I had enough time to play, chasing each other around the courtyard or through the fruit orchard. Hopscotch was another popular pastime.

By the time we entered grade school, early mornings were devoted to dressing, eating, and walking to the school in Radach. After arriving home in the afternoons, Horst and I had specific chores to which we were assigned. It was my job to feed the chickens. Horst was responsible for feeding and watering the rabbits in their hutches. We raised a number of these as a meat source. Hungry hogs also waited eagerly each day for their food.

* * *

Our farm day began at sunup. First, the family ate breakfast together. Mutti would prepare a hearty meal: huge, warm slices of rye bread, lard and salt to be used in place of butter, and blue plum jam. As soon as this meal ended, Pappa left the house to feed the horses and harness them. Our horses were large and powerful. We farmed with horses. The plow was guided across a field as the horses pulled it behind them. They stood each morning patiently as Pappa readied them for the day ahead.

Then, it was off to the fields. Our fields stretched out as far as I could see. Pappa grew potatoes, rye, oats, and sugar beets. Lots of potatoes. Lots of rye. Potatoes were a staple of the German diet. People used rye and wheat flour to make a delicious, hearty, brown bread, another German favorite.

Pappa had several sources of farm income.[3] In the fall and early spring, it was not unusual for farmers from other nearby regions to come through Radach. They would buy our seed potatoes and take them home to plant on their farms. Horst remembered how these same farmers would often trade us their wheat for our rye. Their soil was different than ours, and it was challenging to grow rye where they lived. The abundance of sandy soil in the Radach area led to many successful rye crops.

The wheat Pappa received from these migrant farmers was used to make flour.[4] Radach boasted three different flour mills. Pappa was one of their valued rye suppliers. Following the rye harvest, my dad would set aside a portion of the grain and store it. The rye would be sold later in the year for a premium price due to high demand. Pappa knew how important it was to get the most money for your product.

* * *

As we lived on a farm, we always had enough food. We raised chickens, turkeys, ducks, and geese. We did not have beef because our cows were milk cows. Mutti and Pappa milked them until Horst and I were old enough to help. We had pork. We raised several hogs and were allowed to butcher two a year. The fatter they were, the better because then we had more lard.

As we did not have a refrigerator, Mutti would can meat. She canned *everything*. It was the fastest, easiest method of food preservation. Smoking was another method Mutti used to preserve meat. Big slabs of ham and bacon were salted and then smoked. She also made sausage.

Our orchard offered a constant supply of fruit from a variety of trees. We had little blue plums, apples, pears, and lots of cherries. We canned the cherries with the pits in them. As Mutti worked in the fields, there was simply no time for pitting cherries. So, you are eating the cherries, and you have to spit out the seeds.

Forests dotted the area of Brandenburg between the small towns, like Radach, that were only about a mile or a half-mile apart. We got around everywhere by bicycle, on foot, or by wagon. We often hunted mushrooms in the forests. The perfect time to find the little delicacies was on a morning after it had rained the night before. Because we lived on a black-topped road, you would see the ladies coming out of town on such mornings, armed with their baskets for the mushroom hunt. Mushrooms grow that fast. They pop up overnight.

Several times a week, Horst and I would venture out with our own little baskets to collect mushrooms for Mutti to can. I had to know what I was picking. Often, my little brother would dig up inedible (poisonous) mushrooms. It would be my job to sort those collected by Horst and throw out the bad ones. I would not even take them home when Horst picked the wrong kinds of mushrooms.

I would say, "Out, out, out."

And Horst would say, "But my basket is about full."

And I would say, "I know, but these aren't any good."

The same applied for hunting wild blueberries. You had to know what you were picking. The nearby forests were full of them. Mutti would pack a sandwich for our lunch. We would then grab the cans used to collect the fruit and head out to spend most of the day, like Forty-Niners looking for Gold Rush nuggets.

Wild blueberries are little, not plump like those you buy in the store. We would sit there in the patch and fill up our cans. It took us most of the day. And since Horst was color-blind, he would pick unripe red and green blueberries.

My favorite picture of my mother

I would just let him take them home. Mutti would often say when Horst presented his filled can to her, "Oh, here we go."

My Mutti was amazing and took care of so many different responsibilities on our farm. She worked in the fields alongside Pappa, Horst, and me. When we were digging potatoes, Mutti would be out there until ten o'clock in the morning. Then she would leave and fix lunch for all the people that might be helping. There might have been as many as ten. She would have worked half of the night before to prepare part of the meal ahead of time, like peeling the potatoes. She could not go home at ten o'clock and have the vegetables ready. One of Mutti's dishes began with cooked meat. Then she would cut up cabbage and potatoes and add them. That was often our main meal.

Mutti was an excellent cook. She learned her culinary skills as a young girl right out of grade school in the kitchen of the Schloss, the home of the Baron von Senden and his family, who lived in Radach. The Baron's estate had nearly fifty rooms. He employed dozens of servants in his household. There were cooks, nannies, and people who cleaned. Half the population of Radach worked in the Baron's fields. My mother learned to cook with the chefs who cooked for the Baron. She acquired additional skills at a culinary school to which the Baron sent her when she was sixteen.

Mutti baked rye bread at least once a week for our family, and this was a task our mother took very seriously. Pappa grew the rye and then took it to one of the mills in town to grind into flour. She would feed the bread starter the night before. Early the next morning, Mutti would get up and mix the dough in a great big, wooden trough, which Horst described as "humongous."[5] She used

My parents (last couple on right) at the wedding of Onkel Hermann and Tante Martha; Cousin Gunter and me holding hands in front

about two-thirds of rye flour and about one-third wheat flour. After mixing the dough, she would work in the yeast. Once ready, Mutti would shape the soft dough into ten to twelve individual loaves, setting them a small space apart atop the wooden kitchen table and leaving them to rise for at least three to four hours. Each loaf was probably about twelve to fifteen inches long. When I was a little girl, they always looked so big to me.

The kitchen was in a building separate from the main house.[6] A vast brick oven was built out through the back wall of the kitchen. An iron door about three feet square allowed access from the interior of the kitchen while sealing off the heat within. Mutti mainly used pine branches to fuel the oven. As the dough rose the morning of the bread-making day, the fire in the oven would be stoked and left to get hot.

Mutti used a long-handled wooden paddle to place bread in and remove it from the oven.[7] This tool, about five feet long from the handle to the broad end, allowed her to put food in the oven without getting burned. When Mutti thought the oven temperature was right, she would get a piece of wheat straw and place it in a crack in the wooden paddle's surface. After opening the door of the oven, she would extend the paddle inside. Mutti would move the paddle around, making slow, horizontal circles with the larger end of the oversized utensil. When that wheat straw turned brown, and the burning wood glowed a pale white, she knew the oven was ready.

Plump loaves of dough would be placed one by one atop the plank of the spatula and then fed onto the oven's brick cooking surface.[8] The interior of the oven was large enough to cook all the loaves at one time. Mutti, the consummate culinary expert, always knew when the bread was ready to take out. Once the loaves were baked, our mother would take them out to a little bench on a porch. Each loaf would cool propped against the wall. Once the rye bread was cooled, they were then placed on shelves of a wooden storage cupboard in the kitchen and covered with hand towels.

How wonderful that rye bread made our house smell![9] After the first loaf came out and was cooled, Horst and I would each get to cut an end off. We would put some butter or honey on it and eat it. That was the biggest treat we had! Both Horst and I agreed that the smell of fresh-baked bread was our favorite memory of our mother's cooking. It was particularly appetizing when we got home from school on a day when Mutti had baked bread.

Our immediate family consumed most of the rye bread Mutti baked. Between the four of us, we could eat practically one loaf per sitting. Mutti also used the bread to make lunch sandwiches. Summertime was always a busy season due to harvesting. Our mother might make as many as twenty to thirty sandwiches for all the hired workers who helped Pappa on the farm. It took a lot of bread to feed all of us.

* * *

Regular church attendance and worship were part of our Schindler family routine. We were Evangelical Lutherans, as were most people living in our northern region of Germany. We attended Radach Church. Although I do not remember much about Sunday School, we had catechism class on Wednesdays. Horst and I both went to that. One time, my brother got in trouble, and the pastor spanked him, which would not have been unusual. Once we got home, I made the mistake of telling my parents. As Pappa was a strict disciplinarian, Horst got spanked again. My dad was not kind about punishment and spanked hard. *One time was enough*, I thought. I never told on my brother again.

My parents had a deep faith, although it was not a subject often discussed, mainly because there was little free time. Pappa and Mutti were working *all* the time. Yes, we prayed at night. But my parents were so busy, living their lives each day consumed them.

* * *

My world, contained in the environs of Radach and our farm, was happy and carefree. I was blissfully unaware that Germany was still struggling to recover from her devastating defeat suffered at the end of World War I. A financial depression was making it difficult for many to make ends meet. I was also ignorant of the fact that Germany's political structure was quickly morphing into something sinister and evil. By the time my fifth birthday arrived in the spring of 1934, the man with the funny little mustache who yelled a lot had firmly established himself as the leader of Germany, giving himself the title of Führer.

Never in my wildest dreams could I have imagined the future events that would forever change all our lives.

CHAPTER TWO

In the Eye of the Storm

W hen some 1.5 million soldiers of the German *Wehrmacht* invaded Poland on Friday, September 1, 1939, a war began that would engulf not only our country but also the entire world.[1] Known by its code name *Fall Weiss* (Case White), the operation stunned the terrified Polish population. Dark clouds of *Luftwaffe* airplanes filled the skies, endless divisions of foot soldiers marched in stride, and thousands of armored tanks roared through town and countryside alike as this enemy force surged forward, cutting its way effortlessly like a hot knife through butter.[2]

Not quite a month before the war's start on August 23, 1939, Germany and the Soviet Union had signed a Non-Aggression Pact, a document the press would refer to as the Hitler-Stalin Pact.[3] The agreement ensured Germany and Russia would not attack one another and that control of any conquered eastern European territories, located between the two countries, would be evenly divided. Hitler, never good at keeping his word, would sever this agreement in less than two years.

Hitler had two main reasons for wanting to conquer not only Poland, but other countries as well: Poles were considered racial underlings, and the Reich wanted to acquire more room for the natural growth of its population. *Untermenschen* was the term used by the Nazis to describe peoples they believed to be inferior, either racially or socially.[4] History records that this mindset of the Führer and the leaders of his inner circle would influence programs of the Reich employed against many other peoples and nations, including Poles, Russians, and Jews, just to mention a few, painted with this unfortunate moniker.

The rural location of our Schindler family farm kept us isolated and protected. The summer of 1939, in the weeks leading up to the war, was the first time that I remember seeing the *Wehrmacht* soldiers. Many, heading for Poland, marched out on the road that ran in front of our farm. I could see them from the potato field where I was working.

Pappa and Mutti worked incredibly hard to make sure Horst and I lived a somewhat normal life despite the storm of Nazism that had already been swirling around us since I was a small girl. The Nazis needed farmers, and although Nazi officials would visit our farm from time to time, we were otherwise left alone.

Life for Horst and me consisted, as it always had, of carrying out our daily chores—working in the fields alongside Pappa and Mutti, attending school, and attending catechism classes on Wednesdays and church on Sundays. This secluded life we enjoyed was yet another of God's many mercies.

* * *

I was ten-and-a-half years old in the fall of 1939 and had just started the fifth grade. Horst and I attended Radach Grade School. We would walk to school to meet our friends after completing our morning chores. My best friend, Gerda Schmidt, and I shared everything. My favorite subjects were reading and writing. In this particular academic year, I knew we would be practicing our handwriting. The writing in German schools had changed the year before when I was a fourth-grader, from the old German script to "international" script, a form of cursive penmanship in which the letters flowed into one another.

The German school system in the early 1930s ran pretty much the same way it did in the days of the Weimar Republic. After kindergarten, children attended *Grundschule* or "ground school," which consisted of the next four grades.[5] Children living in more rural areas, as I did, were allowed to continue and complete four more years of education in the same school system.

I suppose the subjects I learned during my elementary school days were the same as most children are taught: history, math, language, and science. In addition to reading, writing, and arithmetic, I was also taught to crochet and knit in school. These needle-art skills kept my hands busy and helped me pass away the hours on days when my help was not needed in the fields.

Despite what the history books state, I do not have memories of being taught lessons in Aryan racial superiority. I do remember raising my hands with

Mildred's birthday party with friends. Mildred, *second from left.*

German Alphabet Script

my classmates in the required "Heil Hitler!" salute. I also remember a framed picture of the Führer hanging on the wall of our classroom, but there were no printed pictures of him appearing in the front of our textbooks. I do not remember hearing disparaging remarks about Jewish Germans.

The only unpleasant memory of those elementary and early secondary school days is of one severe teacher, in particular, who stands out. This lady's husband was in the war, an S.S. (*Schutzstaffel*) officer deployed to Africa. The S.S. or "protection squad" was responsible for maintaining the security of the Reich.[6] They also terrorized many in our country, as well as in European territories occupied by Nazi Germany. This man was probably in the *Waffen-SS*, which was the armed military S.S. division that saw actual combat.[7] This lady was unkind to me and others. She was probably very frustrated over the fact that her husband was away in the war, and she took it out on us. She was very strict.

Even though membership in the *Hitlerjugend* (Hitler Youth) had been required for all German males of Aryan descent since the passage of the Law on the Hitler Youth on December 1, 1936,[8] Horst was too little to join. He would have only been four-and-a-half the winter of 1936. The same decree stated that by a young man's tenth birthday, he would be registered, his racial background investigated, and, if found acceptable, would be drafted into the *Deutsches Jungvolk* (German People). This group groomed young men for the *Hitlerjugend*.[9] Since Horst's birth, but especially by the time he turned ten, our family had been living on the family farm, hidden in plain sight from German authorities whose job it was to examine the rosters of local youth groups.

There were also two youth organizations for young women: the *Bund Deutscher Mädel* (League of German Girls) and the *Jungmädel* (Young Girls). The latter was for girls between the ages of ten and fourteen and, like the boys' *Deutsches Jungvolk* group, provided preparation and training for membership in the *Bund Deutscher Mädel* group, in which girls were required to join from ages fourteen to eighteen.[10]

Three years later, the Second Hitler Youth Law was put into effect on March 25, 1939, and made it mandatory for all German males between the ages of ten and eighteen to join the *Hitlerjugend*.[11] If not, a youth could be removed from his or her family, made a ward of the state, or even sent to prison. This Law and others were not enforced for either Horst or me in the years that followed, yet another sign of God's protection over our family.

Neither Horst nor I was a member of any of these Nazi youth organizations, and I do not remember any school friends who were. Although I was aware of the Hitler Youth, it was always described to us as very similar to the Boy Scouts. Parents in our little town of Radach were against these organizations due to the local political disagreement with what Hitler was doing. The rural location of our village was once again a saving grace.

By the time I reached the upper grades, I attended school in Klein Kirschbaum, a town four kilometers (almost two-and-a-half miles) away. I completed the seventh and eighth grades there. I had to walk through the forest to get there. It was not unusual for my friends and me to see animals, like deer and wild hogs, on our way to school. Pappa always warned me not to try to catch the baby pigs, especially in the spring, when litters were common. He told me to let the little pigs pass, so the adult hogs with sharp tusks would not attack me.

The school had a rule that students were to walk to school, as not all had bicycles. Those of us who had one would often offer a ride to classmates, who would sit on the handlebars or perch behind on the seat. We would hide the bikes at the first farm before we reached Klein Kirshbaum so that we would not get into trouble.

Confirmation, the formal recognition in the Lutheran church that a young person had come of spiritual age, was another highlight of my eighth-grade year, sometime between August 1942 and May 1943. Family photos that survived the war show me standing by the front steps of our home, wearing a new black dress, made especially for the church service. It was a very auspicious occasion for all my friends in the class.

How nervous I was during the confirmation service! We were sitting in front, and all the people were looking at us. We had to know our scriptures. Reverend Althausend tested us in front of everybody. Pappa was a deacon in our church, and I especially did not want to disappoint him.

My formal education ended in May 1943, with the completion of my eighth-grade school year. After this age, a young person either went on to a trade school or went back home to work in some capacity. Those that advanced to trade school were either young men or those whose parents were Nazi party members. I was neither. Mutti was so disappointed, as she had wanted me to learn to play the piano and to sew and cook, skills that I would have acquired in a trade school setting. Mutti became my new teacher, schooling me in lessons I would put into practice for the remainder of my life.

* * *

Farming was a hard way of life, as everything we did was by hand. Pappa did have horses, which helped him plow the fields. Otherwise, the burden of

All dressed up for my confirmation service

tilling the rye fields, weeding the garden, harvesting the rye wheat, and planting and digging up the potatoes was carried on our collective shoulders.

Besides all Pappa did to keep our farm running, he also helped run the farms of six or seven other female neighbors. These women did their best to take care of the fields, as their husbands were fighting for the Reich. Many nights, Pappa came in well after dark, returning from one of those nearby farms.

My dad was a well-respected leader, both in our community and in the Radach church. He and Mutti both expected a great deal from Horst and me in terms of our behavior. Although Pappa was a strict disciplinarian, both Horst

Outside the Radach Church with Reverend Althausend and my confirmation class

and I respected him tremendously and wanted to be the best children we could for him.

Mutti had many responsibilities as the wife of a farmer. She spent so much of her time working in the fields. Cooking our meals also kept her very busy. There was precious little time to make my clothes. As a result, a lady who lived in Radach made most of my dresses; we bought the rest in Drossen.

If there was any spare time, Mutti would often spend it praying. She had a deep, abiding faith in God. Often Horst and I would find her in a room of the house, seated off by herself, with her head bowed. We would stay as quiet as possible and head outdoors to play, leaving Mutti to her conversations with her Lord.

* * *

I was Mutti's little helper around the house, copying what she did and trying my best to do the same. Cooking. Cleaning. Making my bed. Setting the table. My mother was a patient teacher, and I tried to put into practice what she taught.

When I was about six, Pappa taught me how to plant potatoes. Pappa and some of his hired workers would have already dug the holes. Horst and I, armed with baskets filled with cut-up bits of potatoes, would walk along the rows, dropping a piece of a seed potato into each hole. As I grew older, one of my main jobs was to walk behind the *lister*, the horse-drawn plow implement that pulled potatoes out of the ground. Once the plow dug the furrows, Horst and I would take baskets and walk along the rows to collect the newly-uncovered vegetables. Our filled baskets would then be placed in the bed of a big wagon and hauled away.

During the winter, Pappa stored our potatoes in a large hole in the ground, located out behind the barn. The pit was several feet deep and lined with straw. Once filled, the potatoes were covered with a mound of straw, creating a tent effect. Dirt covered the straw, keeping the potatoes safe over winter until Pappa sold them at the market.[12]

Horst and I were close, as we were only two years apart. He was a kind boy who always looked out for me. Horst worked hard with Pappa to take care of our farm. Mutti doted on him. However, he was often getting into some kind of mischief. "Ornery" is my favorite word to describe him.

One of my favorite stories about Horst is when he and our cousin, Klaus, thought it would be funny to take some of our chickens and put them in a barrel. The boys had this grand idea that the chickens would produce lots of eggs, and perhaps they could sell them for a little pocket money. Well, they scooped up those poor chickens, dropped them into a barrel, tamped down the lid, and promptly forgot all about those birds. By the time the boys remembered, all the chickens were dead.

Another time, Horst sicced our German Shepherd, Lux, on the mail carrier. Pappa asked him, "Horst, did you do this?"

"No, Pappa," Horst would reply.

Horst loved Mutti's cooking, as I did. His favorite dish that she cooked was *Hefeklösse*, a sticky bun made with yeast, the recipe for which could also be used to make dumplings. The bun was served with a cooked blueberry sauce spooned over it. Mutti made it often for my little brother. Maybe that is what helped him grow so big and tall.

* * *

Christmas was always a special time for our family. Horst and I looked forward to the holiday each year. The celebration began early in the month on December 6 with the observance of *Nikolaustag*, St. Nicholas Day.[13] Children all across Germany would leave an empty shoe or house slipper outside their bedroom door the eve of December 5. One of the primary duties of St. Nicholas was to reward children who had been good and punish those who had not. If Horst and I were good, there would be some candy or coins in our shoes. If we were naughty, we would get a stick. I never got a stick, but Horst did *many* times. As a result, he was on his best behavior between St. Nicholas Day and Christmas.

My family and I always observed the tradition of attending a candlelight church service on Christmas Eve, December 24. Upon our return home, Horst and I would delight in discovering gifts left by *Weihnachtsmann* or "Christmas Man," as we called him. Also known as "Father Christmas,"[14] this figure would somehow manage to slip in and out of our home undetected. We never did figure out how.

Christmas would not be the same without all the mouth-watering food prepared for the holiday. Many delightful hours were spent with Mutti in the kitchen as I helped her prepare holiday treats. I watched as Mutti made the syrup, and filled the crocks with all that she baked. Some of my favorites were *Pfeffernüsse, lebkuchen,* and *springerle.*

Pfeffernüsse (also spelled *Pfeffer neusse*) is a holiday iced spice cookie that is a staple of German Christmas celebrations. Brown sugar, cinnamon, and cloves provide rich flavor for these treats. *Lebkuchen* is a German gingerbread. *Springerle* is a type of licorice-flavored shortbread, due to the addition of anise seeds in the recipe. The dough is rolled, cut, and then stamped with a mold to create an imprinted design on each cookie. *Springerle* cookies are often iced or painted in some way to highlight the embossed pattern.[15]

Nothing thrills me more at Christmas than singing the age-old carols. Some of my favorite lyrics are from Joseph Mohr's beautiful "Silent Night:" "Stille Nacht, Heilige Nacht, Alles schläft; einsam wacht." Our family had no idea that the memories of those last few Christmases we shared would have to last us a lifetime. All in our little world would not be calm and bright for much longer.

CHAPTER THREE

The Terror All Around Us

Now seventy-five years after the end of World War II, facts of the brutalities, carried out against German Jews, are both documented and well known. The Nazi regime carried out this reign of terror against these noble people in the years between 1935 and 1945.[1] Referred to as the *Holocaust*, this term comes from a word meaning "destruction of life by fire." However, many Jewish historians prefer the term *Shoah*, from a Hebrew word meaning "catastrophe."[2]

Many German Gentiles lived, during this time, in larger urban areas, and as such, would have had more interaction with German Jews. Those that did may have been aware of state-sponsored cruelty aimed at Jews, acts taking place in plain sight. Our family lived in an isolated, rural area. We did not have Jewish neighbors, as no Jewish families lived in our little village of Radach. My parents did not talk to us about what was happening. Maybe they were trying to protect Horst and me.

However, a strong Jewish community existed in the nearby, larger town of Drossen, located six kilometers (about four miles) southeast of Radach. The courthouse was here. Drossen also boasted many shops and stores, mostly owned by Jewish merchants. Pappa often traveled to this city to transact business. Sometimes he would take Mutti, Horst, and me with him. I distinctly remember one Jewish family with whom my father traded. This relationship created some of my fondest childhood memories.

Pappa and Mutti would bundle up Horst and me and pack us into the sleigh. Pappa would then drive us all to Drossen for a shopping trip. Although the trip was not too long, Horst and I would be half-frozen by the time we had reached the store. Because it was cold, it was not possible for Horst and me to wait outside in the sleigh. At one particular store, the shopkeeper's wife would take my brother and me to the back of the store while our parents selected their purchases. Waiting for us would be warm yeast buns covered in butter and drizzled with honey. A cup of hot milk accompanied the bread. What a treat!

Then, one year, we rode to Drossen in the sleigh with Pappa and Mutti. The welcoming merchant family who had always greeted us before was gone, and their store was dark, the jagged edges of the shop's broken windows glinted in the sun as if teeth in some gruesome smile. An eerie feeling settled over Mutti, Horst, and me, as we watched Pappa stand silently in the street in front of the shop. We immediately realized something was dreadfully wrong, as my dad turned around sharply and stomped back to the sleigh. His footsteps on the frozen ground sounded ominous and hollow. All he would say was the storekeeper and his wife were gone.

Horst and I looked at each other in surprise. Neither of us said a word. I still remember the questions that bounced around in my head, as Pappa tightened the harnesses. *What has happened to these people? Why has someone damaged their store? Why would someone do this to them?* What my brother and I witnessed was beyond our comprehension.

My father's life was grounded in the principles of honor and respect. The fair, honest way in which my Pappa conducted his business is part of what drew others to him. Although too young to understand the significance of the scene in front of me, I could read my father's expressions as he prepared the sleigh for our trip home. Anguish and disgust flashed across his face, only to be replaced by hard, flinty anger as if something he feared had somehow come to pass.

I never saw my Pappa at a loss for words. He had *always* been able to help Horst and me make sense of confusing or frightening circumstances, reassuring us with his gentleness and compassion. As he turned the sleigh around, heading toward Radach, my father looked as though he were struggling to hold himself together. This one time, Pappa had no words.

I have no way of dating this particular encounter. Still, it could have occurred near *Kristallnacht*, the "Night of Broken Glass," a full-scale vandalization carried out on two separate evenings in mid-November 1938 against Jewish synagogues and businesses. My parents *never* discussed the events of that trip to Drossen with Horst and me. The question of whatever happened to that dear Jewish family, for which I have not received an answer, still tugs at my heart.

* * *

I learned about the formation of the Weimar Republic, the German state established in 1918 after World War I's end, in my elementary school social studies lessons. As a little girl, I also remember studying about the Versailles Treaty and its significance as the instrument that ended the Great War. However, it was beyond my third-or-fourth-grade grasp to fully understand the very public humiliation and international shame Germany began to suffer, even as the ink dried on the treaty documents. The disgrace of the country's defeat—forced to acknowledge blame for causing the war, ordered to dismantle the country's military, acceptance of crippling economic sanctions, and removal of formerly German-controlled territory—created an atmosphere which would spawn an evil beyond imagining.

Adolph Hitler appeared as the head of the *Nationalsozialisticsche Deutsche Arbeiterpartei* (Nationalist Socialist German Workers' Party) in July 1921. Formerly the German Workers' Party and more commonly known as the Nazi party, this newly reorganized political group and its organizer promised great things for not only its party members but for all Germans. Except Hitler's vision was for a few, not all.

Hitler dreamed of creating a thousand-year reign, which would be the envy of the world, partly due to the purity of its people. According to this diabolical dictator and those who consumed his ideology, individual German citizens were declared unfit for no other reason than their lineage and faith. Long before the start of World War II, Hitler and his henchmen were working on ways to rid themselves of Jews and others, which they considered *Untermenschen*. Even now, this word makes me cringe, mainly because of my vivid memories of the Drossen merchant's demolished store.

Not until I was a grown woman, with a family of my own, did I learn, with shock and embarrassment, of the many laws enacted in pre-war Nazi Germany that placed limits, in ever more restrictive ways, on every aspect of life for German Jews. These laws ran a broad gamut—from matters about ownership of working farms to the right to vote to denial of German citizenship to those of the Jewish faith or lineage. Shortly after *Kristallnacht* in late 1938, it became mandatory for German Jews to wear a yellow Star of David on their clothing and place a sign on the door or window to mark their businesses with a "J" for *Juden*, the German word for Jew.

Almost two months before my thirteenth birthday, S.S. General Reinhard Heydrich convened the Wannsee Conference on January 20, 1942.[3] Fifteen Nazi officials met secretly to discuss a systematic plan, the "Final Solution of the Jewish Question," to determine once and for all how to achieve Adolph Hitler's dream to rid not only Germany but all of occupied Europe, of its Jewry. What began slowly as harassment of German Jewish citizens in the late 1930s, progressed into laws limiting the civil rights of these same citizens in the early 1940s, and finally resulted in the full-scale extermination of almost six million Jews.

* * *

I was devastated to learn, years later, the extent of the horrific, unspeakable deeds carried out against German Jews, while helping my children with their history lessons and in a country half the world away from the one in which I had grown up. Thinking back on my parents' silence on this subject, I realized with startling clarity that they had been protecting my little brother and me. Shame doesn't even come close to describing how sick to my stomach I still feel to this day, about the atrocities carried out by the wicked Nazi regime. My lack of awareness of the terror all around us is one thing that haunts me most about the years I grew up in Germany.

My prayer is that when human beings, of whatever faith, see society around them headed in the same direction, they will do all in their power to prevent this evil from happening again.

A German Lutheran pastor, Martin Niemöller, wrote one of my favorite quotes about this period:

> "First they came for the socialists, and I did not speak out—
> because I was not a socialist.
> Then they came for the trade unionists, and I did not speak out—
> because I was not a trade unionist.
> Then they came for the Jews, and I did not speak out—
> because I was not a Jew.
> Then they came for me—
> and there was no one left to speak for me."[4]

How I wish those who knew had spoken out, but I understand why they did not. Had I been in those same shoes, I would like to think I would have had the courage to say something.

CHAPTER FOUR

"Little Girl, Feed the Chickens"

L iving on a farm offered our family many opportunities to remain self-sufficient. For one, we could grow our food, even though we had to use ration cards for specific items like sugar and shoes. Other than the occasional Nazi official that might wander out to check on us, we were pretty much left alone. As the war dragged on, however, life became a little more complicated.

The German government began rationing for its citizens in August 1939, one month before the war commenced.[1] Five main categories of goods—clothing, food, leather goods, shoes, and soap—were to be purchased with the *Lebensmittelkarten* (ration cards) that would become precious to so many.[2] We still had to use money when buying food, even if we used ration cards to make the purchase. Various food items covered by ration cards included bread, cooking oil, dairy products, fruits, fruit-related foods (such as jellies and jams), meat, and sugar. Pappa and Mutti usually drank coffee with their meals, but over time, even coffee became just about impossible to get. As the war went on, people used inventive ingredients to produce a coffee-like substitute, including acorns, chicory, oats, and roasted barley.[3] Our coffee was a combination of roasted oats and barley.

Perhaps beginning in the spring of 1942, once America joined the Allies in their fight against Hitler, we would see more and more fighter planes flying overhead while making their runs.[4] Because of this, once the sun went down, we closed the shutters and drew the shades before turning on the lights.

Even though we were able to grow our food, it was not only ours to enjoy. The German government demanded we give back to them a significant portion of our food—rye, potatoes, milk, and eggs. We had to give the government a certain amount of milk per cow—the same with eggs. The government expected us to provide them with sixty eggs per hen per year. If a hen died, the quota still had to be met.

When I was about eight or nine, during the middle of one day, a Nazi soldier in a brown uniform appeared at our farm. Although I did not know the man's name, his face was familiar, as he lived in Radach. I was outside, all alone. Mutti and Pappa must have been in the fields working.

The soldier looked at me and said, "Little girl, feed the chickens."

I remember being scared and thinking, *Why do I want to feed the chickens this time of day?* That was a chore usually Horst or I performed. We would open the coop first thing in the morning and allow the chickens to wander all over the farm for most of the day. Toward evening, we would feed them. We would scatter food for them—barley or rye or whatever we had for them—and then we would call them. I would go, "Putt, putt, putt, putt, putt, putt, putt." Here they would come running from all directions. Once fed, they would all go into the coop for the night.

The soldier's question still puzzled me. But I was an obedient child, and I did what the man asked me to do. Unbeknownst to me, the soldier was trying to get a headcount of our chickens to make sure we were giving enough eggs to the government. What I did not know at the time was Mutti kept a crate of chickens hidden in the hog pen in one of our barns, so that we would have enough eggs for our use. The soldier was unaware of this fact also, and so got an incorrect, much lower count of our brood.

We usually kept a couple of hogs. During the war, we butchered a few throughout the year, and we would do our best to make the meat last. Even though we did not usually eat beef, there were a few times during the war when Pappa and Horst butchered a calf, long after dark, to provide fresh meat for us. Mutti's vegetable garden helped put something green on our plates, at least for two meals in the day.[5]

* * *

Several years after the war started, perhaps in 1942 or 1943, a Polish boy, Jan (pronounced *Yahn*), came to live with us. The Germans had captured him for repeatedly cutting telephone wires. He and the other boys with him were warned that if they did not stop resistance efforts against the German army, they would be captured and sent to Germany to work on farms. The practice of enslaving captured civilians, both men and women, was frequently practiced by the Germans. As more and more of the male population went off to war, the result was a tremendous void left in the workforce, especially on farms. As farming was held in high regard by the Reich, considered a necessary component of building and maintaining a strong nation, many of the young men captured in occupied territories were sent to Germany, expressly as farm laborers. According to research from the United States Holocaust Memorial Museum, Jan would have been one of 1.5 million Polish citizens deported.[6]

The day Pappa came home with Jan, Mutti said, "What were you thinking? I can't believe this; he can't speak German. How are we going to get along?"

Pappa shrugged his shoulders and said, "Well, he can work on the farm."

This Polish teen could not speak a word of German, but we managed somehow to get along. Jan was a year older than I. Over time, Horst and I began to think of him as an older brother.

One day a Nazi official walked into our home unannounced to check on the Polish teen's status. We had Jan sitting at our table eating with us.

The Nazi officer said, "What's he doing sitting at the same table with you? He's a prisoner. He will sit at a table by himself."

We had to put Jan at his own little table nearby. That infuriated my mom and made her feel terrible for Jan. Now, can you imagine? That is what the Nazis were doing to us. They would just appear out of nowhere. I was so surprised to see this man in our house. Now, that was unnecessary.

Jan's primary responsibility was to work with Pappa in the fields. Over time, he became my dad's right-hand man. He also helped Mutti and Pappa milk our cows. Both my parents always treated him like family. Jan, however, was not the only extra member of our family.

By the time I was about twelve and still in grade school, an older teenage German girl named Alma came to live with us. She was one of those girls that either her parents did not want or she had run away from an unhappy situation. Either way, my mom and dad took her in. She lived in a room on the second floor of our house.

One of Alma's responsibilities was to milk the cows. Our five cows lived in the barn, and we never put them out to pasture. They had to be milked twice a day and also fed and watered. She also worked along with us in the fields.

Alma was easy to talk to, as she and I both spoke German, unlike Jan, who spoke only Polish. If we went into town or out for a ride, especially during

Playing in the snow with Alma, *seated on sled*

winter-time in the sleigh, Alma would often come with us. She would also watch Horst and me if Pappa and Mutti needed to go somewhere for a grown-up function or into town shopping. Horst and I came to think of Alma as an older sibling, just as we did with Jan.

* * *

For many of you reading this story, the world of the early-to-mid twentieth century in which I grew up must sound like a place straight out of the screenplay for a movie. No television. No Internet. No instantaneous communication. During the 1920s, 1930s, and 1940s, the primary way most people gained information about the world was either through reading a newspaper or listening to the radio.

The Germans, masters of propaganda, used this technology at every opportunity. Capitalizing on the creative genius of Italian inventor, Guglielmo

Marconi, the Nazis used this method of cost-efficient, mass communication to hypnotize many unwitting souls living within Germany's borders. Joseph Goebbels, Hitler's squirrely Minister of Propaganda even had a low-cost radio, the *Volksempfänger*, designed. Known as the "People's Receiver," this little box was easily affordable to be purchased and placed in every German home.[7]

We had a radio, but Horst and I did not listen to it very much. Our parents did, but they probably waited until long after we were asleep to turn it on. Pappa worked very hard to protect his children from all the horrible things happening within Germany and in other nearby countries.

The radio would soon bring us news of several attempts made on Hitler's life. All of us, especially Pappa, hoped one of them would be successful.

CHAPTER FIVE

"They've Missed Him, Again!"

My Pappa had a strong dislike for Hitler and the Nazi party. I do not know if my dad ever did say, "Heil Hitler." He would have died. I mean, that is just how he felt. Pappa had been spared years earlier from service in the German *Wehrmacht* due to his occupation as a farmer. Local officials pressured him in the time that followed to help the party in any way possible. "My father was not a Nazi and often criticized the policies of the party. The police were on the lookout for him and twice they warned him."[1]

No one truly knows the numbers of German citizens who were not Hitler fans. Pappa thought things would get better once Hitler was gone, but that day never came. The working people liked him. He promised everyone a *Volkswagen*, "the people's car." Hitler was tough on farmers and people that worked for themselves, but the people who worked in factories went along with him. They thought Hitler was doing good.

I am still surprised that I lower my voice when talking about this subject, now seventy-five years after the end of the war. The farmers and the shopkeepers could see right through the German leader. My dad did not think Hitler was doing a good job. Neither did my mom.

* * *

Several photographs of Pappa in various uniforms have survived. With the assistance of many, I have tried to determine what type of uniforms they were, all to no avail. There is one particular picture of Mutti and Pappa standing together in front of the apple tree by our home. The uniform looks like that of a Nazi soldier. An armband was visible on the left sleeve of his tunic just above the elbow. Mutti, however, had taken an ink pen and scratched out whatever was on the armband. She wrote an illegible word across this same area of the photograph. Its meaning would remain a mystery to me (see page 220).

Perhaps the pictures of Pappa in uniform were taken in the last year of the war, after the formation of the *Volkssturm* or "People's Militia" was created on September 25, 1944.[2] The German public first learned of this home guard militia-style group on October 18, 1944. Able-bodied German males between the ages of sixteen and sixty were required to join. There was no standard uniform, only whatever the member could find in the way of a discarded military uniform. Regardless of dress, each *Volkssturm* member wore an armband, in colors of red, black, and white emblazoned with the words, *Deutscher Volkssturm Wehrmacht* (German People's Storm Defense Force). The band was worn on the left sleeve of the outfit. Some historical archives show armbands worn below the elbow, others above.[3] The *Volkssturm* armband may have been the one in my parents' photo, on which Mutti had scratched out the armband. Each *Volkssturm* member was required to have "a rucksack or backpack, blanket, field bag, messkit, canteen, cup, knife, fork and spoon."[4] I do not remember seeing Pappa in a uniform, ever seeing one hanging in a closet in our home, or ever seeing an equipment backpack as the one just described.

As a younger man, my Pappa had immigrated to the United States in 1922 and worked there for several years. He married Mutti in that same period and returned to Germany six months after I was born. As I neared adolescence, I became aware that the Nazi authorities were keeping an eye on my dad, as they knew he had lived in the United States.

Pappa often went to Radach to meet with other farmers or attend town meetings. He and Mutti were aware that Nazi officials would be watching those meetings and reporting back to their superiors. Mutti would always remind Pappa before he left, "Don't say *anything* when you go to the meeting. Don't lose your temper." Although he kept it in check, my dad had a temper, especially when riled up about subjects he felt deeply about, like the welfare of his family or his strong disagreement with Germany's government structure. Mutti was afraid Pappa would not come home, because the Nazis might take him for some reason, for something he said.

One of the reasons that Hitler and his government went unchecked for so long is that they had created such a state of fear and intimidation in German citizens' minds. The most insignificant action could result in an arrest. Distrust was ever-present among friends, co-workers, neighbors, even family members. One learned very quickly to keep one's opinions, especially about the government, to oneself. If you did not, you might find yourself in jail or worse. My mom and dad were afraid of what was happening in Nazi Germany, but they could not say anything publicly for fear of what might happen to all of us. You could *not* say anything.

The only person Pappa could talk to about political matters, other than Mutti, was his very close farm neighbor. Those two would visit with each other privately, but they could not talk to others like we do in a group. We were afraid to be noticed or say something for which Nazi officials might punish us. It was not necessarily against the law to meet in groups, but the fear of being overheard was always with us. I never heard any conversations between Pappa and his friend, our neighbor. My dad kept that very quiet. I do remember my parents talking together off in the corner of a room in low, hushed tones, but Horst and I would shut it out. I never gave it much thought.

Mutti and Pappa never discussed any fears or worries about the Nazi government in front of Horst and me. They worked very hard to protect us. As the years of the war raged on and news of worsening conditions made its way to our farm, my parents never discussed the possibility of leaving Germany or moving back to the United States. It would have been much too dangerous. Besides, when you have a farm, you do not leave it. Our farm had been in our family since the 1600s. Pappa was not about to abandon it.

In the years between January 1933, when Hitler declared himself Chancellor and his suicide near the war's end in April 1945, there were five different attempts made on his life. You might be familiar with the name Claus von Stauffenberg, a Nazi colonel, who masterminded the last assassination plot against Hitler.[5] He was portrayed by the actor Tom Cruise in the 2008 film *Valkyrie*, which detailed the operation known by the same name. The names of four other men, who also plotted against Hitler's life, should be remembered as brave and true—Maurice Bavaud, Georg Elser, Henning von Tresckow, and Rudolf von Gertsdorff.[6]

We would often spend evenings on our farm listening to the radio as the day would begin to wind down. Mutti might be washing dishes or Pappa working to sharpen a plow blade or repair some small pieces of broken equipment. Horst and I would be sprawled out on the floor, looking through books or coloring pictures. I remember one particular evening when the news broadcast detailed a failed attempt on the Führer's life.

My dad almost crawled into the radio. "They've missed him, again!"

I could not believe it, but he had said it out loud.

Although we did not talk about it, each of us in our family was secretly praying that someone would stop this madman. Time was running out.

PART II

The Merciless Russian Onslaught

"World War II had no parallel in history.
It was waged without rules or mercy.
It assumed a life of its own, as though it would go on forever.
Yet at the same time
it was waged with malevolent intelligence.
No one in Europe escaped it."

—From *Voices from the Third Reich*[1]

CHAPTER SIX

The Red Wave

By the fall of 1944, more and more Allied bombers were flying over our farm. We could sometimes see them, although we were not worried about them; they were going to Berlin. To avoid being identified, the planes flew over rural areas. Gesturing up to the sky, Pappa would point out the bombers as they flew over. "Here they're coming! Here come the Americans!" he would say. I remember the planes made a dull, roaring sound. They were going, "Whoo, whoo, whoo," very much like the sound of a thrashing machine. It would not be until years later that I learned that other Allied planes flying over our farm sounded differently because their payload had already been delivered.

Marie, one of Pappa's sisters who lived in Berlin, and who was known affectionately as Tante (Aunt) Mariechen (pronounced mah-REE-kheeyn), would occasionally come for a visit. We would sometimes hear bombers in the air nearby while she was with us, and inevitably the subject of air raids would come up. Tante Mariechen would say to Horst and me, "I need to take you children home with me for one week and let you find out what we go through every night when we have to go down in the shelters." She and every other Berliner were weary by this time, after experiencing Allied bombing raids for over four years.

By the early spring of 1945, the tide of war had turned against Germany. No one knew for sure, but rumors about a possible Russian invasion swirled all around us.

January 1945

The rumors were not the only sounds we heard. On many days, we heard loud booms that sounded like thunder. Mutti would say, "It's January. Why do we hear thunder? This sound is *not* thunder. They're [the Russians] closer than we think." We were hearing Soviet artillery going off in the distance, the sounds of which emanated from a different direction than the one from which the Allied bombers usually came.

The black-topped road stretching out in front of our house was a byway on which many travelers passed. The presence of Ukrainian refugees grew from a trickle to a flood, as so many of them were making their way westward, frantically trying to outrun the Russian army they said was headed our way. Mutti, ever hospitable, would often serve them coffee or offer something to eat.[1]

Many of the refugees begged us to join them. "Do not stay here," they said. "We have lived under the oppression of the Russians for all our lives. You will not like it."[2] Perhaps we should have joined these people, but how do you leave everything behind?

One morning we were sitting at the breakfast table. Through our window, we could see the Baron's coach fly past our home, headed down the black-topped road at a frantic pace, the frightened horses harnessed to it racing as if to outrun a specter. Later, we learned that Baron von Senden and his family fled their home when notified Russian troops were close. They left food on the table; abandoned all furnishings. They took nothing with them.

The German propaganda on the radio would always state, "We're holding the line." However, the streams of people passing by our house every day did not instill much confidence in that statement.

Threats made by Nazi officials had kept Pappa from packing us all up and heading to safety. One of them told my dad, "You do not leave."[3] They told him that if we did, they would shoot our horses, even while hitched to a cart or wagon. A dead horse would not be much good to anybody. Sometimes out of a sense of frustration, Pappa had whispered to us about trying to head west. He thought if only we could reach the Americans, they could help us get safely to the western side of Berlin. You did not discuss a possible escape with anyone outside your own family. Nazi officials controlling our area would have been on the alert for news of any such plan made by local townspeople.[4]

One day near the end of January, Pappa gathered our little family together and told us, "We are not staying out here. We're going into town." He and Mutti had decided it might be safer for us to stay at night with family friends, as our location a half-mile outside of Radach left us isolated. This family worked as shepherds for the Baron. Alma and Jan would also come with us.

We felt safer somehow being in this larger group of several families. These few days were spent waiting and watching and trying our best to fill our minds with anything but thoughts of the Red Army that might be getting closer. Mutti and Pappa had to go back to our farm each morning, early before sunrise. Alma and Jan would accompany them to help feed the animals and milk the cows. Late each afternoon, they returned to milk the cows again. The four would walk back to join us in our new living quarters once completing their chores. Horst and I stayed behind with the other families in town when Pappa and Mutti left on these daily errands. We were all wondering what was going to happen, as we knew the Russians were close.

Thursday, February 1, 1945

On this particular morning, Pappa, Mutti, Alma, and Jan had gotten up before sunrise for their morning tasks. When Horst and I woke up, we could not find our parents. Now fifteen, my next birthday was only one month away. Horst was thirteen. We were not little children anymore, but it was still very disconcerting to awaken to find our parents missing.

I told Horst, "We're going to go find Mutti and Pappa. Let's go. You and me together."

On the way home, on the outskirts of Radach, we could see a Russian tank heading down the black-topped road toward us. The chain on the tank's treads made a horrible sound on that paved surface. Two soldiers lay on top of the tank. I mean, they were just lying on the tank with their guns. And here are two kids walking. We were scared.

Horst and I were walking off in the ditch on the side of the road, kind of along the electric pole lines so that we would not be in their way. The soldiers look tired. They did not do anything except stare at us as the tank rolled past.

As we got closer to the farm, we could see all these soldiers milling around the grounds. There was a big hole in the slate roof of our house. A shell from one of the tanks must have hit it. Horst and I ran past the uniformed troops to find our parents.

"I shall never forget those tall, broad-shouldered, grim-faced Russian soldiers carrying guns—they were so tall they had to bend over to get into the front door of our house. They were all between 20 and 30 years old."[5] I can still see the face of the first one that walked in. I remember how surprised I was by the size and physique of the soldiers because Hitler kept telling us in radio addresses that Russia had none left but old men and young boys. None of these were old men, but neither were they young boys. Lots of them had smallpox scars. They must have survived an epidemic when younger. Their faces also bore very stern expressions. Of course, they were fighting troops.

When I got to the house, I took off my winter coat and laid it on a chair. Not finding my parents inside, I ran out into the courtyard behind the house. You will never know how glad I was to find Pappa and Mutti out in the kitchen.

After a long hug, my mother said to me, "What did you do with your coat?"

I said, "I laid it on a chair in the house."

"Well, you better go get it. There are soldiers in and out."

* * *

As I walked into the room where I left my coat, a Russian soldier was walking out the doorway on the opposite wall of the room, my jacket in his hand. I did not dare say, "Give me my coat back." The man was pilfering anything he could get his hands on. There is no way he needed my coat. I should have kept it on. It was with a heavy heart that I returned to my mother in the kitchen.

Mutti was so shaken up by all the chaos erupting around us. She was forty-seven, and Pappa was forty-six. Suddenly, their world had been turned upside down. Horst and I also found ourselves in a surreal situation. "We had no idea what would happen. It was like overnight there the Russians were, and there were no German soldiers to defend us."[6]

The days dragged on as if in slow motion. Pappa tried his best to stick with his daily routine, but it was much more challenging now, with a Russian soldier following close behind, a gun pointed at his back.[7] I wonder how my dad held his anger in check, as he loved us all so much. How hard it must have been for him to be unable to shield his family from these Soviet marauders.

The soldiers got drunk much of the time that they were at our farm. One day, they were tromping through the barn building that contained the kitchen. Maybe they were looking for food stockpiles, as they had gotten into the second story rooms where the grain was stored. Laughing and yelling, they poured molasses down the stairwell, then ripped open a featherbed and scattered the feathers from inside it all over the sticky liquid. Mutti was especially upset because it had taken her a long time to prepare the molasses, and the soldiers had wasted it on purpose. On another day, the Russians tromped around the farm shooting all the turkeys, ducks, and geese we raised for a meat source. Mutti cried more hot, angry tears.

Three distinct divisions of the Red Army had been unleashed only three weeks earlier to begin their march through Poland and on into Germany toward Berlin—the First Belorussian Army Group, the Second Belorussian Army Group, and the First Ukrainian Army Group. After looking through history books and carefully studying military maps of this period, it was most likely troops of the First Belorussian Army Group, under the command of Marshal Georgy Zhukov. They were nearest the vicinity of our little village of Radach and invaded our home that fateful February morning.[8] The presence of these unwelcome strangers ruined our days like dark, ugly ink stains splattered across a freshly laundered white shirt.

I lost track of time between the arrival of the Russian soldiers and when they forced our family to leave our home. During that awful time, Horst and I stayed close to Mutti and Pappa and close to one another. We just knew it was day time and night time. We now knew what war was like, as the Russians had brought it to our door.

Friday, February 9, 1945

This morning, the Russian soldiers told us we had to leave. They gave us only two hours to collect belongings and gather what we could. Then we were forced out of our home. Our belongings, along with those of six other families, were placed in a one-horse-drawn wagon. Each individual had a suitcase or bundle of clothing. This same thing was happening down the black-topped road to the entire population of Radach, about six hundred people.

As we headed out on our trek to an unknown location, one group of armed soldiers would walk in front and another behind us to make sure no one managed to escape. They told us the German Army would not let the Russians into Berlin, so we were being taken to Poland. Pappa whispered to us that he had heard the Germans were holding the line against the Russians at the Oder River.[9] The first day we walked about three or four miles east "to a place half way between Berlin and Poland. There we had to live in a barn, the only place for us."[10]

Mid-February 1945

Over the next few weeks, Red Army soldiers escorted us through several small towns, seizing the residents, always herding our group northeast. Villages in this part of Germany were only about one to two miles apart. We would stay in a town for about a week, and then the Russians would force us to leave. Our group got larger the further we went. Through the years, I have tried to remember the names of those different villages. That information still eludes me.

The weather was bitterly cold, as winter held the landscape firmly in its grasp. While making our way from town to town, we were horrified to see elderly people lying on the side of the road, grandmas and grandpas that had died. Since there was no time to bury them nor any sympathy given to do so, these poor souls were simply laid in the ditches beside the road and covered with blankets. "And babies died, too, in the cold. We didn't have babies or grandmas or grandpas. It was just the four of us. Our parents just tried to keep us together."[11]

Jan and Alma were taken along with us when the Russians forced us from our home, but while being shuffled along from town to town, we became separated from Alma. We never did find out what happened to her. Somewhere in those same first few weeks after that fateful first day of February, the Russians took Jan into the army. He cried because he did not want to take a gun. I bet they shot him.

As our group grew in size, we would begin to hear stories of how our new acquaintances had fared when encountering our Russian hosts. One of the stories told was of young men forced to fight with the Soviet army. Although tall and well-built for his age, Horst had terrible eyesight and wore very thick glasses. This condition was indeed a godsend, as the Red Army might have conscripted him as a forced laborer.

At least our family of four was together. Little did we know how short our time together would be.

CHAPTER SEVEN

Losing Pappa

T he days ran together in a jumble. February 1, the day the Russian troops invaded our farm and forced us to leave with them, seemed forever ago. Nothing seemed to make sense anymore. Now Pappa, Mutti, Horst, and I were being herded northeast toward Poland, along with all the people from our little village of Radach and more people from other towns, all scooped up like fish in the net the Russian army had cast for us. It had now been about four weeks since that awful day when our world turned upside down.

On March 5, we were in the fourth town we had come to since leaving Radach—a little village called Trebow, located somewhere close to the Polish border. The Russian soldiers came around to where groups of people were sitting or standing and began pointing at different men, reaching out to grab others, and motioning for them to step out from the crowd. They took my father, along with fifty other men, to feed and herd cattle. Kurt Stark, a seventeen-year-old young man from our village, who had been a year ahead of me in school, was also taken. The Russians told us Pappa and Kurt would only be with them for about three days.

Even though my dad and Kurt were of different ages, they were both strong, healthy men. The Russians were looking for these kinds of laborers. Though that exact day is now hazy in my memory, Pappa and Kurt must have had enough time to talk with each other and devise a plan.

Pappa said, "Kurt, let's stay together. That way, if something happens to one of us, we can let our families know what happened to the other."

My friend, Kurt Stark, who was captured along with my
Pappa in March 1945

Before my dad and Kurt climbed up into one of the big trucks waiting to
take them to wherever the cattle were, my mother ran to get a warm scarf for my
Pappa. It was freezing that day. I do not know if the scarf was hers or if someone
standing nearby offered it. Mutti and Pappa had only a very few minutes to
share any type of farewell.

Pappa told her, "Keep the family together."

* * *

Here is my recollection of that earth-shattering day from a first-person
account I was able to share in 1947, which appeared in our church's denomina-
tional newspaper:[1]

The Russians took my father away, saying that he would be gone for only three days on a job. But no word has ever been heard of or received from my father since that time. He has completely disappeared from this earth as far as we are concerned. My great uncle, age 74 years, who was also taken by the Russians, described some of the things my father had to endure at the hands of the enemy.

It is terrible to think that my father had to suffer like this. But the Russians took off most of his clothes except his trousers, and then beat him merciless until the blood ran down his back. My uncle said that this was the punishment inflicted on him because one of the Russian officers had scratched himself on a needle which my father carried on his coat lapel. (This would have been a threaded needle Mutti placed under the coat's lapel in case her husband needed it.) Another article written many years later adds a little more detail to the story: "No word has been heard from him [Pappa] since except through my great-uncle who was taken the same time but was released the next day due to his age," Mildred says.[2]

* * *

I can only wonder how it must have been for Pappa, afraid for his life and yet more frightened and concerned for ours. Kurt Stark survived the war, and almost thirty years later, in the early 1970s, I was able to reconnect with him while on a trip to Germany. That is when Kurt told me about the plan that he and my dad had made, the deal to stay together. Kurt shared that he and Pappa had been able to stay together for a while, but after some time, they became separated when they were loaded back into the trucks. After that, Kurt never saw my dad again.

Kurt said it was a horrible time. You did not rear back, fight back, or react in any way to treatment from Russian soldiers. And my dad did *not* have that much patience.

The greatest tragedy of this horrific experience is that we never really found out how and when my father died. Across the years, speculation of where my dad's life ended offered possible scenarios in many different locations, including Moscow, Siberia, and Poland.[3] At least when a loved one dies, the cemetery provides a place to go to be able to feel close to them or to pay one's respects. There is no such place that marks the final resting place of my Pappa.

My mother later received a letter from the Red Cross, saying my father died in Poland. Since the Russians never asked for names of the people they took as

47

The way I remember my Pappa

workers, how would they know who Pappa was and where he died? It was all so callous and inhumane.

Somehow God gave Mutti, Horst, and me the strength to keep going. I am not sure how we did it to tell you the truth. Mutti lost her better half and the love of her life. Horst and I lost the central guiding figure in our lives in those tender, vulnerable teenage years. I was fifteen; Horst was thirteen. We each lost so very much that day.

Fritz Robert Schindler was such a marvelous, strong, principled, honest, loving, faithful, and true man. Our home was a safe place, and we knew he would always protect us. He filled our lives with so much love and security. I like to think the best of him lived on through Horst and me.

I never got to tell my Pappa goodbye.

CHAPTER EIGHT

A Mother's Fierce Love

I n those first days following Pappa's abduction, my mother must have been beside herself with fright and worry, although I do not remember her appearing so. Mutti was in charge of our family now. She would need to muster every ounce of daring creativity to fulfill the assignment Pappa tasked her with—to keep the family together.

As the days dragged on and it became more apparent that we might not be seeing Pappa anytime soon, Mutti, Horst, and I worked extremely hard to keep ourselves busy, stay focused, and to stay together as my dad had wanted us to do. My Mutti loved her children with a fierce love, one that gave her courage in these challenging days.

The Russian troopers were like wolves, always prowling around us. Not for a minute did Mutti miss the stares of one or two of them focused on me. She was also well aware of the attention these barbaric foreigners focused on other young women. Rumors of brutal assaults, carried out by the soldiers against women in our group, ran up and down our company like shivers down one's spine. Mutti was desperate to come up with a plan to keep me safe and keep the wolves at bay.

At any moment, Horst or I could have been subject to the unwelcome attention of our captors. My little brother, just beginning to grow toward his adult height, was tall, slender, and more muscular than his lithe frame implied. His icy blue eyes looked like giant orbs, floating behind the soda-bottle, thick lenses of his glasses. Mutti urged him to play up his optical difficulties.

That is what we think kept the Russians from taking Horst. They probably thought his eyesight was too weak for him to shoot like a soldier, which was another godsend. He also did not know much about shooting. Since you were not allowed to have a gun in Nazi Germany, Pappa had buried all the firearms he owned. Horst would have been a little boy when this happened. If the Russians had discovered a weapon on Horst, they would have taken him or even killed him.

Russian soldiers thinned out our group every few days and either took men, like they had taken Pappa and Kurt, to work in labor camps or on building projects or took women to work in laundry camps. I was afraid the soldiers would take my mother and brother from me and that I would be all by myself. Young men close to Horst's age were also occasionally dragged out of our column and given a gun. They then marched off to accompany the Russian soldiers on some task, possibly even forced to fight against the German army. The soldiers' attention to Horst seemed to have waned, at least for the moment.

Keeping her only daughter under wraps was going to be a little more difficult for Mutti. Each morning she would begin her ministrations of disguise, a makeup job that would have made any theatrical company green with envy. My cheeks were rosy, so Mutti would pat flour all over my face to make me look pale and sickly. Then she would rub lard on my neck. Once all the grease was applied, she would wrap a rag around my neck. The dirty cloth, coupled with the lard's rancid smell, gave my neck the appearance that there was some sort of rash or wound there. By the time Mutti finished fastening the length of fabric around my neck, I could not even turn my head.

I was sitting there with a stiff neck. The soldiers would look at me and pass by. I have wondered many times if I could have done that for my girls. My mother was forty-seven in the spring of 1945. Mutti's demure appearance belied the iron will that lay within.

Early each morning, the soldiers would wake us up and have us on the march soon afterward. We probably walked several kilometers each day. They would commandeer some poor farmer's barn as a place for our bedraggled party to sleep, out of the night air.

Mutti was ever mindful of the wolfish intentions of our Russian hosts. On nights when a pile of hay served as our mattress, she would create a "nest" for me, concealing me within the hay. Mutti and several other women would then sleep over me.

My Mutti loved Horst and me with a fierce love that gave her courage in these impossible days. Her disguises for me seemed to be working perfectly, but the situation we all found ourselves in was far from perfect.

CHAPTER NINE

Hitler's Soap

One morning the Russians came looking for laundry workers earlier than expected. Unfortunately, Mutti had not yet had a chance to camouflage me. Before we knew what was happening, a soldier stepped forward and grabbed my arm. With a rough jerk, he pulled me toward him from where I was standing.

"You, come," he growled, nodding in the direction of a frightened group of girls, women, and men gathered nearby.

Mutti, Horst, and I stared at each other across the space between us. It may as well have been the distance to the moon. Our eyes telegraphed silent messages of love; our hearts were burning within us at the injustice of it all. My worst fear was losing my family. As the soldiers led me away, I did not know if I would ever see my mother and brother again.

Pappa had been gone more than ten days, and now I was being carted off to God-knows-where by the Red Army. Mutti sobbed as I clambered up into the bed of a wagon and plopped down beside another young girl that looked to be about my age. There were probably close to fifty young women and ladies taken with me. Most were teens, but a few of them were mothers, their young children pitifully crying as they were left behind. I knew none of the females taken with me except one. A female cousin of mine, ten years older, was also somehow in the wagon with me. Although she did not live in Radach, she may have been living in a nearby town with her parents. She was married, but her husband, a soldier in the *Wehrmacht*, had been away. The Russians also took about ten men, probably required to turn the cranks on the laundry machines.

The soldiers explained that we would be taken twenty kilometers away (about twelve miles) and would only be there for three days. A chill ran down my spine. That is what they had told Pappa, too; he would only be gone from us three days. As the harness leathers cracked over the backs of the horses hitched to our wagon, a great sense of foreboding washed over me. With my every backward glance, my mother, brother, and all of the people taken with us grew smaller and smaller. In front of me lay an uncertain future.

* * *

Finally, we arrived at a town in which there were no local people. No civilians, only soldiers. Our captors herded the women into one building that would serve as our sleeping quarters, and the men were marched off to another. This ladies' dorm of sorts had been someone's home before this terrible time. Our beds consisted of boards nailed onto supports in the wall, the makeshift beds forming both a lower and upper row, like bunks. Scratchy lumps of long straw served as our mattresses. None of us had any belongings with us, only the clothes on our backs. I scrambled up onto an upper bunk, hoping to place as much distance between me and this horrifying situation in which I now found myself. Exhaustion rocked me to sleep.

The next morning, they escorted us some distance away to another building, another unfortunate, lifeless former home now serving as a laundry. Those in charge explained our duties to us. Most would be washing clothes, cleaning shirts for the Russian soldiers; remaining prisoners would work in a makeshift garden, planting potatoes to feed both our hungry Red Army jailers and us. A piece of soap, half the size of a bar of Lava soap, was given to each laundry worker. They were familiar, as they were ration soap we had used all through the years of the war. We would be given a new piece of soap after washing twenty shirts.

"This is Hitler's Soap," the Russian soldier told us, as she held up a piece of soap. "You will wash one hundred shirts per day. Make it last," she said in a menacing tone, gesturing once more with the white bar and demonstrating how we were to use a wooden washboard.

On this first day, I washed thirty-four shirts. Because I did not meet the quota, I had to stay past dark at the laundry facility and work by the light of a kerosene lamp.[1] On the second day, I washed seventy-two shirts. On the third day, eighty-three shirts. If we did not get the shirts clean enough, one of the female Russian guards would slap us across the face with a wet shirt. The washboards were hard and rough, not smooth like the metal washboards Mutti used at home. My hands quickly became chafed because they were always wet and because of contact with the harsh, lye-based soap. By the third night, my hands hurt so badly I could not sleep.

Irritation to the skin of our hands was not our only physical ailment. Lice presented another set of problems. Probably already present in the filthy straw on which we lay every night, the vermin now crawled all over our heads and burrowed in our clothing. None of us had any extra clothes, and neither did our captors offer any. The only means to bathe they gave us was a water-filled trough in front of the house in which we slept. You could wash your hands up to about your elbows and reach up and wash off your face and the back of your neck. Cleaning any more of your body was impossible, as a male soldier stood guard, pointing his gun at us. He was standing right there. So how else could you?

We ate three times daily, each meal consisting of potatoes cooked in some fashion. Breakfast provided potato soup with rancid bacon. Our noon meal offered mashed potatoes and rancid bacon. Potato soup served with a piece of Russian black rye bread was the entrée at supper. Although I did not like potato soup, I ate it anyway. When you are hungry, you do not have the luxury to be picky.[2]

The Russians forced us to find our dishes. Various plates and utensils lay scattered on the ground in the town where we were staying—more evidence of Russian cruelty. I held my nose while digging a plate and broken cup out from underneath a pile of manure. As I rinsed the pottery in the water trough, I prayed the germs would be washed away along with the filth.[3]

Each morning, we would line up in a long line. A female soldier would walk down the line in front of us and say, "You and you and you, wash." Those of us she had pointed to would have to go to the laundry line.

On this fourth morning of wash duty, a Russian female officer barked orders in front of us. She wore an *ushanka*, a winter cap with ear flaps to be tied up over the top of the head.[4] I can still see the red star of the Russian army emblazoned on the front of her hat. (Now, when I see one of those caps, I want to throw it away. I never allowed my boys to have one because all I can see is Russians in my mind. I do not have anything good to say about the Russians. We did not like the Nazis, but we *really* did not like the Russians.)

When she pointed to me, I stepped out of the line, held out my hands, and said to her in German, "Look at my hands!" Rubbing against the edge of the hard washboards wore off almost all the skin from my hands. They were red and bloody. I shook my head from side to side, making my "no" emphatic. I knew if I refused to obey an order, the female officer in charge would shoot me. But I did not care.

I looked at her defiantly and thought to myself: *I don't know if my mother or brother is still alive. My dad is gone. You don't even know my name. What's the difference? Go ahead and shoot me.* Once again, God protected me. The female officer pushed me back in the line and took the next girl. Her hands looked as bad as mine, but she did not say anything.

Now that the Russians had pulled me from wash duty, my new assignment was planting potatoes in the fields nearby. It was perhaps early April by this time. Although frightened and all alone, I was able to find some comfort when working my hands into the rich, dark soil each day. How many times had I done this same thing in the fields of our farm in Radach? Never in my wildest dreams could I imagine how perfecting Pappa's planting lessons would prepare me for what now lies before me.

I planted the potatoes about eight inches apart or so, the way my dad taught me to when I was a child. Engrossed in what I was doing, I was surprised when the sharp thump of a riding crop stung my shoulder. I looked up to see a soldier astride a horse. He was so close that his horse could have stepped on me. I did not say a word. You did not say anything; it would only make matters worse. He told me, in words and with hand motions, that I needed to plant the potatoes further apart, perhaps about eighteen inches or so from each other. While he was still there, I performed the task the way he had shown me. The minute he left, I went back to the way I was planting before. More potatoes for the Germans!

Days rolled on in a numbing procession. The soldier, who had come by to teach me the Russian method of planting potatoes, obviously was not that interested in my progress, as he never came back to check on me again. In addition to my field duties, as was the case with many other female workers, I was later tasked with cleaning the soldiers' quarters. Thoughts of Mutti and Horst filled my mind as I pushed a dirty rag back and forth to dust the worn tables and chairs. Prayers for Pappa accompanied the whisk-whisk sound the broom made as it scratched its way across the dirty floor.

* * *

Somewhere in those days between Pappa's disappearance and my internment in the laundry camp, I reached my sixteenth birthday. Sweet sixteen. Without a calendar to mark time, the day slipped past, as ground mist burned away by the rising sun. No one noticed. No one knew.

Looking back now, after all these years, it is obvious how God protected me during those agonizingly long three weeks I served in the Russian laundry camp. While growing up on the Schindler farm, I had become well acquainted with the cycle of life and death, having witnessed the frequent birth of a drift of piglets or the loss of one of our cows to disease or old age. A sense of self-sufficiency had been honed within my character because I was used to walking or biking almost everywhere I went, either to school or to work in the fields farthest from our house. Countless hours spent working hard alongside Pappa, Mutti, Horst, Jan, and Alma had developed strong muscles within my arms, legs, and back.

Now, however, this intractable situation required mental stamina as well as physical endurance. This ordeal forced me to dig deep and draw upon the tensile strength God had been developing deep within my spirit, upon waking every morning in this abominable camp. Despite all I had learned of life in these short sixteen years, I was still innocent. Pappa and Mutti had protected me well from many harsh realities, some of which I was now learning in this unwanted object lesson. I had never before witnessed such brutality carried out by men against their fellow human beings.

The night brought a terror all its own. The armed male guard patrolled the area around our sleeping quarters. His presence, while preventing us from escaping, ensured that other soldiers looking for female company would be undeterred in their search. There were women in the laundry camp who did not fare as well as I did, females who unfortunately were selected to be the recipient of unwelcomed advances by these barbaric soldiers. I was thinly built. The soldiers seemed to like the girls and women who were a little heavier and bustier than I was. I had also selected an upper bunk, which possibly made it harder to drag me out into the night.

Statistics on the numbers of German women who were sexually assaulted by soldiers of the Red Army are mind-boggling, defying comprehension of such brutal behavior. Historians estimate some one hundred thousand German women were raped in the city of Berlin, once the Russian occupation began. Some two million women throughout the rest of Germany in the spring of 1945 suffered this same ignominious fate.[5]

Somewhere within these three weeks, my cousin left the camp. I am not sure how she escaped, but one day, I realized that she was not there anymore. The soldiers may have mistreated her. All I knew was that she abandoned me.

Mutti was praying for me, wherever she might now be, and God was not only hearing, but answering those prayers. How thankful I am to Him for sparing me from suffering this type of violence at the hands of my Russian captors. How I wished I could have prevented many women in our laundry camp detail from enduring what must have been a horrific and humiliating ordeal.

* * *

It would not be until some years later that I learned that the First Belorussian and the First Ukrainian Army groups began their assault on Berlin on Monday, April 16, 1945. Two days later, forces of the Second Belorussian Army joined them.[6] Perhaps seven days or so later, our Russians captors told us that our services were no longer needed. They were now heading to Berlin, and we were free to go.[7]

Go where? To whom would I now go? In which direction was home? It had now been a little over three weeks since that fateful day when the soldiers had torn me from where I stood that morning in the crowd with Mutti and Horst. My mother and brother could be all the way to Poland's eastern border with Russia by this time. And where might Pappa be?

What in the world was I going to do now?

CHAPTER TEN

Needle in a Haystack

We were stupefied when the Russian soldiers told us we could go home, all the girls, women, and men who had been laboring in this laundry camp under armed guard. But where was home? Where was the town from which they had taken us? We had been carted off with a horse and wagon. From which direction had we come? We hurriedly left the laundry camp, eager to vacate our place of confinement.

Four of us girls took off. I do not remember exactly. We told each other we would go back to the town where we were pressed into laundry service. Well, which way do we go? We did not know. We walked into thick forests and back out into open fields along the roadside. We wandered on foot for several days, finding shelter under cover of trees—small, wooded areas set back from the road. How long we traveled once we left the laundry camp, I do not know.

We had no food that we had brought with us, as our Russian captors controlled even our access to nourishment. As each day passed, the rumbling in the pits of our stomachs grew louder. Even though it was now sometime in mid-April, it was still too early to find berries in the forest.

Although I was grateful for the company and for the fact that I was not alone, I never knew the names of these three girls who now were also searching for their families. The hopelessness surrounding me extinguished any curiosity to discover the stories of the women whom the Russians captured along with me. It took every ounce of mental energy I possessed to keep myself from breaking down.

When we got to the edge of the first town we came to, soldiers met us and told us, "No civilians in the town." Disappointed, we struck out for the next village. I took full advantage of every opportunity to walk up to any adults I saw out on the street or standing in a yard and ask if they had seen my mother. I would describe Mutti and would also include a description of Horst.

In this second town, I explained to one of the ladies, "I'm looking for my mother. She's short and kind of stocky. And I have a thirteen-year-old brother who wears thick glasses."

Dorothy Grothusen, a reporter for the *Ellsworth County Independent Reporter,* wrote many articles about me and my wartime experiences. Through those interviews, she became a trusted, treasured friend. The following is her description of how Mutti, Horst, and I were reunited: ". . . Mildred located her mother and brother, after describing them to a woman she met. Her description of her 13-year-old brother wearing thick eyeglasses jogged the woman's memory and she [Mildred] was guided to a house. There, she found her mother, cooking over a fire in the yard."[1]

God performed a miracle for all of us that day in the spring of 1945. How in the world do you make sense of three members of one family reunited in a foreign, war-ravaged country, members who have been separated for almost a month, living among thousands and thousands of other refugees? There is no *other* explanation for my finding my mother and brother, *but* that God led me to them. I will never know how many hours and days Mutti had stood cooking over that fire pit, desperately hoping I would appear on the road in front of her. This day, God answered our prayers.

* * *

I called out to Mutti from a long way away, but my mother had already seen me. We stood some distance apart, but, in our hearts, no space existed. We were crying tears of great joy and relief, tears pent up for too long, which now streamed freely down our faces.

My mother was an incredibly smart woman, blessed with both common sense and God-given wisdom. These wartime experiences had provided her with many lessons she could have learned no other way. Even from a distance, she could tell that I was filthy and probably covered in lice. I had not changed my clothes or taken a bath in almost a month.

As I got closer to the yard where she stood, Mutti said, "Oh my, Mildred, you are dirty, and you've got lice."

Continuing to walk towards her, I thought to myself, *How does she know this?*

My mother pointed to a shed that was visible, far back in the rear of the yard. "You go into this shed here," she said. "You can't come in the house. We've got to get you cleaned up first. Eighteen people are sleeping in one room, like herring packed in this big house. We're full; all of us refugees. You can't come in there because you've got lice."

Dutifully, I followed Mutti into the shed. Once inside, I removed my clothes. Looking around, I spotted a tarp tossed over a stack of boxes. I reached for it and wrapped it around me. Mutti immediately took the clothes that I had been wearing outside and threw them into the fire. While I waited, my mother heated some water over the fire burning out in the yard.

Once ready, Mutti brought a big container of hot water for me to clean up. She stepped back out the door of the shed and retrieved a bundle. In her hands, she held some of Horst's clothes. He must have had an extra change of clothes because that was what I ended up with—a pair of ski pants and some kind of shirt or top. She also handed me a clean towel and a bar of soap.

Mutti said gently, "I'll give you some time to yourself," nodding to where steam was rising from the large pot. "That's not something you've had much of lately." With that, she disappeared through the door of the shed and closed it behind her.

Filth and grime caked every inch of my body. *Oh, my word,* I thought. *What is that smell?* It took me a few seconds to realize the awful stench filling the room was wafting up from my own body. It threatened to make me gag. Funny, how I never even thought about how badly I smelled those weeks at the laundry camp. After two to three rinses, the water in the container was now a disgusting dark brown shade. *Better there than on me,* I thought, looking at the dirty water. Cleaning my hands and arms proved to be a little difficult, as sores and cracks covered them. Those weeks in the laundry camp had taken their toll on my body.

By the time I had closed the last button of the borrowed clothing, Mutti had returned to the shed with a small container in her hand. Motioning for me to sit on an overturned wooden crate, she bent down next to me and carefully rolled my sleeves. As my mother reached into the little pot and brought out a glob of grease with her fingertips, the questions in my eyes were quickly answered. Mutti gently massaged the ointment onto the dry, damaged skin. Once she completed her mission, she delicately rolled down the sleeves of Horst's shirt.

"Now, Mickchen," Mutti said, tears brimming in her eyes. "That should make you feel better." She then explained that I would have to spend this first night in the shed until the lice were gone.

Now began the delousing process. Mutti had me lean over and began to pour vinegar all over my head. After soaking my hair with the sour-smelling liquid, she wound my hair on my head and tied a large rag tightly around it. Soon, I could feel the lice running all over my scalp.

"I can't stand it," I cried. "Take it off." I stamped my feet on the ground, the sensation of tiny bugs unnerving me.

Mutti said, "No, no," reaching out to keep the head rag in place.

"It's burning," I said more emphatically, this time slapping at my head. The skin on my head was sensitive from having scratched it almost continually since my arrival at the laundry camp.

"You've got to keep the rag on till morning," my mother explained. "You must keep your hair covered and the cloth tied around it."

Mutti stood and wiped her hands on the edge of her skirt. "I'll be right back with a bowl of oatmeal and some bread. You must be starving."

* * *

Later that afternoon, the creaking sound of the shed door opening startled me. I turned to find Horst's beaming face staring back at me, sunlight reflected in the lenses of his glasses.

"Mickchen," Horst called out, his voice thick with emotion.

I stood but stayed in place within the shed. "Stay there, Horst," I replied. "I don't want the lice to get on you. How much I want to hug you."

"I know, Mickchen," he replied.

I was trying so hard to be brave, but it was tough. As I looked across the small space separating us, I could not believe how much my little brother had grown in less than a month.

"How beautiful you look," Horst said teasingly. "Mutti and I have been praying for you," a more serious tone was now marking his words. "Our prayers have been answered."

Suddenly I was aware of what a fright I must have looked like to him. Reaching up to adjust the rag tied around my head, I offered, "Thank you for sharing your clothes with me." I stood a little straighter and tried to look as dignified as possible.

His smile never wavering, Horst said, "I'll see you soon, sister dear." He stepped back and closed the shed door. The reunion with my little brother would have to wait.

The stinging sensation lasted most of the night. Finally, just before I drifted off to sleep, I realized that the lice were not scampering across my scalp anymore. I guess the vinegar had helped.

The next morning, when I awoke, I was so delighted to find my Mutti beside me. It had not been a dream. She brought a comb with her and took it out of her pocket before unwinding the knotted, damp rag from around my head. If the Russians had just cut my hair, it would have helped prevent the lice from taking up residence on my scalp. There was never a way to keep it clean or to brush or comb it while at the laundry camp. Unpleasant as it was, I endured this homemade remedy. The vinegar did the trick.

Once deloused, I was allowed in the house. How good it was to be able to hug Horst finally. The other refugees living there with him and Mutti greeted me warmly. The residence where they had found shelter had belonged to a baron or someone of higher rank. The high ceilings overhead added to the vastness of the large, spacious rooms.

I never did know if those other girls ever made their way back to their families. I only knew that I had. God had orchestrated this remarkable series of events, too wonderful for me to have imagined. The warm, peaceful feeling, created by my reunion with Mutti and Horst, cloaked me like a soft, downy quilt. I never again wanted to feel any other way.

* * *

Russian forces stormed their way into the heart of Berlin on Monday, April 30, 1945.[2] Perhaps some of them were the soldiers who had only three months earlier invaded our farm, taken Pappa, forced me into slave labor in a laundry work camp, and made refugees of my mother, brother, and me. These invaders accomplished what Adolph Hitler once claimed impossible. Later this same afternoon, Russian troops took control of the *Reichstag*, the German parliament building, and raised the red and yellow-sickled flag of Russia.

Later, all of Germany and the world would discover that the arrogant psychopath, who believed Germany's glory would last for a thousand years, was indeed a puny imposter. Unable to accept the reality of his failure, Hitler committed suicide almost thirty feet below the very ground where tanks of the Russian victors were now rolling. A master manipulator, he had even convinced Eva, his former mistress and new wife, to join him in *their* final solution.

The next day on Tuesday, May 1, officials in the town where we were seeking refuge told us we were finally free to return home.[2] Could this be true? Mutti, Horst, and I stared at one another in disbelief. Soon, hugs and shouts of joy accompanied tears we wiped from our eyes. After saying our goodbyes, we gathered what little we had, stuffed our meager possessions into makeshift bundles, and struck out on foot to make our way home.

Could we even find our way back to Radach? If we did, what would we find there? Maybe Pappa would be waiting for us? These and many more questions bombarded my mind, taking up far too much space for clear thought.

But it did not matter.

We were going home.

CHAPTER ELEVEN

The Last Few Bricks

The Russian takeover of Berlin on Wednesday, May 2, would soon make international headlines. Meanwhile, we were making headlines of our own. Each new stretch of the road before us brought us one step closer to home. We traveled for some four or five days, sleeping at night under cover of trees, as I had done when searching for Mutti and Horst. Many others passed us in these days, those displaced and made homeless by this terrible war. Weary smiles and hands raised in silent greeting were shared as we passed each little group, these very common courtesies reminding us of the dignity that still lay within each of us.

It was the middle of the morning the day we reached the familiar fields of our Schindler farm. We would later discover that we were one of the first families in the Radach area to get back to our home. A jumbled heap, visible in our front yard, grew larger and larger with each step Mutti, Horst, and I took. Once we stood directly in front of our house, we could see this small mountain was an enormous pile of all our belongings the Russians had thrown outside. *What in the world?* I thought.

When we reached the doorway of our home, the three of us stood there, dumbfounded. It was difficult for us to accept what our eyes relayed to our brains, the images we had to acknowledge as our new reality. The Russians had turned our home into a laundry like the one from which I had just come. I almost cried, looking at our beautiful, hardwood floors.

"Ach du meine Güte!" exclaimed Mutti. "Oh, my goodness!"

Horst and I were speechless.

Once again, Dorothy Grothusen's words perfectly captured the moment. "It was a terrible homecoming. Everything was gone . . . the livestock . . . all their belongings, all those things they treasured—like the beautiful wardrobe chest Mildred's father made for her as a birthday gift . . . Their house was filthy."[1]

Several articles written about my war-time experiences detail the damage incurred. "'Our fine home had been used as a wash house, and round holes had been bored into the floor for the water to run out. When we stepped on the floor water would seep out through the holes.'"[2] One huge opening had been cut in an outer wall just below a window, presumably to let water out. Filthy, black mold covered the walls.[3]

Little furniture remained in the house. We wondered if the Russians had used it for firewood. We hoped to find some of our belongings within the pile heaped up in our yard but were only able to unearth several mattresses and some clothing articles. We later found a bed and a chair in the village. We assumed the Russian soldiers might have taken the better furniture for their officers, for use in the homes commandeered as headquarters.

* * *

The late afternoon sun was our only illumination. Mutti was insistent on going out to the barn at the rear of the house. Horst and I followed her through the back door and across the courtyard. We both looked at each other as we walked, wondering what we might find next.

The barn looked as disheveled as the house. Broken pieces of equipment and feed sacks lay about the floor. Mutti kicked straw around with the toe of her shoe. Raking her hands through her hair, she intently stared downward, as if to locate a specific spot. After a few minutes of looking around, she went to her knees toward the center of the barn floor.

"Help me," she implored as she began scraping back straw and dirt with her hands.

Horst and I immediately joined Mutti on the floor, mimicking her movements.

"What are we looking for?" I ventured.

Mutti stopped for a moment, sitting back on her knees. She reached up to brush a piece of straw that had gotten tangled in her hair. "Food," she answered, the light of hope beaming in her eyes.

Before the Russians came, Pappa and Mutti had stored canned pork sausage, cured hams, and bacon in large, metal trunks usually used for transatlantic travel. My dad and Jan buried the chests beneath the barn's dirt floor and then covered the spot with hay and straw.

We went back to digging with our hands, but it quickly became apparent we would need something more substantial to move the dirt. "Go find me a rake or a jagged piece of wood, Horst," Mutti said, not even looking up from her task. "We've got to be able to dig."

After a few minutes, Horst returned, proudly holding the broken leg of a chair he had found in the rubbish pile in our front yard.

Mutti made her way to her feet and brushed off her skirt. "Horstel," she said, employing her pet name for my brother, the intensity of the digging evident in her labored breathing, "see if you can dig out a little hole in this place?" pointing to the spot we had all uncovered. "I'm sure this is where Pappa buried the trunks."

In about ten more minutes, we heard a thumping sound when the piece of broken wood in Horst's hand struck the solid object buried beneath the barn floor. Mutti, Horst, and I immediately went to our knees, each claiming a spot around the small crater excavated with the discarded chair leg. The digging continued in earnest.

We wrestled two oversized, suitcase-like crates out of the hole in the barn floor, by the time we had completed our arduous task. When the latches were unclasped, and the lids lifted back, we found the cases crammed with whole jars of canned meat and carefully wrapped bundles containing cured hams and bacon slabs. Our mouths were watering just thinking of the feast we would have.

"We're going to be very careful with this," Mutti said, looking first at me and then at Horst. "We will use this a little at a time, so it lasts."

Although it was now dark, the rising moon offered a lamp by which to complete our task in the barn. The holes, where we found the trunks, were filled with dirt and covered with straw. Horst and I made a game of trying to see who could kick up the most massive pile. The three of us were able to push the two cases over to a corner of the barn floor. We huddled in this corner for our first night back home. Not at all sound, but we were safe. At least for now.

* * *

The next morning, we shared a meager breakfast of hard, crusty bread, which Mutti had somehow managed to make last for four or five days. We had all decided we would wait to break into the smoked meat, although it was tempting. Mutti had another mission for us to accomplish on this day.

Mutti led Horst and me from the barn and out into the courtyard. The morning sun seemed to dispel the images of the Russian intruders who had violated the sanctuary of our home. Smaller piles, of discarded wood and such, lay about this area, similar to the heap in our front yard. Mutti just stood there, her hands on her hips as she surveyed the destruction all about her.

Throwing back her shoulders, Mutti looked at both of us and said, "Come with me."

This time, Horst and I followed her back to the house. Mutti pulled open a door that was barely hanging on by a single hinge. She passed through the opening, heading down a set of stone stairs that led to the basement under our home. My brother and I followed behind wordlessly.

The air in this underground room was dank and musty. Only a little light was available from two small windows cut in the upper edges of the wall. Our eyes slowly adjusted to our dimly-lit surroundings. This brick-floored basement had been one of Pappa's favorite storage places. Items kept here remained cool and dry. Now the brick-patterned floor looked as if a giant had picked up the bricks, one by one, and tossed them around the room like one might throw a child's bean bag toy.

Horst and I waited to take our lead from Mutti, who was now glancing silently about the room. Our nostrils were full of the earthy smell of dirt. After a few minutes, Mutti headed over to one corner of the little room to a small area of undisturbed bricks. It looked as if whoever had been tearing up this room had been interrupted. We followed our mother's lead and began to pick up the bricks, as she was doing, and moving them more to the center of the room.

"Your Pappa knew the soldiers were coming," Mutti said, continuing to move bricks out of the floor. "We never told you this because we didn't want to worry either of you. There were important items hidden here under this floor, although I'm not sure they're still here."

Again, Horst and I looked at one another in amazement.

"Horst," Mutti continued, "would you please go to the barn and bring me the broken chair leg we used last night to uncover the food trunks? I think we're going to need it here."

Shortly, Horst returned with his prized piece of wood and handed it to Mutti. By the time he had gotten back from his errand, I had been able to remove one of the last few bricks in the corner. A neat little stack of the ones we had moved now lay behind us. Mutti used the jagged piece of turned wood to dig in the dirt and dislodge an undisturbed brick in this particular corner of the basement, just as Horst had done the night before in the barn. As she lifted the baked clay brick from the basement floor, a spot of sage green canvas peeked through the dirt underneath it. Excited, Mutti used her hands, digging like a terrier trying to uncover a bone, frantic to dislodge the prize awaiting her.

Horst and I held our breath as Mutti drew out what looked like a pouch of thick, worn farm cloth, the kind used to cover our plow in bad weather. The packet was about the size of a loaf of bread. Mutti gently brushed away the dirt, like she was rubbing talc across the tummy of an infant.

"Danke Gott," Mutti exclaimed, as she hugged the small pouch to her chest. "Thank you, God!"

Our God had once again made Himself evident amid this horrific ordeal of World War II. Horst and I watched as our mother unwrapped the cloth. What treasure lay inside! Mutti's and Pappa's marriage certificate. My birth certificate and my baptismal record book, containing a picture of me as a baby. The land transfer from my grandfather giving Pappa the farm. A stash of German marks (probably worthless by this point). A small jar containing the only family jewelry heirlooms we possessed: a marquise-cut ruby and rose gold ring, a gold necklace of Mutti's, and Pappa's gold pocket watch and chain.

By nightfall, Mutti had constructed a small, hidden pocket near the waistband of her dress, using a needle and thread she had with her. The family jewelry would stay on her person in this hiding place for the next few years. Many years later, Mutti would have to have an operation to repair a hernia caused by pressure placed upon her abdomen by the pocket watch.

Although Horst and I could not truly comprehend the magnitude of the moment, our mother had a smile once again on her face, and all seemed right with the world.

* * *

Unbeknownst to us, Germany had formally surrendered to Allied forces on May 7, shortly after we arrived back at our farm. It would be some time before this news reached us. Any radios in our little corner of the world were long gone. Tell-a-friend was the only other method of long-distance communication available, and most of our friends knew as little as we did. Fellow Germans rejoiced throughout the land that Hitler was now gone, the years of his reign finished, just as the Munchkins rejoiced in *The Wonderful Wizard of Oz* with the news that the wicked witch was dead. The three of us—Mutti, Horst, and I—were a bit numbed and much too tired to care about the significance of this event. All we knew was we were home, and we were free.

Items, hidden by Pappa, now recovered from under the brick basement floor

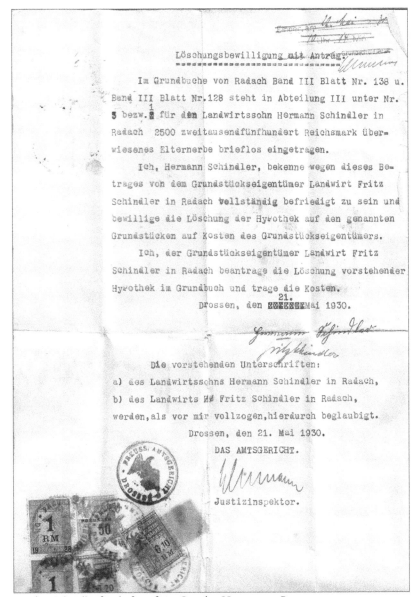

Deed to Schindler family farm from Grandpa Hermann to Pappa

Schindler family farm inventory list (translated on right)

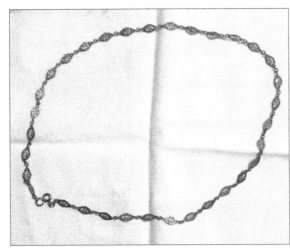

Mutti's gold necklace

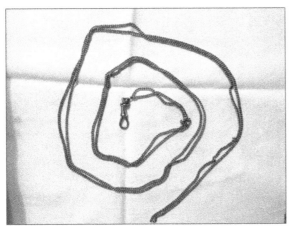

The gold chain to Pappa's
pocket watch

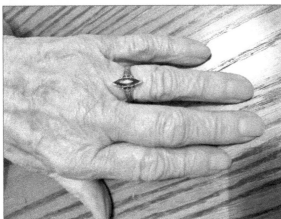

Mutti's marquise-cut ruby
and rose gold ring

My parents' marriage certificate

My baptismal record book: "In Memory of Your Baptism"

The only surviving baby picture of Mildred

STANDARD CERTIFICATE OF BIRTH

STATE BOARD OF HEALTH
DIVISION OF VITAL STATISTICS
STATE OF KANSAS

DO NOT WRITE IN THIS SPACE

405   1628

1. PLACE OF BIRTH

County of ....Barton....

Township of ....

or City of ....Great Bend, Kans.......... street. Reg. No. 50

(If birth occurred in a hospital or institution, give its NAME instead of street and number.)

2. Full Name of Child ....Mildred Schindler....

3. Sex of child: ....Female....
4. Twin, triplet or other....
5. Number, in order of birth....
6. Legitimate? ....Yes....
7. Date of birth ....March 11.... 191 9

8. Full name FATHER ....Fritz Schindler....
14. Full maiden name MOTHER ....Anna Gerlach....

9. Post-office address, street No. or R. F. D. No. ....Great Bend, Kans. RFD 2....
15. Post-office address, street No. or R. F. D. No. ....Great Bend, Kans. RFD 2....

10. Color or race ....White....
11. Age at last birthday ....29.... (Years)
16. Color or race ....White....
17. Age at last birthday ....31.... (Years)

12. Birthplace (city or place) (State or country) ....Germany....
18. Birthplace (city or place) (State or country) ....Germany....

13. Occupation Nature of industry ....Farming....
19. Occupation Nature of industry ....House wife....

20. Number of children of this mother (Taken as of time of birth of child herein certified and including this child.)
(a) Number of children born alive and now living ....1....
(b) Number of children born alive but now dead ....0....
(c) Number of children stillborn ....0....

CERTIFICATE OF ATTENDING PHYSICIAN OR MIDWIFE

I hereby certify that I attended the birth of this child, who was ....born alive.... at ....8 P.... m. on the date above stated.
(Born alive or stillborn.)

* When there was no attending physician or midwife, then the father, householder, etc., should make this return. A stillborn child is one that neither breathes nor shows other evidence of life after birth.

Signature ....[signature]....
....Physician....
(Physician or midwife.)

Given name added from a supplemental report ....
(Month, day, year)
Address ....Great Bend, Kans....
Filed ....3-16.... 191 9 ....[signature]....

Registrar
Registrar

Mildred's American Birth Certificate

During these first days back on our farm, Horst would often leave to explore our fields or tromp through the nearby woods. One day, Mutti and I looked up to see Horst leading a horse into the barn area with a halter he had braided from a grapevine pulled from a tree. The ribs of the poor animal were all sticking out. How long it had been since he had eaten was anybody's guess. Although he was a bit skittish, perhaps having escaped a Russian army camp, the poor creature quickly adjusted to his new surroundings in our barn. Horst worked hard each day to pick grass and wild onions for him to eat.

On another outing, Horst returned through one of the fields where we usually planted the rye and saw a shoe sticking out of the ground. As we had practically nothing in the way of clothing or material possessions, he was delighted with his find. When he got closer and bent down to pick it up, he was horrified to find that the shoe was still on the foot of the body of a dead Russian soldier buried in a shallow grave. I am not sure if Horst ever walked through that field again.

* * *

Over the next few days and weeks, neighbors and relatives returned home to Radach, beginning the process, as we were, of putting their lives back together. Because the soldiers had so damaged our home, we moved in with a kind relative living in town. We spent our nights in the company of family and our days at our farm.

Some of the treasures excavated from the rubbish heap the Russians had left in our front yard were packets of spinach, lettuce, and carrot seeds. By now, it was probably late May or early June, and the weather and the dirt were just right for planting a garden. Horst and I kept the garden weed-free. Like proud parents, we carefully watched our little garden grow. After a few weeks, we had fresh greens ready for our dinner table.

Although we had the stores of canned and smoked meat, we consumed them in moderation. Food was still scarce, and there was not much variety in what we ate every day. There were some days we picked grass and plants from the ground to eat. Horst was more than familiar with having to eat boiled grass during those weeks spent living in a house, much like the Baron's house, with the other refugees. Due to my confinement in the laundry camp, I did not enjoy that delicacy. Horst had learned to tolerate it, and I learned quickly to follow his lead and develop a taste for it. Although this was not what we were accustomed to eating, we were grateful to be alive and thankful God had supplied us with food of whatever kind.

We spent the days of summer laughing with friends and extended family, tending our garden, and working to repair our house as best we could. The hot sun warmed not only our faces but also our hearts. Something akin to contentment began to accompany us more and more each day.

We had no idea how few of those days we had left.

PART III

Evading Stalin: Daring to Survive

"O God, where hearts are fearful and constricted,
grant courage and hope.
Where anxiety is infectious and widening,
grant peace and reassurance.
Where impossibilities close every door and window,
grant imagination and resistance.
Where distrust twists our thinking,
grant healing and illumination.
Where spirits are daunted and weakened,
grant soaring wings and strengthened dreams.
All these things we ask in the name of Jesus Christ,
our Savior and Lord.
Amen."[1]

CHAPTER TWELVE

Polish Ticket to Berlin

Horst and I would make a game each morning of racing each other along the black-topped road stretching out from Radach and see which one would be the first to climb the broad steps in front of our home. Mutti would follow behind at her own pace. As the summer sun shone brightly above, the two of us worked in the garden and helped Mutti with various chores, like scrubbing mold off the walls and patching holes in the floor.

Every day, without fail, all three of us managed to find time alone to keep watch for Pappa. We were *always* hoping beyond hope that we would see him: appearing in the courtyard or coming through the fields or stomping his feet at the back door before he entered our home. Our hearts were sore from bearing this heavy burden, but it was one of love, so we carried on. One day, Pappa would return to us.

On the morning of Tuesday, July 17, some four hundred thirty-five kilometers away (two hundred seventy miles) in Potsdam, west of Berlin, the "Big Three," including American President Harry S. Truman, British Prime Minister Winston Churchill, newly-elected Clement Attlee, and Soviet Premier Joseph Stalin, met at the Cecilienhof Palace, a grand estate built by members of the Hohenzollern family, one of the ruling families of old-world Germany.[1] Together, these world leaders, along with a cadre of staff and auxiliary personnel, would hash out a series of agreements, two of which would determine Germany's immediate governance and detail the dispensation of former German-controlled land to its western neighbor, Poland.[2]

A newly established entity, the Allied Control Commission (ACC), would maintain control of former Nazi Germany in this period immediately following the war from its headquarters in Berlin. This entity had representation from each of the four Allied powers.[3]

Germany was carved into four Zones of Occupation to be controlled by each of the four allied nations who won the war—the United States, Great Britain, France, and the Soviet Union. The ACC would coordinate with each sector. The eastern third of Germany became the Russian Zone; the other two-thirds of the country subdivided into the American Zone, the French Zone, and the British Zone.[4]

Each of the four sectors had a capital. Berlin was also separated into four divisions. The Soviets controlled the eastern part of the city; the Americans took charge of the southwestern portion of Berlin.[5]

Poland, which had been pulled apart during the war like a rope caught in the teeth of a large dog, was now more than ready to begin the complicated process of re-establishing itself. Squeezed between Germany and the Soviet Union for the six protracted years that marked World War II, Poland also suffered destruction in many of its finest cities, loss of national treasures, and humiliation due to construction and maintenance of many Nazi concentration camps. The Poles had no more patience.

* * *

Mutti had not been feeling well. Perhaps she had a summer cold from which some in Radach suffered. Maybe it was some digestive issue caused by our inadequate diet. I think she had nervous exhaustion. The knowledge that our mother was now the sole breadwinner and *the* single parent of two adolescent children, living in a ruined house, with no money and no hope of any and no end in sight to the situation at hand, had taken its toll. Even though Mutti put up a good front, she must have realized deep within herself, as the months wore on, that Pappa would *never* come back to us. She was heartsick, and her body was finally showing the outward signs of what had been taking place within her troubled soul.

For weeks now, Mutti had spent hours in bed in the small bedroom we shared in Radach. She had agreed to let us bring her out to the farm with us occasionally. Horst and I had fashioned a cushion from old coverlets in the bed of a hand cart we found in the corner of the barn. Once settled, we took turns slowly pulling the cart down the black-topped road, careful not to jostle Mutti in any way. Once we got to our house, Horst and I helped our mother walk to the house. She would spend the rest of the day lying down on a pallet we had made for her inside the back door.

Horst or I would drag a chair out into the yard so that Mutti could sit and watch us work in the garden. The sunshine and fresh air were beginning to bring some color back into her ashen face. Remembering times past, she remarked to us on several occasions, "I wish Jan was here. I always thought he could have taken over our farm. He knew so much about it."

My brother and I were so proud that the vegetable seeds we planted earlier in the summer were now ripe, nutritious plants. We wanted Mutti to see the results of our hard work. In the middle of the afternoon, Horst and I finished weeding the vegetable garden, while Mutti was taking a nap. We had just come back to the house after filling a basket with fresh spinach we had picked for our mother when we heard strange voices we did not recognize.

We were startled to see soldiers at the side gate between the house and the livestock barn. A group of four or five men in uniform stared at us. Horst and I stood very still on the back steps, aware that Mutti was lying just inside. Each of the men was armed, although their weapons were not pointed directly at us.

The tallest of the group, probably their leader, stepped forward and said something gruffly in a language neither Horst nor I could understand. A second soldier, acting as an interpreter, spoke out in German, "This is Poland now. The Russians gave this land to us. You must speak Polish and become a Polish citizen if you want to stay here. Otherwise, you are to leave."[6] Horst and I looked at each other in astonishment. *Polish? What in the world was he talking about?*

Although Horst was taller than me, I was the older sibling. A protective feeling washed over me as I stood up straighter and looked the taller man squarely in the eye. "Sir," I said in the politest voice I could manage. "Our mother is sick, and she is not able to travel now."

The interpreter relayed my response.

The leader made a menacing motion with his rifle, now pointed too near me for comfort. Once again, he spoke a stream of words I could not understand.

"I shoot her," the interpreter translated. "Zastrzelę ją."

Horst and I moved closer to each other, our backs blocking the soldiers' view of the inside of the house. Suddenly, we felt a hand upon our backs and knew at once it was Mutti. We turned to make room for her on the step. Pale and haggard, she tried her best to face these new intruders bravely.

The soldiers stared at Mutti, their disinterest and disdain apparent on their faces.

"Ask them," Mutti said to us, "if they'll give us one day to make our decision."

I once again faced this unfriendly officer. "Sir, my mother asks that you give our family one day to talk with each other. We have a huge decision to make."

The shorter interpreter shared my response. The taller man did not look very pleased.

"Very well," the interpreter replied.

"Sir, one more thing you must know," I said. "The Russians destroyed the inside of our home. Although we are here this afternoon, we return to Radach each night to sleep in the home of family members. That is where we will be tomorrow morning."

Once again, one of the soldiers translated my statement. The taller soldier nodded affirmatively.

The translator replied, "Tomorrow."

* * *

By the time we had wheeled Mutti back to Radach in the hand cart, darkness had settled all around us. The family members with whom we were staying were greatly relieved to see us coming through the door. The soldiers had also paid an unwelcome visit to the people living in town. All of us were in the same boat. Our group's mood quickly became somber and tense, as we discussed the ultimatum the soldiers had given us. We knew nothing of the Potsdam Conference or of the signed agreements which had, once more, changed the course of our lives. We only knew that, in less than six months, we were being forced from our home once again.

My son, Kenton, would later say of this time, "It was hard for my mother to leave home for the last time, knowing that all they owned and worked for was no longer theirs."

We talked late into the night, many in our group offering suggestions of scenarios that would allow us to stay. First, it was the Russians who had come and told us, "Go, go!" Now, it was the Poles. *What kind of a choice was it when your only option was to lose your identity, your language, and your national honor to stay in your house?* In the end, that was a choice none of us was willing to make.

Mutti, tired and weary from the whole ordeal, looked at Horst and me before speaking to the others, "We're leaving. I'm not going to stay."

The soldiers returned to Radach the next morning, barely allowing us time to finish our breakfast. As before, the tallest soldier stepped out in front of the group, the shorter interpreter at his side.

"Your decision?" the interpreter demanded.

One of the other adults in our town spoke for the group, "We have decided to go."

The taller officer grunted when told by the interpreter of the choice we had made. He spoke to the shorter man and nodded for him to share his response.

"We leave in one hour," the interpreter said.

None of us could hardly believe what we had just heard. One hour? We spent the next sixty minutes frantically putting on any extra clothing we had, layering the pieces one on top of the other. The women, only allowed to pack a handbag, busily stuffed whatever valuables they could fit within the small purses.

At the hour mark, the soldiers returned, this time accompanied by several others, all of whom held rifles in their hands. They rounded up all the townspeople of Radach in a group, soldiers on either side. Horst and I joined the crowd gathered. We loaded Mutti into the hand cart, the cushion of coverlets once again wrapped around her. Jabbing at us with their guns and uttering Polish commands, the soldiers set us to walking westward.

We walked most of the day, six to seven hours at least, most in our group too shocked to waste energy on conversation or idle chatter. The soldiers allowed us very few breaks. Horst and I took turns pulling Mutti's cart. She had said very little since we left Radach, and she appeared to be asleep much of the time.

At least we are together, I thought, looking with concern at the frail figure of my mother, curled up like a child inside the little wagon. *That is something.*

The sun was hovering near the horizon by the time we reached the town of Frankfurt on the Oder River. Truman, Stalin, and Attlee, Great Britain's new Prime Minister, had signed an agreement on July 26, during the second week of the Potsdam Conference, which established the Oder-Neisse line as the western boundary between Germany and Poland.[7] What none of us understood on this particular day was that with the stroke of a pen, our little village of Radach ceased to exist and in its place, the newly-established town named Radachow, Poland was born.

Near the end of this summer day, all the Radach villagers were escorted by Polish soldiers to the bridge over the Oder River. Standing on either side of us, they urged us on to the bridge. Our group, scared and tired by the frightening events of the past few days, huddled close together.

"Now, go!" The command was given once again through our interpreter. The soldiers adjusted their guns and stared grimly at us.

We began the walk across the bridge, once more heading toward a destination about which we were unsure. We knew, beyond a shadow of a doubt, that the war had turned our lives upside down. Radach and our beloved farm home, more casualties of war, had simply disappeared from the map of our lives.

* * *

There were times of the day when Mutti seemed more alert and talkative than others. During these periods, the three of us bounced ideas off each other in the hopes of making some sort of an organized plan. Wandering the countryside was going to get old quickly. While engaged in one of these conversations, Mutti threw off the coverlet and worked to pull herself to a sitting position. An expectant light gleamed in her eyes, one Horst and I had not seen in a long while.

"Your Pappa's sister, Mariechen, lives in Berlin. She and Onkel (Uncle) Hermann might be able to help us." Satisfied with this pronouncement, our mother burrowed down in the bottom of the hand cart once more.

Horst and I looked at one another and nodded in agreement. Berlin, it would be.

What became of the other residents from our little village of Radach, I do not know. Horst and I pulled Mutti along in the hand cart. During the day, if we saw cabbage or carrots in a field, and we did not see the farmer who owned the land, Horst and I would race over and grab whatever we could.[8] At night, Mutti would urge us to sneak out into nearby planted fields to dig up potatoes that we could eat. Horst and I would fill up our pockets with as many as we could gather.[9]

The roads teemed with fellow refugees. The closer we got to Berlin, the more crowded they became. Horst and I were beside ourselves with worry about Mutti. It seemed like an eternity since we had crossed the Oder bridge. The trip to Berlin took us four long days. During the last three, we had no food. We were so hungry.[10]

When we first arrived in Berlin, we made our way to the home of my aunt and uncle. Marie and Hermann Bohm shared a small, two-bedroom apartment with their children—daughter Waltraud and son Klaus. They were overjoyed to see us and to learn that we were safe. In those first hours of our arrival, Mutti and Tante Mariechen shed many tears for the husband and brother they had both lost.

Although Tante Mariechen and Onkel Hermann were hospitable, their quarters were cramped. Mutti tried to put on a brave face, but Horst and I knew she needed medical attention. After about a week, the three of us said our goodbyes and made our way to the nearest refugee camp. After being processed, waiting in many lines, and answering countless questions, we were finally allowed to accompany Mutti to a private room she was provided, as she was ill. Once settled in, Horst and I would take turns sitting near her as she slept. There seemed to be an abundance of doctors and other medical staff. I am not sure, though, if they had what was needed to cure our mother. Mutti's heart was broken, and her spirit bruised and battered.

Horst and I prayed she would recover.

CHAPTER THIRTEEN

Saved This One Time

I t was perhaps the third week in August by now. In the last few weeks, the world had been stunned by the daring shown by the new American president. Germany had capitulated three months earlier in May. Japan, fiercely proud, still refused to surrender. Playing the one card he had been holding close to his chest, President Truman put into practice a last-resort plan. His authorization of the bombing of two Japanese cities ushered the United States and the rest of the world into the atomic age.

On the morning of Monday, August 6, the B-29 bomber, *Enola Gay*, piloted by Colonel Paul W. Tibbetts, Jr., dropped its payload, a 15,000 ton, TNT-equivalent atomic bomb nicknamed "Little Boy," on the Japanese city of Hiroshima.[1] One hundred thirty-five thousand people died.[2] Japan, seemingly unmoved, still refused to surrender. Three days later, on the morning of Thursday, August 9, a B-29 bomber, *Bock's Car*, piloted by Major Charles Sweeney, emptied its cargo bay, releasing a second 21,000 ton, TNT-equivalent atomic bomb nicknamed "Fat Man," on a second Japanese city, Nagasaki.[3] Fifty thousand people died.[4] Five days later, on August 14, Japan, cowed with humility, surrendered.

Even before the war's formal end, with the signing of surrender papers by Japanese government officials on the USS *Missouri*'s deck, plans had been put in place to take control of former Nazi Germany. These programs would establish a modicum of order with which the German people themselves could put the pieces of their shattered country back together.

* * *

Reconnecting with Tante Mariechen and her family had become a more important reason for travel. Although we were now safe in the refugee camp, with access to food, clean clothes, and medical care, this was not a place in which we cared to stay for an extended period. Mutti was getting stronger but was still not yet back to her old self. We pleaded with the camp authorities not to send us to a location within the Russian Occupation Zone. We asked them to send us to the American, French, or British Zones. Our cries went unheeded.

Once again, we found ourselves on the move. This time, we were sent some two hundred forty-five kilometers (one hundred fifty-two miles) northwest to the city of Nienhagen, near the Baltic Sea in the German administrative district of Mecklenburg. We found lodging in a house with four other refugee families, with whom we shared a kitchen. Memories of the February 1 invasion of our lives by Russian troops were still fresh. The three of us were wary, as we were still in the Russian Occupation Zone and not safe from danger. This strange new normal was a hard adjustment for us all.

Fall was on its way, and the air was crisp and cool. By this time, both Horst and I had found work for hire, performing menial labor in nearby local farmers' fields. Instead of money, our employers gave us food. At least we had something to eat. We were grateful. While we worked each day, Mutti rested. She still had not completely recovered from her illness.

One day in early October, the mayor of the town came to Mutti. He told her that Russian officials had demanded that he send thirty girls from Nienhagen to work in Siberia. They would send for twenty more after the first of the year. How grateful I will always be to this gentleman, although his name, after all these years, escapes me. The mayor was a very kind man and was aware that our mother was not well. He was also probably savvy enough to understand that the causes of her ailments were as emotional as they were physical. Before he left that day, the mayor promised Mutti that, although he could allow me to stay with her during the coming winter, he would be powerless to prevent me from being sent to the work camp with another group of girls in the new year.

Horst and I dug potatoes and harvested crops by hand. While we worked, Mutti sat in our room, plotting an escape plan for me. Just as she had done six months before when using flour and grease to create a disguise for me, she hatched another ruse to keep me out of harm's way. Mutti knew she might not ever see me again if I was taken to Siberia. The plan established, my mother waited until the perfect time to put it into action.

* * *

Mutti waited to orchestrate my escape plan until the train had left the station on December 26, 1945, carrying on it thirty young women from Nienhagen. Agonizing images of the families of the equally distraught young women just carted away whirled through her mind, as she walked from the train station to the mayor's office. Mayors were high-profile officials within the various administrative districts, as they had the power to decide who was allowed to travel and who was not, who was issued special passes and who was not.

Mutti gave an Oscar-winning performance on this second visit with our town's mayor. She persuaded him to grant his official permission and allow me to travel to the American sector of Berlin to go to my aunt's house to retrieve "winter clothes" which were being stored there for us. Pappa's sister, Mariechen, did indeed live in Berlin. That much was true. There were, however, no "winter clothes." That part of the plan was merely an excuse for the train ticket. Again, Mutti was protecting me.

* * *

The morning of February 3, 1946, dawned cold and clear. I had hardly slept the night before. I folded my last piece of clothing, placed it in the bag, and closed the small valise. The train ticket lay on a small table. It might as well have been a snake. Just as I was about to button my blouse, Mutti's voice in the dimly-lit room stopped me.

"Mickchen," she said, coming over to where I stood. "I want you to take this with you. It is a *very* important document." A folded piece of paper was in her hand. Before I could even say a word, she reached over and placed it inside my brassiere. "You may need this," she continued, as she pinned the paper in place.

"Mutti, I *don't* want to go," the words barely audible as they tripped over the lump in my throat.

"You *have* to go." Mutti's words were gentle, yet unwavering, as I fastened the last button on my blouse. There would be no argument. "When you get to Tante Mariechen, she may be able to help you find a job. I know she will help you in any way she can."

We spoke but a few words as we walked from the house to the train station. Mutti had packed some food for me and wrapped it in cloth. I carried her care package in one hand, my small suitcase in the other. The city was awake, people already out on the sidewalks headed to work or appointments of the day. People hurried past us, oblivious to our situation. Angst and frustration were building up inside me like water boiling in a kettle. I did *not* want to leave.

Mutti and I said our goodbyes, so much still unsaid between us. In these last months, the color had returned to my mother's face, and she seemed more like herself than she had been in a very long while. As she held me tightly, it seemed as if she were trying to press her very heart and soul into me, sharing whatever strength and courage she had with her only daughter.

Placing my foot on the first step of the train car was one of the hardest things I have ever had to do. I did *not* want to make this trip, but Mutti had said I must. Respect was a cornerstone of the Schindler family. One of the most important lessons Pappa and Mutti had taught me was to be an obedient daughter. My mother had told me to do this, to make this return trip to Berlin to see my aunt, and I was going to do what she said. As the train wheels creaked and steam bellowed from the engine, I waved out the window to my mother.

I prayed I would see my Mutti again soon.

CHAPTER FOURTEEN

Game-Changer

I ran my hands over my coat, brushing off little pieces of lint that had gathered while on the train from Nienhagen to Berlin. The trip, other than long, had been uneventful. Checking the slip of paper which I held in my hand, I confirmed I was at the correct address. I took in a deep breath and knocked on the painted, six-paneled door before me. The sound of heels, making their way across a wooden floor, could be heard inside. The metallic sound of a safety chain, removed from the inside of the door, was audible. The apartment door swung open, and Tante Mariechen beamed at me.

"Mickchen," my aunt said, wrapping me tightly in a warm embrace. She pulled me inside, closed the door of her apartment behind us, and was careful to replace the chain.

Once again, I found myself in their small but immaculately-maintained apartment. The sunlight streaming through sheer curtains seemed to whisper a welcome.

Marie "Mariechen" Schindler Bohm was Pappa's little sister. She was also the second oldest of three sisters and the fourth of six children born to her parents. The first child born to Hermann and Marie Schindler was a son, Richard, who was killed in World War I. My Tante Anna was born next, followed by my Pappa, Tante Mariechen, and my dad's younger brother, Hermann. Tante Ida was the baby of the family.

It had been some time since I had seen my aunt. My heart ached as I listened to her talk, the resemblance to my Pappa uncanny. The fact that her daughter,

Two of Pappa's sisters, Mariechen (seated) and Ida (standing) taken in front of the Schindler home. Grapevines grew on a trellis by the house. The blocking style was much like modern-day cement stucco.

Waltraud, worked as a housekeeper for the interpreter at the American consulate here in Berlin was one reason why Mutti had sent me on the train. She had hoped Waltraud might help me find gainful employment.

After a hearty dinner with my relatives, Tante Mariechen made a bed for me on the couch in the living room. "Sleep tight, Mickchen," she said, standing in the doorway. "We are glad you are here safely."

Lying in the dark, I wiped away hot, angry tears, no longer prevented from escaping the confines of my eyes. I swallowed a sob before it made a sound. I was trying to be brave for my Mutti, but it was so hard. I also wanted to be strong for Tante Mariechen and Onkel Hermann. In one month, I would be seventeen. Prior to the harrowing events of the year before, my parents and I

Pappa's sisters Mariechen Schindler (left) and Anna Schindler (right) on the paved road in front of the Schindler home in rural Radach, Germany. This is one of the few photos of the Schindler farm home and parameter fence. Bicycles were the family's main mode of transportation.

My aunt, Ida Schindler, with pigs on the family farm. Pork was a meat source, along with chicken. Girls wore aprons all the time, even to school.

had never been separated for any lengthy period. As my eyelids closed under the weight of exhaustion, my last thoughts were of Mutti and Horst.

* * *

Several days later, I accompanied my cousin to the American consulate, which was located just inside the Soviet sector of Berlin, about a twenty-minute walk from the apartment. Waltraud had made some inquiries on my behalf regarding employment. The woman for whom she worked had told her to bring me to an appointment at her office. Remembering Mutti's words, I had brought along the "*very* important document." I tucked the folded paper safely into the pocket of my coat. I gazed in amazement at all the damage evident around us as we made our way through a maze of sidewalks. Proof of the calling cards sent by both American and Russian bombers was all around.

The meeting with Waltraud's boss went very well. The lady was friendly, her grey eyes sparkling with warmth and kindness. After a few minutes of conversation, she asked Waltraud to take me to another office to begin the process of applying for a job. I dutifully followed my cousin into the hallway.

A line had formed outside the office to which she had directed us. Waltraud and I caught up with each other while waiting, the line inching forward every five minutes or so. Eventually, we found ourselves in front of a desk staffed by an American official, his suit crisply pressed. Although I had never seen an American before, this particular man exuded a calm, trustworthy air.

"Bitte dokumentieren," he said in German, but the accent was one with which I was unfamiliar. "Document, please."

Waltraud turned to me, smiling as she urged me to present the paper Mutti sent along. I pulled the folded piece of paper from my coat pocket and handed it to him across the desk.

The consulate official slowly unfolded the paper, careful to make sure he did not cause any more damage to its weathered surface. He read the words on the form and then appeared to reread them. For the longest time, he stared at the document. Then he looked up at me, a broad smile dawning upon his face.

"'My dear girl, you ARE an American citizen.'"[1] He seemed quite pleased with what he had just told me, although I could not understand a word of his English. He repeated the phrase in German.

Waltraud, who worked for the interpreter, looked at me and then at the official, quickly returning her incredulous gaze to me. "Do you understand what he just said to you?" she said to me in German.

"Nein, nicht ein wort." I replied. "No, not a word."

"Du bist ein Amerikaner!" My cousin slowly repeated the words that were to change my life, "You are an American!"

The American administrator seated at the desk turned around and called out loudly to a few people working on paperwork behind him. Suddenly, it seemed that they and many others in the office came running over to the desk where Waltraud and I stood. A heated exchange ensued as the helpful gentleman held my birth certificate high in the air like it was a winning lottery ticket. After a few more minutes of conversation between these consulate staff members, Waltraud and I were escorted to a private office and told to wait there. We whispered to each other until the door opened, and a smartly-dressed woman entered to take a seat behind the desk. Accompanying her was the consulate employee for whom Waltraud worked.

For the next thirty minutes or so, Waltraud's boss, the interpreter, helped translate questions that the woman asked.

"Are you *sure* this is your certificate?" the woman began.

"Ja," I replied. "Yes."

"Are you *sure* you didn't find it?" the woman asked next, pointing toward my birth certificate before her on the desk.

"Ja," I replied.

"Is it possible that this document belongs to a family member or perhaps a friend of yours?"

Waltraud repeated her question to me.

"Nein," I said.

"Have you got another type of identification paper?" the woman queried.

"Nein," I said, shaking my head for emphasis.

"Why do you want to go to America?" the woman asked.

I looked at Waltraud as the interpreter translated this next question. I was confused.

"Ich bin hergekommen, um arbeit zu finden. Ich dachte, dieses dokument könnte helfen," I replied. "I came here to find work. I thought this document might help."

My cousin conveyed to the nice lady across the desk that, before today, I was unaware that the document Mutti had pinned inside my bra before I took the train to Berlin was my birth certificate. She also explained that she had brought me here to meet her employer in the hopes of finding a job. Upon hearing this, the woman behind the desk picked up the phone and placed a call.

* * *

In the next few weeks, I spent many hours in interviews at the American consulate, ones very similar to the one just described. A staff person assigned to my case spoke both German and English. Her presence in these interviews was a tremendous help and a source of encouragement. I wanted to get back on the train and travel to Nienhagen to rejoin Mutti and Horst. It had been explained to me, however, that for my safety, I would need to remain here at Tante Mariechen's apartment, located in the American sector of Berlin.

I spent many additional hours waiting for admission to those interviews. While sitting on the bench in the third-floor hallway of the consulate, I pondered the peculiar status of my birth that had brought me to this place. It may seem strange to someone in this twenty-first century that my family could be ignorant of the significance of my birth certificate. It was a different time in 1946, and the world was not as cosmopolitan as it is today. Although my parents had never hidden the facts of my birth, specifically that I had arrived in this world on U.S. soil, it took the crucible of war to turn this legacy of my birth into a game-changer.

Tante Mariechen, Onkel Hermann, Waltraud, and Klaus had been very kind to me. My aunt and her family had come to visit us many times on the farm. Waltraud and Klaus came to stay with us every summer. All of them tried to make me as comfortable as possible. When I had arrived in early February, I had very few items of clothing in my small bag. I would soon need more. Waltraud was almost four years younger than me, so her clothes were not a good match. Tante Mariechen, though, had some old clothes which she gave to me. Others, I was able to purchase at a local thrift shop. The living room sofa had amply served as my pallet, although it meant my aunt and her family had to tiptoe into the kitchen if waking before I did.

It was evident that quarters were getting tight, and purchasing enough food for all of us was becoming an issue. Even though the war was over, supplies of food and other items were sometimes not easy to obtain. Something was going to have to change, though I could not have imagined how.

* * *

Consulate officials told me at one of my weekly meetings that I would be able to travel to the United States, once my identity was positively established.

"Aber ich will nicht gehen," I told the staff person, who had just interpreted this bit of information for me. "But I don't want to go."

"You've *got* to go," said another kind lady across the desk. "You're the only American citizen in your family. You can have your mother and brother come later to join you."

When asked if I had family members living in the United States, I replied, "Ja, die Schwester meines Vaters, ihr Ehemann, und Tochter. Sie leben in Great Bend, Kansas." (Yes, my father's sister, her husband, and daughter. They live in Great Bend, Kansas).

With the aid of the staff interpreter, I was able to fill out an information request form, which the consulate then mailed to Pappa's sister, Tante Anna Herb, who was living in Great Bend, Kansas, with her husband, Charlie, and daughter Margaret. She explained that this document, sent to my aunt, requested her to secure a certified copy of my birth certificate and mail it back to the American consulate in Berlin. It would possibly be two or three months before we heard anything.

I returned to Tante Mariechen's apartment to wait.

* * *

One day about nine weeks later, Waltraud returned from her housecleaning job at the American consulate interpreter's home. After hanging up her coat, she fished a note for me out of her pocket. I was still struggling to understand English and certainly could not read it. I asked her to tell me what the note said. She opened the envelope and unfolded the small piece of paper.

"Das Konsulat hat soeben die Kopie Ihrer Geburtsurkunde erhalten, die Tante Anna geschickt hat." As she read the note, a slight smile played across her face. "The consulate has just received the copy of your birth certificate that Tante Anna sent."

Finally, they'll believe me, I thought. Relief washed over me. "Anything else?" I asked her.

"Ja. Sie haben morgen früh um halb zehn Uhr einen Termin im Konsulat, um Ihren Fall zu besprechen," Waltraud replied. "Yes. You have an appointment at the consulate at nine-thirty tomorrow morning to discuss your case."

The next morning, I made my way from my aunt's and uncle's apartment to the American consulate. I climbed the stairs to the third floor, to the office where I had first met with the staff interpreter and the nice consulate lady almost three months before. Both of these helpful people were waiting for me. Their smiles immediately put me at ease, as they told me that I would indeed be able to travel to the United States, but it might take a while.

After our meeting was over, the staff interpreter accompanied me to a nearby Displaced Persons (DP) camp to fill out paperwork, which took about three hours to complete. Once I finished the paperwork, I went back to Tante Mariechen's home to wait.

A knock on Tante Mariechen's front door the next morning announced the arrival of a telegram which had been sent to me. I was wide-eyed, as my aunt read the words printed on it: I was to move to the DP camp to await my return to the United States. My time with Tante Mariechen and her family had come to an end, but how thankful I was for all the love, support, and assistance they had given me. There is no way I would have made it through all the many meetings at the consulate without Waltraud at my side.

* * *

I said my goodbyes to my extended Schindler family. Telegram in one hand and my little valise in the other, I began walking toward yet another temporary home.

I could only imagine what lay ahead.

CHAPTER FIFTEEN

My American Roots

As I passed through the front door of Tante Mariechen's apartment building, I felt like a salmon swimming upstream, waiting for a chance to step onto the sidewalk and into the steady flow of passersby. I quickly fell into the same pace as those around me. The only other choice was to get run over. The sound of my shoes, falling in measured strides against the sidewalk beneath them, formed a rhythmic pattern. It was not long before I was lost in thought, reaching back into the corners of my mind trying to remember precisely what Pappa and Mutti had told me about my American roots.

The assassination of Archduke Franz Ferdinand, heir to Austria-Hungary's throne, on Sunday, June 28, 1914, sparked a military conflict unlike any other the world had seen. On Tuesday, July 28, Serbia found herself facing a declaration of war issued by the Austro-Hungarian Empire in retaliation for the crime committed by a Serbian national. Allied nations of Belgium, France, Great Britain, Russia, and Serbia pitted themselves against the Central Powers of Germany and Austria-Hungary. World War I, also known as the Great War, raged across Europe for the next four years.[1] The United States entered the fight on Friday, April 6, 1917, when Congress signed a Declaration of War. The sinking of the *Lusitania*, a British passenger liner destroyed by a German submarine, prodded a sleepy America into action once they learned American citizens aboard also perished.[2]

My father, Fritz Robert Schindler, grew up in Radach, Germany, and was fifteen years old the summer the war began, too young to be conscripted. His father, Hermann Carl Gustow Schindler, was forty-seven and perhaps considered too near age forty-nine, the generally accepted upper limit for military service. My grandfather, Hermann, was also a farmer. As such, he was much more valuable to his country, producing food stores for the military and the German people.

World War I's fighting took place in two theatres: the Western Front and the Eastern Front. By the height of the war, some one-hundred countries had joined the fight. As time wore on, the Central Powers stretched their militaries and their treasuries much too thin. Some 80 percent of Germany's male population at the time was serving in the war.[3] My father would have been one of these soldiers had he been old enough. Approximately one out of every eight soldiers died in World War I, so there is a very high probability my father would not have survived the war.[4] By the fall of 1918, both of the Central Powers saw the handwriting on the wall. Austria-Hungary signed armistice papers on November 3; Germany did the same on November 11. The Great War was finally over.

Some seven months later, the Paris Peace Conference was held at Versailles, the opulent palace of France's King Louis XIV. The "Big Four" attended: Georges Clemenceau, the Prime Minister of France; David Lloyd George, Prime Minister of Great Britain; Vittorio Orlando, Prime Minister of Italy; and Woodrow Wilson, President of the United States of America. The carefully worded papers, signed at the meeting, came to be known collectively as the Treaty of Versailles.[5] Even as the ink began to dry after the treaty's signing on Saturday, June 28, 1919, a cloud of ignominy was settling over disgraced Germany. The former Weimar Republic had to accept full responsibility for the war, fully dismantle its military, and pay war reparations of 132 billion marks, roughly the equivalent of $269 billion.[6] The shame of being called to account in such an international forum created a depression in Germany, both economically and within the hearts of its people. Economic conditions in the country became quite dire in the years following the war.

Although I do not have letters written by my dad from this time, I have surmised that he must have decided to leave home and try to make his way elsewhere. America was the "shining city upon a hill" to which many from across the globe were flocking in the early 1920s. My father decided he would also throw his hat in the ring. The *Hansa*, the ship that carried my father from its port of embarkation in Hamburg, Germany, arrived in New York Harbor on Sunday, June 4, 1922. Pappa's passenger ID was 605085011129. One of 1,551 passengers, he was twenty-three years old.[7] Oh, how I would love to know what he thought when glimpsing the Statue of Liberty for the first time.

My Pappa, Fritz (seated far right), on the deck of the *Hansa* when coming to America in 1922

A photograph shows Fritz seated with a group of fellow passengers on the ship's deck. A handwritten note on the corner of the picture lists a "Karl Priefer and wife." These may have been new friends made while on the voyage to this brave, new world. The chain of the pocket watch, the same one later buried by my father beneath the brick floor of our basement toward the end of World War II, is visible in the photograph.

Fritz ended up in Hudson, Kansas. Again, I do not have any idea of how he got there. It was not uncommon for representatives of various companies to position themselves along the docks of New York Harbor, waiting for the ships bringing new immigrants to this land. Once processed through Ellis Island, these new arrivals would be eager to find employment. The representatives would then make contact, perhaps even arranging for food, temporary lodging, and transportation, if immigrants signed a work agreement. This explanation is one theory of how my father arrived in Kansas.

Recollections of my first cousin, Margaret, whose father, Charlie Herb, was the farmer for which my father worked upon his arrival in Kansas, form another theory. She remembers her parents telling her that Fritz came to the

United States with the Priefer family, who then went on to make their home in Albert, Kansas. Albert is a small town in Barton County, located thirty-nine miles northwest of Hudson, where Margaret's father was living. It may be that Fritz and Charlie met and became business associates, as they were both living in the same general area.

Hudson is a small town located in Stafford County, the county immediately south of Barton County. After making the acquaintance of Charlie Herb, a local bachelor farmer also of German heritage, Fritz and Charlie quickly established a strong friendship. Charlie needed a farm assistant upon whom he could depend. Fritz had farmed all his life and possessed a wealth of expertise and a strong work ethic. Fritz was also a bachelor. A young woman still living in Germany, Anna Gerlach, had caught his eye, but there were no immediate plans for the relationship to get any more serious. This new immigrant farmer would have the luxury of focusing all his attention on his new job.

Fritz was exceptionally skilled in the art of *thrashing* wheat, a means of using a horse-drawn piece of equipment to separate the wheat from the chaff. "The header barge was the wagon that transferred the loose, cut wheat to an area where it was piled up or stacked up. The header was pushed by the horses to cut the wheat. Sometimes an implement would also shock [to place stalks of wheat in vertical stacks] the wheat and make small bundles. All of this would be done when the

Thrashing Crew in Hudson, Kansas, in 1926

wheat still had some green and was not quite ripe. If it were dead ripe, precious kernels would have fallen out of the heads of wheat. Since thrashing machines were expensive, crews would go from farm to farm, thrashing the stacked wheat. There was probably one thrashing machine for every thirty farms."[8]

This central portion of Kansas had rich, dark soil and abundant rainfall. Situated in the middle of the Central Plains, this was America's heartland. Charlie's farm was quite a success, partly due to Fritz's efforts. The friendship between the two men continued to grow. Fritz, gregarious and out-going, quickly made friends with many others in the area.

Almost three years later, in the spring of 1925, Charlie would travel back to Germany, the country of his birth. While there and upon my Pappa's recommendation, Charlie met and fell in love with Anna, my dad's older sister. She returned to America with him, and they were married.

* * *

Fritz had established himself in America. Although he had many friends and was making quite a reputation for himself as a skilled farmer, he was lonely. He and my mother, Anna, must have written to each other since his arrival in the summer of 1922. None of those letters exist, so my imagination has had to fill in the blanks. Charlie's coming back home the summer of 1925, with a wife—Fritz's sister—on his arm, must have also been a contributing factor to Fritz's deciding that perhaps he, too, needed to make a proposal of his own.

My mother, Anna Elizabeth Gerlach, arrived in the United States aboard the ship *Deutschland* when it docked in New York City on Monday, November 1, 1926.[9] Fritz had been pacing for hours by the time the ship's debarkation process was finally allowed to begin. Now twenty-eight years old, Anna had arrived to start a new life, as had my father four years earlier. Fritz and Anna made their way to the Office of the City Clerk after they found each other amidst the crush of people teeming all around. In the municipal building in the borough of Manhattan, they were married by Mr. J. J. McCormick, Deputy City Clerk of the city of New York.

Mutti hunting in the snow

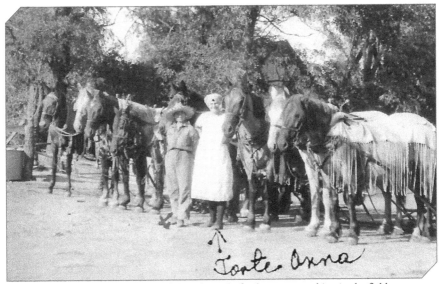

Tante Anna

My Mutti (left) and Tante Anna (right) at the end of a day spent working in the fields

Fritz and Anna Schindler (left) and Charlie and Anna Herb (right)

W. Zubrowsky and Gail Pavramo served as witnesses. What a wonderful "Welcome to America" present![10]

* * *

My parents, Fritz and Anna Schindler, lived with Charlie and Anna Herb for the next three years, building a good life for the two couples. Not only were they heart friends, but they were also family, as Charlie was now married to Fritz's older sister. Laughter and good-natured teasing were a part of the camaraderie among the four. The two Anna's developed a loving friendship that would last for the remainder of their lives.

Somewhere in the fall of 1928, Fritz and Anna received the happy news that a little one was on the way. The Schindler family was about to expand. At eight o'clock on the evening of Monday, March 11, 1929, I arrived in this world and was shortly afterward placed in the loving arms of my mother, Anna. My parents gave me the name Mildred Anna Schindler. My first name may have been a tribute to a Mildred Fischer, the wife of a farmer, who was friends with the Schindlers and also lived in Hudson. My mother may have liked the name and gave it to me as a tribute to the country of my birth. My middle name came from my mother. Although perhaps a little older than other first-time parents,

Mildred's infant baptism certificate

my father being twenty-nine and my mother thirty-one at the time of my birth, I can think of no better people with whom God could have blessed me.

I am still amazed at the wealth of documents, letters, and photographs related to my life that have survived. One of these treasures is a beautiful little booklet, "In Memory of Your Baptism." The Concordia Publishing House, a Lutheran company in St. Louis, Missouri, published the keepsake, written entirely in German. My baptism took place on Sunday, April 14, 1929. According to the memorial booklet, the baptism took place in Great Bend, although the name of the church is not listed. Charlie and Anna Herb, my paternal uncle and aunt, were noted as godparents.[11]

Sometime within the next few months after my birth, a letter from Germany arrived for my father. The message within conveyed the sad news that my paternal grandmother, Marie, had died and that my paternal grandfather, Hermann, needed my father to return home to Radach to run the family farm. The Schindler family had owned this land for almost three hundred years.

My father did not want to go. He loved our life here in Kansas. One of the local farmers had recently told Fritz that he wanted him to consider running his farm once the man retired. An offer to purchase land and a firmly established business did not come along every day. Fritz had a huge decision to make. My mother also was not very keen on the idea of returning to Germany. Many more modern conveniences were available here in the United States. Anna feared they would return to life under more primitive conditions. Laying aside his hopes and dreams, my father, ever the obedient son, decided to do as his father had asked and return home to run his family farm some five thousand miles away.

* * *

Friends and family threw a farewell party for my parents. A photograph from the party shows many of my father's friends, dressed in their best suits, standing in front of a row of well-maintained cars. The men looked prosperous and confidant. Fritz and Anna were giving up a great deal to return to a place they never thought they would live again. However, God had other plans.

As I consider the dire circumstances that developed in the United States over the weeks, months, and years following my family's return to Radach, it is evident that God used the move to shield us from both physical and financial ruin. The Great Depression began in October 1929, overnight wiping out fortunes, both big and small. The Dust Bowl destroyed the American plains' vast swaths, including the Stafford County, Kansas area, in the years between 1930 and 1936. The Smoot-Hawley Tariff Act, signed into law by President Herbert Hoover on

Pappa (center with Bible in hand) at a farewell gathering before returning to Germany in September 1929

June 17, 1930, raised taxes on many imported agricultural products. As a result, thousands of U.S. farmers lost their ability to make a living.[12] Meanwhile, we were half the world away, building a new life on the Schindler family farm.

* * *

The outstretched arm of a soldier suddenly appeared in front of me. "Miss," he said. "You can't go in until I see your papers."

Although I had no memory of the journey I had made across Berlin to the entrance of this DP camp, here I was. The thoughts of my parents and their American journey had served as a sort of magic carpet, now delivering me safely to my destination.

I opened my bag and retrieved my birth certificate and another identification document provided by the American consulate. I presented both to the soldier. Once he had surveilled them, he handed the papers back and stood aside. "Welcome," he said. He tipped his hat as I walked through the gate.

The idea that a simple piece of paper could make such a significant impact on my life was only beginning to soak in.

CHAPTER SIXTEEN

Displaced

As I sat on the cot in the wooden barrack, I felt as if I had passed through some portal and stepped into some strange, new world, like Dorothy must have felt when awakening in the land of Oz. It took a few hours to complete all the paperwork and the process as a new resident of this DP camp. A friendly officer had escorted me to the barracks where I would be staying. A low murmur of conversation buzzed throughout the room; information relayed in a variety of accents and languages. The only voices I wanted to hear were those of my Mutti, my Pappa, and my little brother, Horst. Mutti and Horst were far away, still living in the refugee house in Nienhagen. Only God knew where Pappa was or *if* he was still alive. Words of love and encouragement from them were only echoes now, reverberating within the sanctuary of my heart.

By the summer of my seventeenth year, I had not yet made the decision to follow Jesus Christ as my personal Lord and Savior. However, I was extremely mindful of the many ways He had protected not only me but also the members of my immediate family. The sovereignty of God is a theological concept that is still a mystery to me, the idea that God is in control of *all* the circumstances of my life, not only some. The loss of my father was still a tragedy with which I was struggling to cope, and yet, an unexplainable blanket of peace seemed to surround my soul. As I continued to get used to my new home away from home, I spent a great deal of time pondering the many circumstances of the past two years, many of which were not explainable as mere circumstance. God's fingerprints were beginning to make themselves more and more visible to me.

Many years later, I would learn about the United Nations Relief and Rehabilitation Administration (UNRRA). President Franklin Delano Roosevelt (FDR) hosted an international meeting at the White House on November 9, 1943, which was attended by representatives of forty-four nations.[1] One of the main topics discussed was ensuring the welfare, safety, and care of millions throughout Europe who had been and would continue to be dislocated by this dreadful war. As a result of those conversations, the UNRRA was established. The newly-formed organization's mission focused on providing "economic assistance to European nations after World War II and to repatriate and assist the refugees who would come under allied control."[2] By the fall of 1945, UNRRA was overseeing over two hundred camps in Germany alone, established to care for refugees and those displaced by the war. By the summer of 1947, the number of UNRRA camps across Western Europe had swelled to 762.[3]

Two words by which to describe civilians devastated by the war were given special significance at the meeting. A *refugee,* according to the new UNRRA definition, was an individual who was forced from his or her home country and was unable to return. A *displaced person* was one who, due to war, had been "uprooted" from his or her home. The expectation was that these same individuals would eventually return to their homeland.[4] A *displaced person* was the category into which I fell. Even though I had grown up in Germany and considered it my home, the confirmation of my American citizenship meant I was to return to *that* homeland, the United States of America.

A tiered system was established by which to repatriate the millions who had been dislocated from United Nations' member nations and now lived in UNRRA-run camps. Those receiving the highest priority were those who survived incarceration in Nazi concentration camps. Those helped next were those taken as prisoners of war. The third group were those categorized as displaced persons, due to being used as slave labor by an aggressor nation. This third level of the repatriation process affected me. The fourth tier of the UNRRA repatriation plan was to return Italians who had been displaced by the war to their homes. The fifth and final level of priority addressed the status of "nationals of former enemy states."[5] This lowest rung on the repatriation ladder would impact Mutti and Horst, who would not be allowed to travel to the United States until 1953.

Careful research into these UNRRA-run encampments has led me to the discovery of information about two sites in the Berlin area in 1946. The first of these was the Düppel Center DP Camp, which the U.S. Army established in January 1946. The majority of people in this camp would have been Jewish.[6]

The second Berlin-area center was the Mariendorf DP Camp, opening some six months after the Düppel Center in July of 1946 and located within Berlin's American Zone.[7] This second camp is where I may have stayed, as it would have been closer to Onkel Hermann's and Tante Mariechen's apartment. Its Eisenacher Strasse address sounds slightly familiar. This camp would have also been one which housed many Eastern European refugees. It has occurred to me that I might have been viewed as one of these since our Schindler family farm now lay within the national boundary of Poland. I will never know for sure.

* * *

Although memories of my thirteen-month tenure in the DP camp are vague, the experience must not have been entirely unpleasant. Seven years later, on the morning after my wedding, an article appeared in the local newspaper, detailing this war-time experience. I conveyed my sentiments to the reporter about my stay in the camp—"It was wonderful!"—and how delicious the wieners and sauerkraut were.[8]

Once more, God was making a way for me amid overwhelming circumstances. Although official documents declared me displaced, God knew where I was. My plight had not been kept hidden from Him for one second, nor did it alarm or surprise Him. I would somehow have to find the courage to trust Him, as only He knew what lay ahead.

His plans *had* to be better, as those of mine had long since failed, buried deep beneath the winter snow.

CHAPTER SEVENTEEN

Passage to America

T he United States had been fortunate to have not only one but two strong-willed, courageous presidents from 1939 until 1945, the years in which World War II raged across the world. Though not perfect, both of these presidents were perfectly suited to provide the leadership they offered to the United States during this time. America entered the war late in the game after the U.S. naval base at Pearl Harbor was viciously attacked early on December 7, 1941. But once she did, the United States fought with all her might to end the tyranny of two world despots—Adolph Hitler of Germany and Hideki Tojo of Japan.

When Germany's invasion of Poland in September 1939 ignited the firestorm of war, President Roosevelt was in the White House. He served four terms, the most by any American president. First elected to this highest national office in 1932, FDR then brought the country safely through the Great Depression and the years of economic hardship that followed. He also created the New Deal, which offered employment and buoyed the hopes of millions of Americans still struggling to get back on their feet after the long period of the Depression.[1]

Most Americans were unaware of the physical difficulties the president faced every day, complications caused by polio (also known as poliomyelitis or infantile paralysis), which he contracted in 1921 at age thirty-nine.[2] By the time the bombing of Pearl Harbor occurred, FDR had over twenty years of experience in facing extremely adverse circumstances head-on with courage and fortitude. The battle-testing he endured in his private life provided him with a reserve of inner strength on which to rely in this now very public forum of war. The president's persona was one of confidence and quiet strength.

As no other president had before, Roosevelt made himself personal and accessible through the medium of radio as he spoke to millions of Americans in what came to be known as his "Fireside Chats." From March 1933 until the evening broadcasts ended in June 1944, the nation's families gathered in homes large and small, opulent and shabby, owned and rented, to hear a personal word from their president.[3]

Many organizations created during FDR's administrations remain part of the fabric of American life to this day. Some of these include the Securities and Exchange Commission, the Federal Communications Commission, the Tennessee Valley Authority, the Social Security Administration, the U.S. Housing Authority, and the United Service Organizations (USO). Roosevelt was one of the "Big Three," a triumvirate of world leaders rounded out by Prime Minister Winston Churchill of Great Britain and Premier Joseph Stalin of the Soviet Union. He was also a strategic decision-maker at the Tehran and Yalta conferences, two of three international summits that would make decisions for how millions throughout Europe would be cared for, those who had been terrorized and uprooted by the war.[4]

During a short retreat to his "Little White House" in Warm Springs, Georgia, as he sat for a portrait painted of him, a cerebral hemorrhage struck the president on the afternoon of Thursday, April 12, 1945, and was lost to the world forever.[5] His Vice President, Harry S. Truman, was sworn into office as the thirty-third President of the United States later that same afternoon. Thrust without warning onto the world stage, no-nonsense, straight-talking Truman now had to lead America through what he hoped would soon be the end of this terrible second world war.

A little over three weeks after he took office, the new U.S. president would accept the surrender of Germany on May 7, 1945. Two months later, he would join Churchill (and also Clement Attlee after Churchill's election loss) and Stalin as a member of the "Big Three" at the Potsdam Conference in July 1945 to make further decisions about Europe's fate.[6]

Again, millions like me, either refugees or displaced persons, would be directly affected by Truman's decisions. While at Potsdam, he received word of the success of a scientific test, conducted on Monday, July 16, at Alamogordo, New Mexico.[7] The president's decision to use this newly-developed nuclear technology would lead to Japan's unconditional surrender. The war was finally over. Or was it?

* * *

World War II dragged millions of people in its wake, like bubbles of foam bobbing aimlessly in the sea. Mutti, Horst, and I were three of them. The three of us probably exchanged letters during this period when I lived in the DP camp in Berlin, but those posts are long gone. Mutti and Horst were getting on as best they could in Nienhagen; I was holding on to hope in Berlin. Little did I know I would soon head "home."

America's new President was committed to making sure many of those uprooted by war, especially those in possession of an American visa, would be brought to the United States. Three days before Christmas on Saturday, December 22, 1945, President Truman signed a document, which has since come to be known as the Truman Directive. The words below are from that mandate:

> The WAR has brought in its wake an appalling dislocation of populations in Europe. Many humanitarian organizations, including the United Nations Relief and Rehabilitation Administration, are doing their utmost to solve the multitude of problems arising in connection with this dislocation of hundreds of thousands of persons. . . . The immensity of the problem of displaced persons and refugees is almost beyond comprehension. . . .

> Of the displaced persons and refugees whose entrance into the United States we will permit under this plan, it is hoped that the majority will be orphaned children. . . . Moreover, many of the immigrants will have close family ties in the United States and will receive the assistance of their relatives until they are in a position to provide for themselves.

> These relatives or organizations will also advance the necessary visa fees and travel fare. Where the necessary funds for travel fare and visa fees have not been advanced by a welfare organization or relative, the individual applicant must meet these costs. In this way the transportation of these immigrants across the Atlantic will not cost the American taxpayers a single dollar. . . .

The decision has been made, therefore, to concentrate our immediate efforts in the American zones of occupation in Europe. . . .

This is the opportunity for America to set an example for the rest of the world in cooperation towards alleviating human misery.[8]

One year later, on Thursday, December 19, 1946, President Truman publicly announced his decision to designate four U.S. ships—the *Ernie Pyle*, the *Marine Marlin*, the *Marine Flasher*, and the *Marine Falcon*—to facilitate the transfer of displaced persons from Germany to the United States.[9] In the years between late 1945 and 1947, these four ships would bring some 22,950 persons to America. I was one of 7,650 Gentiles, within this larger group, lent a hand by the president; the remaining 15,300 DPs were Jewish.[10] Truman's commitment to ending the suffering for those he could was made evident through this plan.[11]

According to the Truman Directive, the cost of transporting the affected displaced persons was to be incurred by either their relatives living in the United States or by welfare agencies. I owe a tremendous debt of gratitude to Travelers Aid International, which funded my passage to America. Founded in 1851 by a philanthropist as the Travelers Aid Society, the company's primary goal was to assist those traveling internationally, particularly unaccompanied women and girls.[12] By the time the war had come to an end, the focus of Travelers Aid's provision of humanitarian assistance had shifted to "displaced persons and refugees."[13] How thankful I will always be for their help.

* * *

I had spent almost an entire year living by myself, a seventeen-year-old girl amid several thousand others in the same awful situation. As I have shared before, one of the delays in my return to the United States was the time it took for my Tante Anna to send back a copy of my American birth certificate. Another postponement, although I will never know for how long, was caused by a bituminous coal strike in the United States, affecting transatlantic travel. Due to disagreements concerning wages and benefits, the United Mine Workers of America (UMWA), one of the country's largest labor unions, called for a strike of its members on April 1, 1946.[14] The Krug-Lewis Agreement was signed not quite two months later on May 29 by President Truman and UMWA officials to resolve the argument.[15] Even though the parties reached a supposed compromise, it would be almost the end of that same year before coal mining industry workers returned to business as usual. Two casualties of this stand-off were transatlantic travel and shipping.[16]

It is funny how little details of life events are sometimes filed incorrectly within the confines of our minds. In at least four Kansas newspaper articles about me, written between the years 1948 and 2001, I described the ship that brought me to the United States as having been a former German troop transport named the SS *Lili Marlin*. These articles record that the voyage began from the German port city of Bremen on January 8, 1947. A careful search of records at Ellis Island has led me to the discovery that the actual name of the ship, which carried me to the United States, was the SS *Marine Marlin*. The ship's official passenger manifest clarified the facts of my passage, which brought my hazy recollections into focus. The vessel left Bremen on Friday, January 10, and arrived two weeks later to the day on Friday, January 24. My passenger identification number was 9011868265906, and my passport number was 572. My destination was 1300 Baker, Great Bend, Kansas, the home of my paternal aunt and her husband, Anna and Charlie Herb.[17]

* * *

The day after Christmas, December 26, 1946, I and many other camp residents clambered up into the beds of enormous transport trucks. We were driven by U.S. Army personnel to another camp, probably located in Germany's British Zone, placing us closer to the port of Bremen from which we would eventually board our U.S.-bound ship. Although the DP camp in which we had been living was located within the American sector of Berlin, the remainder of this eastern part of Germany was in the Russian Zone. Russia still relished exercising its diabolical power over those unfortunate enough to be living within the occupation zone, even though the war had ended some fifteen months before. Our party had a considerable distance to travel before we were safely out of this part of Germany. Armed military police accompanied our convoy so that none of the females in our group could be pulled from the trucks and sent to work camps in Russia, as had the group of thirty young women a year before in Nienhagen. I would stay in this second camp near Bremen about three more weeks until I would leave the Germany of my youth.

A day or so before our ship's departure, our group rode by train to Bremen. The weather was cold and damp. I was traveling together with a large group of girls booked for passage on the ship. I had a small American flag I wore on the lapel of my coat. Several of the girls in our group were Jewish. Their facial expressions and lack of conversation led me to believe they were not too keen on me. I tried my best to be pleasant and friendly, remembering it was a hard place for *all* of us to be.

My voyage to America was about to begin. By the time I began the boarding process, I would already be in two American presidents' debt. The first, Franklin Delano Roosevelt, died before I even made it to the land of my birth. UNRRA, created due to his efforts almost three-and-a-half years earlier, was partly responsible for my care since my arrival at a DP camp in the spring of 1946. The second, Harry S. Truman, had, with the stroke of a pen, secured my place on a ship that would carry me homeward, back to the United States of America where I was born.

Departure day finally arrived—January 10, 1947. The gangplank of the SS *Marine Marlin* stretched out before me like a stairway to heaven. There was so much activity on the dock that morning—huge crates of cargo to be stored, almost nine hundred displaced persons trying to board and get settled in their quarters, the ship's crew occupying their assigned stations, the cooks preparing our first meals in the galley. Once on board, we were shown to our rooms. Cabin 13 was a large sleeping area where I would stay with twenty to thirty other girls and women. The bunks were three rows high, their bulky frames commanding the attention of most of the room. The first thing I noticed when we came into the cabin was that a life jacket lay on top of each bunk. That image was kind of scary.

We received outstanding service on the boat. There was plenty of food, and it was delicious. We also got lots of fruit. I especially enjoyed bananas, as we did not have them growing up in Radach. A meal ticket was provided to every passenger. I was amazed at the amount of food and the variety offered to us at each meal.

The trip was frightening. I had never seen the ocean before. We initially had been told that the trip would take only ten days, but it took two weeks. One day I went up on deck for fresh air, but that was a mistake. There were no trees. No birds. No land. I was very lonely. It was hard to wrap my head around the enormous expanse of water stretching out before me with no end in sight, day after day. As there were only water and large chunks of ice to see, I rarely ventured out on deck again.

The passage was incredibly bumpy due to lots of wind. Many of the girls got seasick, but I never did. Because some were too sick to eat, they were kind enough to share their meal tickets with me.[18] On those days, I went through the food line several times.

As grateful as I was for the extra food, there was just so much of it I could eat. I prayed for smoother seas and an end to this voyage.

* * *

We received notification the night before we arrived that we would be in New York City the next morning. The skies above were a bright blue the morning of Friday, January 24, 1947. A brisk, cold breeze blew steadily across the harbor. As the SS *Marine Marlin* drew closer, an enormous statue, which further out in the harbor had looked like a child's toy, now towered above us as we passed by, a gigantic green lady draped in folds of fabric holding in her hand a lighted torch lifted heavenward. Someone nearby whispered in German that this was the Statue of Liberty. I was about to enter "the golden door" closed to many at this time due to strict immigration quotas following the war, but now swinging open widely for me, due to my carefully-saved American birth certificate and the foresight of the country's current president.

A current of nervous excitement surged through the *Marine Marlin's* passengers as we stood on the crowded deck, jostling for places at the rail. The massive ship slowed, then shuddered as the engines were placed in reverse, allowing the gigantic vessel to come alongside the dock. Giant ropes, as large as a man's thigh was round, secured the ship to the pier. Many different languages could be heard all around me. I spoke but only a few words of English. Before we boarded in Bremen, a representative of the American Consulate had taught me to say, "Displaced Person from Germany."

Tears stung my eyes as I wished Mutti and Horst were here with me. The view before me certainly did not look like home.

Once down the gangplank, my feet stepped onto American soil. Although I did not feel any different, I would soon find out what an enormously positive difference my citizenship would make.

PART IV

Awakening from the Nightmare

"Do you who live in America really appreciate your freedom?
You are the most blessed and fortunate people on earth.
You may not realize that, but I do,
since only a short time ago I still lived in Europe.
My coming to America was like an
awakening out of a terrible nightmare!"[1]

—Mildred Schindler

CHAPTER EIGHTEEN

Train Ride to Kansas

Thousands of people teemed all around me, but the spot where I stood all alone on this New York City dock seemed like a harbor from a storm. Suddenly, a tug on the sleeve of my coat let me know I was not alone. An interpreter, who had traveled with us on the *Marine Marlin* had found me. She was pointing to a couple standing off in the distance, who held a large sign with "Mildred Schindler" on it and were also waving their arms. These were the Knappes, friends whom Tante Anna and Onkel Charlie had made over twenty years earlier. I would stay in their home for the next two days.

There was a lot to be done on my first day in America, as the train carrying me to Kansas and Tante Anna, Onkel Charlie, and my cousin Margaret, left in only two days. The Knappes walked me to the offices of a welfare organization, where the final arrangements for my trip were made. I spent a large part of the remainder of that day with a lady from the agency.[1]

What follows is some of what I shared later of my memories of that first day in a first-person account: "'On my first day in America—New York City, to be exact—I didn't believe that you could go into a store and buy things without ration cards. A lady of the Welfare Society helped me to buy a pair of shoes. My, I was proud of them! But my eyes caught sight of all kinds of fruit behind the store windows. I was so excited! This was like heaven! I bought bananas and apples and oranges until I had my fill.'"[2]

The Knappes were very kind. Their apartment was welcoming and warm. I even had a room of my own. Before I knew it, the day of my train trip arrived.

After dressing and enjoying a hearty breakfast, Mr. and Mrs. Knappe walked me to the train station. On our way, we stopped by a corner market, where the friendly couple told me to choose any food items I would like to take with me on my trip to Great Bend. I selected oranges, bananas, nuts, and Hershey's chocolate candy bars. As I had done so many times in recent years, I was about to say yet another good-bye.

Tucked carefully away inside the small suitcase I carried with me were a few items of clothing I had received in the DP camp and several letters from my Tante Anna. Written during the time I lived alone in the center, they detailed the arrangements for me to live with her and my Onkel Charlie in America, the land of my birth. One of the letters contained a picture of my aunt and uncle. Tante Anna said it would help me find them when I got to the train station in Kansas.

The Knappes' bright smiles and waving hands soon disappeared as the train left the station. It was not long before the high-rise buildings of America's largest city gave way to small towns built near the rail line and finally to vast, open pastures of farmland. I watched the scenery whiz past me. *What will I find in Great Bend? Will Tante Anna, Onkel Charlie, and Margaret like me?* Years later, I would learn that the route we followed took us from New York to Chicago and then southwesterly to Great Bend, Kansas.

Just as the passage across the Atlantic had been scary, so was this train trip. Very scary. I knew almost no English. I stayed put in my seat by the window, leaving it only to excuse myself. The gentle rocking rhythm of the train lulled me to sleep that first night, my food bundle serving as my pillow as I dozed against the cold windowpane. My little suitcase was tucked securely underneath my seat. The same interpreter who had helped me locate Mr. and Mrs. Knappe on the pier had also told me what to expect on the train trip. She had said the conductor would come by each morning and take me to breakfast.

Sure enough, on that second morning of my journey to Kansas, I looked up to find the conductor standing in the aisle beside my seat. He said the word *eat* and pointed to his mouth.

I shook my head, "No." Reaching into my coat pockets, I pulled out two bananas and a partially-eaten Hershey bar.

Reaching across the passenger seated next to me, he gently took my hand and pulled me up to a standing position. He then helped me into the aisle and led me to the dining car, my hand still inside his. I stood there, once we were inside this restaurant section of the train. There were people seated on both sides of the dining car, enjoying their breakfasts. A narrow middle aisle separated the tables. The low-level buzz of conversation filled the air. I looked back at the conductor, questions flying through my mind, but he was gone. I thought, *Now, what do I do?*

An empty table was spotted a little further down the aisle. I made my way to it and sat down. The menu atop could have been a jigsaw puzzle, as it looked the same upside-down or right-side-up. The only way I could determine the top of the menu was by the illustrations of food that accompanied some of the meal descriptions. My anxiety was growing by the minute. *How to make sense of this?* I thought.

Just then, I remembered Pappa and Mutti would sometimes speak English when they did not want us kids to know what they were saying. My mother might say to me, "Go get the . . ." in German and finish the sentence, ". . . eggs," in English. Over time, I came to recognize the English word, *eggs*. I spotted a picture of two fried eggs on the menu.

When the waiter came to take my order, I pointed to the words printed next to the picture. While I waited for my breakfast, I wondered if the eggs would be poached, boiled, or scrambled. How surprised I was when the waiter arrived, minutes later, with a tray containing a huge plate heaped with food and a tall glass of orange juice. After placing my order on the table before me, the waiter said something I could not understand, tipped his hat, and was gone. On the plate lay two large fried eggs and several slices of bread toasted a golden brown and slathered with butter. A small container of what appeared to be strawberry jam sat beside the toast on the plate. I took my time, savoring every delicious bite.

By the time I finished my breakfast, I had added one more word to my meager English vocabulary—"fried." That, however, was the last time I went to the dining car. For the rest of the trip, I ate the fruit, nuts, and candy bars the Knappes had purchased for me.

Lost in thoughts of Mutti and Horst, I hardly saw bare-limbed trees and fallow wheat fields flying past my window. *What were they doing right now? Were they worried about me? Had any word of my departure from Bremen been sent to them? How soon could they come and join me?* It had now been almost one year since I had seen my mother and little brother. *When, oh, when, would we be together again?*

The squeal of the train's braking system brought me out of my contemplation as we slowed down to enter the station. Peering through the window, I could see the words, "Great Bend," neatly lettered across the front of the depot. A bubble of nervous anticipation floated in my stomach.

Like Dorothy in the Land of the Munchkins, I was in a strange, new world. Could I finally be home?

CHAPTER NINETEEN

Onkel Charlie and Tante Anna

I stepped onto the station platform from the train car in which I traveled the past two days. Very few passengers got off the train with me. Although I had spent several minutes in the bathroom trying to calm the mess that was my hair, I am afraid my clothes were still rumpled, wrinkles bearing mute witness to the change of clothing I did not possess. While looking at the people milling around me, my left hand made its way into my coat pocket, as I had neither Mutti's nor Horst's hand to hold. Over the past eighteen days, while on this long journey of 5,327 miles, this warm, little burrow had become my hand's retreat. Grabbing the inside lining of my pocket had also become an unconscious response to fear and uncertainty. *I was here safely, wasn't I?* I thought. *Something was working in my favor.*

Suddenly, my attention was drawn to a kind-looking couple making their way through the crowd toward me. I could see the man's face first, and recognized it from the picture packed away in my valise. He was my Onkel, Charlie Herb. A handsome, broad-shouldered man, he had brown, wavy hair and sparkling blue eyes. Standing a little taller beside him was my Tante Anna, a woman who had not seen me since soon after my birth, although I had no memory of her. However, Anna had become very real to me as she was responsible for corroborating the authenticity of my birth certificate eighteen months earlier when I first arrived at the home of her sister, Tante Mariechen. Tears threatened to spill from my eyes as Anna's close resemblance to my Pappa, her younger brother, became evident.

Each of them stepped forward, one at a time, and wrapped me in a warm embrace. I clung to each as if to a life preserver. I gave up the pretense of courage and let the tears flow, having tried so hard to be brave for so long. *Finally*, I was once again with members of the Schindler family.

Standing slightly behind my aunt and uncle was a tall, slender girl who waited patiently, gazing quietly at me with soft, blue eyes. Dark, brown hair framed her pretty face. She was my cousin, Margaret. Charlie and Anna's only child smiled shyly and extended her hand. I placed my hand in hers. Her grip was firm and warm. Although neither of us could presently speak a word of the other's language, I immediately knew I had just made a new friend.

As we left the train station and headed toward the car, Tante Anna held my hand. Every few minutes or so, she would give my hand a gentle squeeze. "Oh, Mildred," she said, speaking to me in German. "We were so afraid you wouldn't come. The information we received from the U.S. Consulate's office told us you

In the front yard of the Herb's house

were to arrive in November. When you didn't come, we were sick with worry." Another squeeze.

"Yesterday was my birthday," Tante Anna continued. "Your presence with us is the best gift ever. We are thrilled that you're here!" she said, blinking back tears of joy.

"Ja, Tante Anna," I said. "Me, too!"

* * *

Charles Fredrick Herb had been born on May 13, 1884, in Untersohlertbach, Nürnberg, Germany. His family immigrated to the United States in 1889, although little information exists about this period.[1] Charlie's father became a naturalized U.S. citizen on May 3, 1898, in the District Court of Kansas; Charlie became the same in 1925.[2] My uncle spent part of his younger adult years working in the steel industry as a sheet ironworker in Philadelphia, Pennsylvania. Census records place him there in 1910 at the age of twenty-six.[3]

World War I commanded most of the world's attention and took the lives of over nine million of the finest men from a host of countries, an entire generation lost between 1914 and 1918. America would be involved for only a little over nineteen months, by the time she entered the fight in April 1917. Before our entrance into the war, there was not a required draft. President Woodrow Wilson signed into law the Selective Service Act on Friday, May 18, 1917, which would begin the process of enlisting and training American men to join in Allied engagements—as a result, three separate enlistment periods opened between May 1917 and November 1918.[4]

The first of these, held on Tuesday, June 5, 1917, required registration for all American males ages twenty-one to thirty-one. Charlie was thirty-three in 1917. The second of these was held one year later on Wednesday, June 5, 1918, for those who had reached the age of twenty-one after the first enlistment date—June 5, 1917. Charlie had just turned thirty-four the summer of 1918. The third and final enlistment registration occurred on Thursday, September 12, 1918. It was on this date that Charlie signed his name on the dotted line.[5] This date was just three months after the second enlistment sign-up, meaning Charlie was still too old to serve. In less than two months, the signing of the armistice on November 11, 1918, ended the Great War. It is unclear whether Charlie went on to complete basic training and serve in some capacity with the U.S. Army. Although not native-born, Charlie dearly loved the country of his choice.

By 1920, Charlie had moved to Kansas, where he would live out the remainder of his life.

It was around the time of his military enlistment that Charlie had also taken up farming. Fertile soil and land as far as the eye could see, coupled with Charlie's hard work ethic, made the perfect combination. Records from the 1920 U.S. Census of Stafford County, Kansas, list him as literate, the employer rather than a hired worker of his farm, and renting rather than owning his home.[6] My father, Fritz Schindler, would have met Charlie in 1922 when he came to Kansas to find adventure. The two soon became fast friends.

Almost three years later, in the spring of 1925, Charlie decided to travel to Germany to search for his family roots. Fritz suggested his friend travel to Radach to meet his parents, Hermann and Marie, and his siblings: Ida, Marie, Anna, and Hermann. Fritz thought perhaps one of his two younger sisters, Ida or Marie, who were still living at home, might catch Charlie's eye. While on the trip, Charlie's attention, however, was captured by Fritz's older sister, Anna. Recently widowed, she had returned to live with her parents after her husband died after being electrocuted in a work accident. Fritz's younger sisters giggled a lot, thinking Charlie's German-American dialect was amusing. Anna, on the other hand, was quiet and thoughtful. An immediate attraction formed between the two.

A note written by Charlie has survived this trip.[7] Here is what I was able to translate from it.

The one who signed below has during his visit in Germany applied for a marriage license at the Civil Court in Radach, Kreis West Sternberg, to the widowed Anna Schröter [Schröeter], born . . . (I was not able to translate this part. Was listing the place of Anna's birth)."

He [Charlie Herb] asks for a document stating that nothing stands in the way of this marriage.

"I was born on the 13th of May 1884 in Untersohlertbach Nürnberg. I am a citizen of the United States, living in Great Bend, Kansas.

At this time, I am in Radach, Kreis West Sternberg. Due to [my] departure, I am asking to send the document right away.

Cash [for the document] is enclosed.

Onkel Charlie's request for the marriage license to marry Tante Anna

The *Albert Ballin* moved out slowly into deeper water after leaving the German port of Hamburg on Friday, May 22, 1925. Onboard were Charlie Herb and his fiancé, Anna Schindler Schröeter.[8] Anna's brother, Fritz, had set out on his adventure from this same port three years earlier. Charlie was now forty-one, and this return trip to his forefathers' country had proved to be exceptionally fortunate. Anna was thirteen years' Charlie's junior. Ship records indicate her visa was #45331 and that she had never before been to the United States. She had seventy-five dollars on her person and did *not* intend to return to Germany. Just as Pappa and Mutti had done, Onkel Charlie and Tante Anna were married in a New York City clerk's office shortly after disembarking.[9]

Learning a new language was Anna's primary adjustment after she arrived in America. What a godsend that Charlie, just as she did, spoke German. It would be talking only to those Anna might encounter at the market or in the church that presented an immediate challenge. Charlie, however, was a patient teacher, as were new friends Anna made. Before long, she was speaking English, accompanied by an endearing German accent.

As both Charlie and Anna were a bit older when married, they entered the world of parenting a little later than most. Adoption was the miracle by which they became parents following Margaret's birth on Saturday, November 7, 1931.

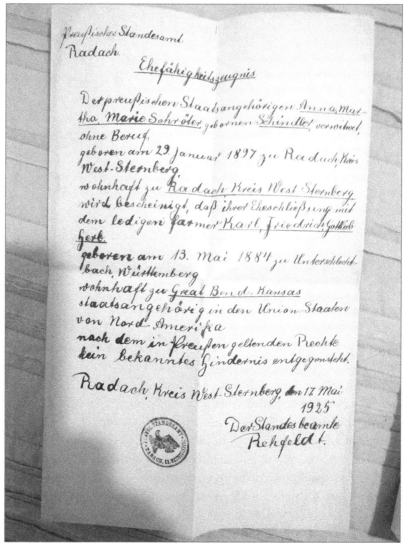

The marriage license of Charlie and Anna Herb (photo by Carol Wilkens Silvernail)

She was the apple of their eye and quickly stole their hearts. Margaret and I, through the years, have become and still are *very* dear friends. She is my family.

* * *

Theirs was the loving home into which I had come to live that January of 1947. From the minute I arrived, Onkel Charlie and Tante Anna treated me as one of their own. It was a welcome relief to know that both my aunt and uncle spoke German. As badly as I knew I needed to learn the language, the combined emotional weight of all I had been through in the past two years left me little mental energy to spare, at least not in those first few weeks after arriving in Great Bend. Decoding English vocabulary was not at the top of my "to do" list.

Margaret was so sweet to share her room with me. She giggled and pulled me through the doorway. She led me around the room to show me how she had cleared space from several drawers in her chest. Hanging clothes had also been moved over in the closet. My pitiful little valise, which had been my companion from Germany, certainly did not contain enough clothes to crimp Margaret's space. As we lay down in her bed that first night, I wanted so badly to let her know how much I appreciated all she was doing for me. The only English phrases I knew, however, were "fried eggs" and "Displaced Person from Germany." Neither of those would suffice.

"Good night, Margaret," I whispered in German, "and thank you very much." I was not quite sure she understood.

"Bitte," came the reply. Margaret's perfect pronunciation of the German term for "You're welcome" warmed my heart. "Gute Nacht."

The bright moonlight streamed through the lacy curtains at Margaret's bedroom window, allowing me to study the various furniture pieces around the room. I was safe and once again with people who loved me, although I did not know them very well. Safety and love would provide a good start. The four of us had the rest of our lives to get to know one another. I turned over and drifted off to peaceful sleep.

* * *

Margaret was a junior at Great Bend High School. After she left for school each morning, Tante Anna would let me know how I might be of help to her. Sometimes it was performing household chores, like folding clean laundry once we took it off the line. Other times, she would give me a cooking lesson in the kitchen, teasing me with a wooden spoon dipped in some delicious-smelling sauce.

Another thing we would do, while Margaret was at school, was to spend hours talking about the life I had shared in Radach with Pappa, Mutti, and Horst. My aunt was hungry for news of her brother, Fritz. My dad and his sister had exchanged letters in the years since 1929. Mutti, however, wrote the majority of the letters, as Pappa would have been too busy. She was able to provide details my dad may not have shared with his sister. Tante Anna let me read a few of those letters. My heart hurt to see my parents' familiar script scrawled across the page, and yet, their words brought them close to me. There were several times we sat and cried together; me for a father, Tante Anna, for a brother. Somehow, it made the burden less heavy to carry as we shared the weight of our grief.

Many days, I helped Onkel Charlie. Much of his farm equipment was mechanized, and the methods of farming much different than the ones we used, as we had performed most of our farm work by hand in Radach. Onkel Charlie grew wheat and raised cattle, pigs, and chickens. A farm girl, born and bred, I quickly found my way around his farm. It would be hard to keep a good girl down.

Before I arrived, Margaret had plenty of time to think about how we were going to get along. One of the ways she found to build a bridge between us was taking me out for a drive several times a week in the family car. The Herbs had an old grey '38 Ford. It was an enormous car with a huge trunk. Although Margaret was embarrassed because no one else's family had a car that old, the Ford still drove and got us where we needed to go. Some days we would run errands for Tante Anna. Other days we would hang out together eating ice cream cones at the drugstore. When we were feeling especially adventurous, Margaret would steer the grey ghost downtown, where we would drag Great Bend's Main Street. Laughter and smiles made up the difference on days when words were hard to find. Some years later, Margaret told me she could tell how happy I was to be in the United States. It was written all over my face.

* * *

Looking back now, I am still amazed at the kindness Margaret extended to me when I first arrived at their house at 1300 Baker in Great Bend. She worked so hard to make sure I had any and everything I needed. Her sweet, unselfish nature ministered to me. Across the years, Margaret has become more like the sister I never had. Laughter and smiles were the first bonds we forged. They remain so to this day.

Onkel Charlie, Tante Anna, and Margaret hold a special place in my heart. My Onkel Charlie taught me so much about honesty and hard work, fairness, and integrity. He loved me unconditionally and always made me feel special like there was no one else in the world like me. He filled that void in my life left vacant when the Russians took Pappa. All in our family, not just me, owe an enormous debt of gratitude to Tante Anna because she preserved any family photographs we have of the almost seventeen years we lived in Radach. Mutti must have taken pictures quite regularly of our family. As soon as she did, she would send a collection of them to Tante Anna.

Enjoying picked
cherries

Pitching hay on Onkel Charlie's farm

Any family records or photos still in our home in Radach would have been destroyed soon after the Red Army soldiers forced us from it. When told you only have two hours to leave your home, you do not grab a picture book or scoop up stacks of photos. Because of Tante Anna, those years of our lives live on through the photographs she so lovingly saved.

* * *

The days turned into weeks and soon melted into months. The calendar said May. *How can that be?* I thought. Margaret's junior year was almost over. She would entertain us, as we sat around the dinner table at night, with stories of what had happened during her school day. Even though I could not speak much English, the fact that I had been living with English speakers had helped increase my comprehension of the language. Sometimes Onkel Charlie would leave the newspaper on the table after breakfast. I would pick it up and find the comics section. The illustrations were entertaining and helped guide me as I picked out a word here and there to learn. However, I quickly discarded this as a way to learn English.

Margaret did not speak much German; Onkel Charlie and Tante Anna spoke it fluently. Not having to worry about what I said or wondering if the person to whom I was talking could understand me was appreciated when I first arrived in Great Bend. But, over time, I began to realize I was not doing myself any favors by hiding behind my German language. Sooner than later, I was going to need to learn English. I also had a financial debt to repay for the remaining balance of my passage to America. A job would also help me in that regard.

One day I worked up the courage to talk to Tante Anna about helping me find a job where I did not necessarily have to speak to do the work, but could still have an opportunity to learn English. She promised she would keep her ears open. A few days later, she handed me a notice from the local newspaper, the *Great Bend Tribune*. Circled on the folded piece of newsprint was an advertisement for a job opening in the diet kitchen at St. Rose Hospital, a local Catholic-run medical center.

Later that same day, Tante Anna and I drove to the hospital. I waited in the car while she went inside to pick up an employment application. Once back at her house, my aunt helped me fill it out. Taking another piece of paper, she would write down the English words that were needed to answer the question, and then I would copy them into the appropriate space. I was exhausted after that little exercise. She returned the application to the hospital the next day, and we began the waiting process.

One week later, the phone rang in Tante Anna's kitchen. I was working at the counter, cutting up fruit for the jam we were making. After a few, "Uh, huh's" and several more, "I see's," my aunt said, "Thank you very much. I'll be sure and tell her."

Hanging up the receiver and turning to me, her smile as bright as a shiny new penny, she said, "Mildred, you've got the job!" Tante Anna then explained I was expected at work at St. Rose Hospital the following Monday.

My English language lessons were about to start in earnest.

CHAPTER TWENTY

Peeling Grapefruit

Tante Anna woke Margaret and me early. Today was one of Margaret's last days of the school year. My new job at St. Rose Catholic Hospital would also begin today, and I could not be late. A mouth-watering breakfast awaited us in the kitchen. We chatted about the day ahead between bites of homemade buttered biscuits and scrambled eggs and sips of piping hot coffee. Soon it was time to dress. Now eighteen years old, I was feeling grown-up. Not having yet received my uniform, I had chosen to wear a plain white blouse tucked into a simple, black skirt. I hoped it would be acceptable.

Although my English had improved somewhat, I was not ready to engage in a lengthy conversation of any sort. Tante Anna agreed to accompany me to the orientation. We dropped Margaret off at school on our way to the hospital. A document from the hospital had arrived in this past Saturday's mail, which Tante Anna said I needed to take with me when I came for work. As my aunt and I walked through the front door of St. Rose, I crossed yet another threshold into a brave, new world. At the front desk, I presented the piece of paper to the receptionist, who then made a phone call and motioned for us to take a seat in the lobby waiting area.

As Tante Anna and I sat there, a series of black and white photographs of the hospital caught my eye. St. Rose Hospital was established initially by seven Dominican sisters, who arrived in the fall of 1902, at the request of several Great Bend physicians. The lack of a competent surgical facility in the town had prompted the doctors to action. Interestingly enough, not one of these sisters had training as a nurse. The last of these nuns, Sister Loretta Feinler, who was both a pharmacist and a registered nurse, would arrive six months later, bringing the medical credentials needed.[1] The facility took its name in honor of St. Rose, the patron saint of Lima, Peru, and South America.[2] By the 1940s, St. Rose was a large, sprawling red-brick facility that served the health needs of the Great Bend community and offered professional health training through its nursing program.[3]

Five minutes later, a lady called me into an office. Tante Anna joined us. I understood probably about every fourth or seventh word she said, but it did not matter. The administration of this hospital had decided to take a chance on me. I would not disappoint them. A few first-day-on-the-job tasks such as filling out more paperwork and being shown around the hospital were first on the to-do list. A staff person assigned to me spoke passable German, which made me feel more at home. As I filled in the forms, Tante Anna helped me keep the various pieces of paper in order. Before leaving St. Rose, we went to the diet kitchen, where introductions were made. Although I did not quite understand everything they said, the ladies' bright smiles and waves of greeting told me all I needed to know.

After our hospital tour, Tante Anna drove me back to her home. The next order of business was for me to pack my clothes and personal items, as I would be living in barracks provided for employee housing on the hospital grounds. Once we accomplished this task, the two of us drove back to St. Rose. The kitchen staff would stay together in a house with one large bedroom. It did not take long for my aunt and me to get my little corner of the sleeping quarters situated to our liking. This crowded room would be my new home. Where would this job lead?

* * *

Since I was assigned to help with breakfast, I had to wake up at four o'clock and dress. My new green uniform looked crisp and sharp with its smart, white collar, as I checked my reflection in the mirror. I wanted to allow myself plenty of time to walk to the main hospital building, as my morning shift began at five o'clock sharp. Upon arriving at the diet kitchen, I was shown to my station, a place along the counter where I would manage several simple tasks. Cards containing English words like "grapefruit," "peel," "plate," "tray," and "bowl" were waiting for me. One of my co-workers, while standing next to me, showed me, through simple hand motions and the use of these pre-written cards, how I was to prepare the food and where I was to place it on the patient trays.

One of my responsibilities was to peel grapefruit, section it, and then place the juicy, pink slices in small bowls. After doing so, I would then place the fruit-filled bowls on the food trays. At that point, another lady would fill the plate with the other components of that day's meal. Once we filled the tray with a plate of food, beverage, cutlery, and a napkin, it would be placed on a shelf of a delivery cart. Then, one of the kitchen staff would wheel it to a patient floor and deliver the meals. I enjoyed my role in helping prepare nutritious meals for the patients of St. Rose Hospital.

All of us in the diet kitchen stayed very busy. Tasks such as washing and prepping meats, fruits, and vegetables, cooking, delivering meal trays to patients, collecting meal trays after each meal, and cleaning trays and utensils kept my co-workers and me extremely busy. I listened to the relaxed conversation shared between the other women, as I peeled grapefruit and stocked the food trays. Although the language barrier was difficult at first, as time went on, I began to understand more and more of what they were saying. Learning to interpret the ladies' various facial expressions and voice inflections added another layer of depth to learning English by immersion.

Since St. Rose was a Catholic-run facility, employees were expected to attend mass in the hospital chapel every morning before work except Sundays. A few of the ladies who worked with me in the diet kitchen were Catholic. One morning, one of them invited me to sit with her during the service. As we entered the chapel, morning light filtered through the lead-glass windows. Candles flickered in the dimly-lit room. I was concentrating so hard on doing the right thing that I did not notice that my co-worker had stopped to kneel and make the sign of the cross before entering the pew. I tripped over her feet and barely saved myself from sprawling headlong into the center aisle. After that, while attending other chapel services, I kept my distance until my fellow kitchen staff worker completed her genuflecting.

* * *

Each of us on the diet kitchen staff took turns for the early morning shift. On this particular morning, I was the sole employee in the kitchen. I had been working alone for about thirty minutes or so when the phone rang. *Oh, dear,* I thought. *Now, what do I do?* Not wanting to shirk my responsibilities, I picked up the phone and said, "Yes?"

An authoritative female voice on the other end of the line began speaking. I only managed to pick out a few words—"diet," "food," and "two trays."

I had no idea what had just been said to me, although I was bobbing my head and uttering, "Yes," every few minutes. Standing there with the receiver in my hand, I thought to myself, *Mildred, why did you answer the call?*

The voice on the other end spoke a few more unintelligible words, and the call ended abruptly. I placed the receiver back in the cradle and went back to my station to finish preparing the trays.

About five minutes later, one of the Dominican sisters appeared in the doorway of the kitchen. Tall and regal in her black and white habit, she was probably the woman who had just called the kitchen. It looked like she was working to suppress a wry smile, just beginning at the corners of her mouth. Next to her stood a shorter young woman in a nurse's neat, white uniform, her starched cap perched atop her head. They looked at one another, and the sister nodded.

The nurse looked back at me and began speaking in clear German, "Are you the new girl here in the diet kitchen? "

Incredulous, I slowly nodded my head. "Ja."

"Do you speak English?" the nurse continued in German.

"Very little," I answered, holding out my hands and forming a small space between them for emphasis.

The nurse turned back to the nun and asked her several questions, which I could not understand. After a few more minutes of conversation, the nurse returned her friendly gaze and asked if I was German.

"Ja," I replied.

She continued, "I've had a couple of years of German in college. Would you like to come to my apartment this evening after work? I live nearby with another girl, and we speak German. We'd both enjoy the visit."[4]

I slowly nodded again.

"Sister Corinna wants to thank you for all your hard work," the nurse told me, still speaking to me in German. She nodded to the nun beside her.[5]

My gaze left the nurse's face to meet that of the nun. Her eyes twinkled warmly. Sister Corinna smiled broadly and nodded her affirmation.

The nurse continued, "Sister Corinna also wants you to know that she desires that you learn as much English as possible to perform your job here in the kitchen. She has asked me to teach you."

"Danke," I said, bowing my head slightly, trying hard to blink back the tears that had suddenly welled up in my eyes.

Once again, God had intervened in the circumstances of my life, this time showing up in the guise of a Dominican sister and a friendly, young nurse. I soon learned that the nurse's name was Dorothy Harder.

Little did I know how much Dorothy's help would come to mean to my life.

Dorothy Harder

Instead of struggling to wake up before dawn to make it to my job on time, I was now practically leaping out of bed. I had a new friend at work, and her name was Dorothy Harder. She was not like anyone I had ever met before. Barely five feet, two inches tall, Dorothy had bright blue eyes and a head full of curly dark blonde hair. She was trim and athletic. Her gold, wire-rimmed glasses only enhanced the constant twinkle in her eyes. She was cheerful and warm and engaging. After only a few minutes in her presence, you immediately sensed the *joie de vivre* with which she lived her life.

Dorothy proved to be a trustworthy friend, ever since meeting her in the diet kitchen, the morning I answered Sister Corinna's phone call. On that first evening after meeting her, Dorothy and her roommate made me feel so comfortable while visiting their apartment. They lived in temporary housing on the hospital grounds, quarters for nurses and other health care professionals. The building was a short walk from mine. Her roommate also spoke German, and it felt good to be able to use the language of my youth, the only language I had known for the first seventeen years of my life. Throughout that summer, the three of us shared many meaningful conversations. Although I never got to know Dorothy's roommate well, she also provided an example of a smart, accomplished, professional woman.

* * *

Dorothy Harder was one of three siblings who grew up in Wetamka, Oklahoma. Dorothy had an older sister, Donna Mae, and a twin brother, Earl.

By the time the twins were in grade school, the Harder family had moved to Valley Center, north of Wichita, Kansas. Dorothy's father was a rig worker in the oil industry, and Mr. Harder was thankful to have this job, as the Great Depression had thrown millions of his fellow Americans out of work. Dorothy's mother was a school teacher. As her children got older, Mrs. Harder searched for the best school district in the area for her family to live. Lorraine, Kansas, was her number one choice, and soon the family settled there. Donna Mae, Dorothy, and Earl all graduated from Lorraine High School.[1]

After high school graduation, Dorothy enrolled in the Bethany Hospital School of Nursing, graduating from the program in February of 1946. She then continued her nursing training as a member of the U.S. Army Cadet Nurse Corps, completing internships at Winter General Hospital in Topeka, Kansas, and at O'Reilly General Hospital in Springfield, Missouri. Dorothy worked extensively with many GIs returning home from the war. In the fall of 1946, she moved to Columbia, Missouri, and enrolled in the College of Arts and Sciences at the University of Missouri, attending classes there for the next three years. She must have been interning at St. Rose Hospital when I met her that summer of 1947.[2]

One of the many talents Dorothy possessed was an affinity for foreign languages. Studying German was part of her program at the University of Missouri. Long before our paths crossed, God had already been preparing Dorothy for what lay ahead. During that same summer of 1947, Dorothy returned to the welcoming fellowship of believers at First Baptist Church of Lorraine. As her daughter, Nancy, shared, "As in most small towns in that era, the church was the center of religious and social activities outside of school."[3]

By the time Sister Corrina and Dorothy arrived to check on me that morning in the diet kitchen, the ears of Dorothy's heart were already attuned to the needs of this young girl.

* * *

Dorothy was four years older than me and quickly became like a big sister, someone in whom I could confide many of the thoughts and feelings that had been bottled up deep inside me. During one of our evening visits, the conversation turned to thoughts of the future. The topic of my returning to school came up. Completing my education was something I had considered impossible, as I was now almost an adult and still struggling to learn English. Although she did not share all the details, Dorothy assured me she had a plan in mind. She said we would talk again when she knew more.

Mildred (left) and Dorothy (right)

After that summer of 1947, when Dorothy and I met and became friends, she returned to her classes at the University of Missouri. A year later, she met a dashing Ph.D. candidate, Francis V. Morriss, who went by the name of Van. He was completing his doctorate in chemistry. The two were married on January 28, 1949. The couple then moved to Las Vegas, New Mexico, where Van had accepted a position on the faculty of New Mexico Highlands University. Dorothy worked at an area hospital for the next year and also served in her free time, as a private-duty nurse, while Van taught.[4]

The year after their first child, Stephen, was born, Dorothy returned to school in January 1950. She completed her undergraduate degree in May 1951 with a major in biology and a double minor in chemistry and German. Shortly after, the Morrisses moved again to Waco, Texas, where Van taught chemistry at Baylor University. During their stay in south Texas, Dorothy and Van's daughter, Nancy, was born in June 1952. The next year the family moved to Kansas City, Missouri, where Dr. Morriss began working with the Midwest Research Institute. Six years later, daughter Mary was born in 1959. Van, Dorothy, and their children would live here for the next eighteen years.[5]

During this season of her life, once her three children were in grade school, Dorothy was employed at St. Luke's Hospital and School of Nursing, where she also taught classes.[6] She also worked to complete a Master's degree in microbiology at the University of Missouri at Kansas City and graduated from the program in 1966. By the mid-1970s, Stephen and Nancy were embarking on their careers, and Mary was entering college. Van and Dorothy moved to Golden, Colorado, in 1977, when a unique opportunity arose for him to help start the Solar Energy Research Institute. One year later, Dorothy completed her doctoral microbiology program. Now the family had two Ph.D.'s. [7]

A few years later, Dorothy enrolled in classes again to complete a Bachelor of Science in Nursing (BSN). Loretto Heights College offered a unique program that allowed the three years of nursing classes, initially taken by Dorothy in her early twenties, to be officially recognized with the completion of a BSN. Throughout the remainder of the years she worked, Dorothy continued to teach, sharing her professional expertise and inspiring others to follow their dreams as she had her own.[8]

Only God knows the countless lives Dorothy Harder touched. How grateful I am that He brought this extraordinary friend to me all those years ago, while I was working in the diet kitchen of St. Rose Hospital. I cannot even imagine the path my life would have taken had I never met her. Dorothy and I have stayed in close contact since that summer of 1947. As each season of life has unfolded, we have shared, through phone calls and letters, the triumphs and tragedies of our lives. Although now living in a retirement center, Dorothy continues to influence my life to this day.

Little did I know the surprises which lay in store for me, doors which would soon swing wide open due directly to the efforts of my dear friend, Dorothy Harder.

CHAPTER TWENTY-TWO

The Dobrinskis

Dorothy and I spent many happy hours together, comfortably conversing in German. Her apartment on the grounds of St. Rose Hospital offered me a sanctuary my living quarters did not afford. As the conversations Dorothy and I shared during that summer of 1947 began to center on more personal matters, Dorothy could tell how badly I wanted to complete my education. It had now been over four years since I had been in a classroom.

One day, Dorothy asked me during one of those visits to her apartment, "Would you like to go to high school?

"I *can't* go to high school," I blurted out, my voice slightly raised in frustration. "I'd have to start in first grade." My English language deficiency was still such a struggle that I assumed that returning to school was impossible. I also had a debt I was working to pay off from my passage on the *Marine Marlin*. The obstacles seemed insurmountable.

A laugh escaped from Dorothy.

I looked at her quizzically.

"No, Mildred," Dorothy said, her calm, gentle voice helping to lower my anxiety. "You won't have to start over. I may know a way you could complete your education."

* * *

Dorothy Harder had done so many thoughtful things for me, but her introducing me to Carl and Esther Dobrinski was one of the most significant. Dorothy and the couple both attended First Baptist Church of Lorraine. Esther had been one of Dorothy's high school English teachers, but by this time, she was a full-time farm wife and mother, who had decided to leave the classroom and care for her two precious little children. Dorothy realized that if my dream of attending Lorraine High School was going to become a reality, I would need a place to live. So, she reached out to her former high school English teacher and her husband, who lived on a farm outside of Lorraine.

Carl had grown up on his family's farm, north of Lorraine. The third of five siblings, he graduated from Lorraine High School in 1932 in a class of ten. Following graduation, he joined his father and began farming.[1] By the time I met Carl, he was growing wheat and raising cattle. He was an extremely hard worker. His daughter, Marcia, recalled years later that even on nights when her father returned home from the fields late, he made it a priority to "horse around" with his children.

Esther had grown up the daughter of an American Baptist pastor.[2] When her father, Wayne Pinson, was called to serve a new church, the family would move to another city. Esther and her family lived in Sedan, Kansas, the year she completed her high school education. She then attended Ottawa University in Ottawa, Kansas, where she majored in English and Social Studies. Her first teaching job, the fall after her college graduation in 1939, was at Lorraine High School. First Baptist Church of Lorraine is the church Esther began attending, and she and Carl met. The couple married two years later in October 1941.

Marcia Dobrinski McDaniel, Carl and Esther's daughter, remembers what her parents told her about how they decided to allow me to live with them:

> Dorothy contacted my mom and asked if she and Dad would think about Mildred coming to live with us and go to Lorraine High School. My mom and dad prayed about it, deciding that they would be able to help her with her studies and English and would welcome her into our home. Dorothy later brought Mildred to church, and that's where my family first met Mildred.[3]

* * *

Once the Dobrinskis had given their okay for me to live with them while completing high school, things started moving quickly. I resigned from my job at St. Rose. The many weeks spent working there had flown by, as if on wings. How much I had learned in such a short period. I exchanged heartfelt goodbyes with the Dominican sisters and my co-workers in the diet kitchen, who all wished me the best. Yet another chapter in my life was ending. A new one, however, was about to begin.

Mildred and the Dobrinski family. *Left to right:* Mildred, Glen, Marcia, Esther, and Carl.

The belongings I had accumulated since arriving in the United States eight months earlier, which still were not very much, were packed into two small suitcases. One of these was the weathered valise that had accompanied me from Germany to Kansas; the second was one Onkel Charlie and Tante Anna lent me. It was so hard to tell my aunt and uncle and cousin goodbye. Their house had become a real home to me. Leaving it meant so much more than merely moving from one physical location to another. It meant yet another adjustment my heart would have to make as well.

My aunt and uncle lived in Great Bend, thirty-three miles southwest of Lorraine. Because I would now be living with the Dobrinski's, it would not be possible for me to walk to their house or pop in after class each day. If they were upset about my leaving Great Bend, they never let on. They always had my best interest at heart and knew how badly I wanted to finish school. But, oh, how I would miss Onkel Charlie, Tante Anna, and Margaret! We had become so close. Margaret said of that time when I lived with their family, "I always thought Mildred would live with us. The fact that she ended up in Lorraine was beyond me. The Lord had his hands all over that."[4]

I had so enjoyed living with Onkel Charlie, Tante Anna, and Margaret. Great Bend, however, was much larger than any other place I had lived. The county seat of Barton County had a population of almost eleven thousand. The

Lorraine community was small, with only about two hundred people living there that fall of 1947. Settled by German immigrants in the late 1800s, the surrounding landscape reminded me of Radach. Lorraine was a stable farming community inhabited by good, honest, hard-working people devoted to their families, their land, and to their God.

Onkel Charlie, Tante Anna, and I had many conversations about the opportunity I now had to complete my high school education. My aunt and uncle agreed and believed, as I did, that the Dobrinski's generous offer to live with them would make this possible. It was time to make a life for myself. I was not going to be able to stay under the care of Tante Anna and Onkel Charlie forever.

I still remember the day that Onkel Charlie drove me to the Dobrinskis. That was the longest car ride. There was so much I wanted to say to this man who had become so dear to me, but the words would not come. Tante Anna had expressed her love and support through her purchase of a beautiful new tan suit I now wore on this momentous day. I was so grateful to Mr. and Mrs. Dobrinski for opening their home to me. Now, that was going on faith—taking in a foreign teenage girl about whom you know nothing! I wanted to make such a good impression when I arrived. The two children—Marcia, age four, and Glen, age two—were playing outside, as Onkel Charlie's grey '38 Ford pulled slowly into the driveway of the Dobrinski home. The front door opened as Carl and Esther came out onto the porch. The children stood shyly behind their mother, but when I offered a sack of lemon drops I had purchased for them, we were instant friends. Hellos and handshakes followed as Onkel Charlie took my suitcases from the car. Once inside the house, Mrs. Dobrinski showed me to the room that would be mine for the next four years.

There was a lump in my throat and a funny feeling in the pit of my stomach as I watched Onkel Charlie's car turn from the driveway out onto the main road. Soon, it disappeared from view. God was asking me to step over yet another threshold. I was nervous; the school year was about to begin. I was not sure how, but I was trusting that, with God's help and Esther Dobrinski's, my return to school would not be a complete failure. Swallowing the lump in my throat, I headed inside to see if I could help Mrs. Dobrinski with dinner preparations.

The bright sound of children's laughter welcomed me as I stepped through the Dobrinski's front door.

CHAPTER TWENTY-THREE

The Most Important Decision of All

T he weight of all that I had been through in the past nine months was sometimes more than I could bear. I crossed the Atlantic Ocean with hundreds of other DPs. Entered the United States not as a visitor, but as a citizen. Traveled to Kansas alone by train. Met an aunt, uncle, and cousin for the first time. Moved in with them. Got to know this family. Turned eighteen. Learned a new language. Took a job in a local hospital. Met new friends. Found a new church home. Moved to another town and moved in with yet another family. Got to know this other family. Began the ninth grade of high school four years older than my peers. Adjusted to the demands of an American classroom. Whew! I get tired just thinking about all that.

Not to mention that within the two years before this one, I was living in a war-torn country. Driven out, along with my family, from our home by enemy soldiers. Suffered the loss of my father. Separated from my mother and brother. Impressed into work in a Russian laundry camp. Reunited with my mother and brother. Allowed to return to our home. Expelled from our home a second time by yet another group of enemy soldiers. Reunited with extended family. Relocated to a refugee camp within a hostile zone of the country in which I grew up. Lived alone for eight months in a refugee camp. I had tried so hard to be brave.

Staying alive had commanded every ounce of whatever survival instinct I possessed. Somehow, in all the craziness and chaos of the past few years, I had been able to do just that—stay alive. But like a balloon that was leaking air, I found it harder and harder to put on a brave face. I was now almost two months into my freshman year of high school, and I was eighteen years old. There was something wrong with this picture. Mr. and Mrs. Dobrinski had been so kind to me. They were extremely instrumental in my not only learning more English but also of mastering some of its more intricate nuances, as I worked to complete my homework each night. I was fast reaching a point where I wanted to throw in the towel on high school. I was overwhelmed. Maybe this was not such a good idea after all.

Sundays were the bright spot in my week, as the Dobrinskis and I would pile in their car and drive three miles to church. First Baptist Church of Lorraine, established in 1878, had been such a welcoming fellowship to me. Many of the young people were now my friends and classmates. The thought-provoking sermons each week told me of God's love for me. Pastor Fred Ferris and his wife had been especially kind to me. Every week, both of them made a point of coming over to where I was sitting to greet me, hug me, and sit down and visit for a few minutes. They seemed sincerely interested in me and how I was doing.

Although funds from Travelers Aid had covered part of the cost, I still had a debt incurred from my passage on the *Marine Marlin*. The money I earned from my job at St. Rose repaid a portion of this debt. Now that I had moved to Lorraine and was attending high school, I did not have a source of income. Esther Dobrinski made a plea on my behalf and asked the church deacons if money from the communion fund could satisfy this remaining balance owed for my trip to America. This particular portion of the church's budget contained dollars set aside to help someone in the Lorraine community who needed assistance. The money the deacons gave to me settled the debt for my transatlantic travel. I was grateful I met the standard.

* * *

One Sunday after church, at a potluck luncheon in the fellowship hall, Mrs. Ferris made her way over to where I was seated.

"Mildred," she said as she bent down beside me. "I wanted to see if you would be interested in helping me at my house on Saturdays from time to time? Esther has told me how much she and Carl have enjoyed having you live with them. She was especially complimentary of your organizational and housekeeping skills."

This request caught me off guard. My cheeks felt hot.

"Well, . . . yes, Mrs. Ferris," I stammered. "I mean, I'm interested in thinking about it. Of course, I'd need to talk to Mr. and Mrs. Dobrinski. Could I let you know something in a few days?"

A warm flush was beginning to make its way up my cheeks. I was not used to being the center of attention. Mrs. Ferris' kind words and intriguing job offer both touched my heart and interested me.

"Fred and I will be waiting," Mrs. Ferris replied. She reached over and hugged me before standing. "We could certainly use your help, Mildred. Take all the time you need."

Her smile washed over me like a soft, gentle breeze.

* * *

The leaves were beginning to turn, and the air was getting crisp and cool when I started my new Saturday job cleaning house for Fred and Inez Ferris. I always looked forward to the time I spent in their home. Most of the time, Mrs. Ferris and their three children were with me, as Pastor Ferris used Saturday mornings to complete work on his sermon in his office at the church. In this minister's wife, I found a caring, compassionate, and kind friend who always made me feel special. I earned three dollars each Saturday that I worked. That was a lot of money to me. While I was glad to have a job to make a little spending money of my own, I used most of what I earned to send packages to Mutti and Horst.

One of the things I enjoyed the most about the time I spent each week in the Ferris home was having an opportunity to be alone with my thoughts. I *missed* Mutti and Horst. There was never a second of the day that I was not thinking of them. Most of the time, however, I was too busy to concentrate on such thoughts. The atmosphere in the Ferris' home was one of peace and calm. The other idea that I was spending more time dwelling on was building a more personal relationship with God.

As I mulled over the catastrophic events I had endured throughout the past three years of my life, I had *no* doubt in my mind that God had intervened in my life and in that of my parents and my brother time and time again. Over and over, God made a way where none existed. I had lived through *too* much to believe that the reason Mutti, Horst, and I were still alive was due to chance or random circumstance. I had witnessed God connect too many of the dots in my life. There was no other explanation *but* God.

I learned a great deal about God while growing up in our Evangelical Lutheran Church in Radach. However, *no one* had ever explained to me the fact that God wanted a relationship with me, that He had expressly designed me (and every other human being) to have a close relationship with Him, and that entering into that relationship was as easy as falling off a log. All you had to do was ask.

One of the blessings of living in the home of Carl and Esther Dobrinski was that I was able to see their faith in God and His son, Jesus Christ, lived out in practical ways every day. Blessings said before meals and family devotions were a normal part of the everyday routine in the Dobrinski household. Esther and Carl also prayed with me. Many days, as Esther handed me a sack lunch before I left for school, she would say, "I'll be praying for you today." The thought that someone was bringing my name before the Creator of this universe made quite an impression on me.

Many nights I would help Esther get Marcia and Glen ready for bed. They would each say their prayers aloud, before being tucked under the covers. Each night while putting her children to bed, Esther recited her adaptation of a popular children's prayer:

"Now I lay me down to sleep.
I pray the Lord my soul to keep.
Watch and guard me through the night.
And wake me up at morning light."

There were many nights I would find myself whispering the same lines as I lay in the dark in my bed. The thought that God would be watching over me as I slept was very comforting.

Now that I had moved in with the Dobrinskis, the only chance I had to see Dorothy Harder was at church. Esther was very involved at First Baptist Church of Lorraine, and, as a result, her family and I were there quite a bit. When getting together with Dorothy at church, I observed in her, as I did with Esther, active, trusting faith in her Lord. In the time that I had come to work in the Ferris' home, I had also had several opportunities for conversation with both Pastor and Mrs. Ferris about asking Jesus into my heart.

After one of those conversations, Pastor Ferris left the room where I was cleaning and went to his study. He returned a few minutes later with a sheaf of papers in his hand.

"Mildred," he said warmly, "these are copies of a few of my sermons. You've asked some very thoughtful questions when we've visited about how you might come to know God better. Maybe you'll find some of the answers for which you're searching while reading these." Pastor Ferris extended the papers toward me.

My pastor, Rev. Fred Ferris, and me (photo by *Baptist Herald*)

"Thank you, sir," I said, feeling as if Pastor Ferris had just entrusted me with a great treasure. "I'll be sure and get these copies back to you very soon."

A slight laugh escaped from the minister. "You keep those as long as you like, Mildred. We're on God's time, not mine." Pastor Fred Ferris' smile was so sincere and genuine. His eyes seemed to look straight into my soul.

I had received a new assignment, one which might prove a whole lot more interesting than social studies or math. For the next few weeks, Esther would read Pastor Ferris' sermons out loud, as my English was still limited. When I had a question about something he had said, Esther would stop reading, and we would discuss the topic until it was understood.

* * *

One day, a few months later, I told Esther, "I'm ready." In early December of my freshman year in high school, I bowed my head and gave my life to the Savior, who had already saved my life many times before. How I wish I could remember the date of my spiritual birthday. It is recorded in Heaven, although lost to me. Over the past five months, I had been with the Dobrinskis, as we prayed as a family each night. Esther Dobrinski had been witnessing to me as my Sunday School teacher. She and I had also had many late-night conversations about what becoming a follower of Christ meant. Although I do not remember what it was about Pastor Fred Ferris' printed sermons that led me to this most important decision of all, I remember being compelled and made so aware that I needed the Lord.

I, along with several others at our church, was baptized on Wednesday, December 31, 1947. The facts of that event are a bit hazy. I do remember being interviewed by the deacons several Sundays before my baptism. Despite the wintry chill in the sanctuary that evening, I came out of the waters warmed and invigorated, a new creature in Christ.

No matter what lay ahead, I knew, beyond a shadow of a doubt, that I had the company of God Himself to go with me every step of the way.

CHAPTER TWENTY-FOUR

"The Best May Still Be Thine"

My freshman year at Lorraine High School began in September 1947. I was the oldest member of my class. I was eighteen, and even though I was four years older than my six other classmates, I was grateful to have this opportunity to complete my secondary education. If Dorothy Harder had not intervened in my life and introduced me to Carl and Esther Dobrinski, I am not sure what I would have done. The school had thirty-seven students in the four grades—ninth through twelfth. Besides the traditional academic subjects of English, history, mathematics, and science, there were various activities outside of classroom studies—music, choir, band, speech, school plays, sports, and Kayettes—offered to the members of our student body as diverse opportunities for involvement.

The Dobrinski farm was about three miles southeast of Lorraine. Carl and Esther and their two children had recently moved from another farm located east of town to this home shortly before I joined them. Most days, Carl had been up several hours and was already working in the fields by the time I got dressed and ready to leave for school. As Esther was extremely busy with child-rearing and household responsibilities, and because we lived out in the country, a "kid hack" picked me up for school each morning and brought me home each afternoon.[1] This funny-sounding term was the name given to adult drivers working for the Lorraine school district, who would pick up students who had no other means of getting to school—approved drivers in the general vicinity. On any given day, my "kid hack" picked up four others beside me.

Though I was not with my family, God had once again provided a safe and loving home where I would flourish during these critical years. Carl and Esther welcomed me, without reservation, from the day I arrived. They were kind and encouraging, and their home warm and inviting. Reminding me of both my Pappa and my Onkel Charlie, Carl worked hard in the fields of his farm all day and returned home at night to share time with his family. It was fun watching him play with Marcia and Glen. Esther's patient tutelage and assistance saved me, as I struggled to complete homework assignments most nights. She was also a marvelous cook. Homemade cinnamon rolls were a special treat we enjoyed practically every Saturday and Sunday. I can still taste her delicious fudge. Esther was also a skilled seamstress who made many of my clothes.[2]

Marcia and Glen were both so cute and lively. Marcia, very observant and smart, even wrote some of her memories of our times together, "Mildred was a willing helper. As a young child, I remember her playing with us and keeping us entertained. She also washed lots of dishes at our house. To get her attention

Posing in the new dress Esther made me

while she was washing dishes, we would untie her apron strings. Then she started tying them in front!"[3] Glen was all boy and liked to stand up at the table while eating. I used to tell him "that if he stood, he'd get big feet and that he should always sit down to eat."[4] Two more children, sons Dale and Kenneth, were born during those four years.

"In God's plan, things happen for a reason," Marcia shared years later when reminiscing about this season of our lives. "I think Mildred's coming to live with us went beyond her desire to learn to speak English and go to school! I think that Mildred coming to join our family was part of God's plan for our family."[5] The friendships fostered with members of the Dobrinski family exist to this day. Marcia, Dale, Kenny, and I still keep in touch. Sadly, Esther, Carl, and Glen have passed away.

* * *

One of the things I liked best about living in Lorraine was the predominant ethnic heritage shared by many in the town. Founded in 1877 as a German settlement, this farming community of approximately two hundred people was reminiscent of Radach, although much smaller. "'When I first arrived in Lorraine in the late summer [1947], I wanted to dig potatoes. It was a craving for me for I worked on the potato farms in Germany. So I was told to go out and help dig potatoes. But as I filled the buckets with the newly dug potatoes, I found myself transported back to Europe with the back-breaking grind of work over there. Before I knew it, I had taken off my shoes and stockings and was working barefooted as I felt the clean strength of the earth on my feet.'"[6]

Carl Dobrinski's parents were both of German ancestry, although his father's family had been in the United States longer than had his mother's. His mother, Theresa Preuss Dobrinski, grew up in East Prussia and had immigrated to this country with her family in the late 1880s as a young girl.[7] Her husband, who was also named Carl, was born in Ohio to German immigrant parents and had moved to the Green Garden Township (the name of Lorraine's initial German settlement) years earlier.[8] Although she spoke with a thick German accent, Theresa Dobrinski spoke German and English fluently. Carl and his four other siblings would have learned both German and English while growing up. Most of my classmates also came from a proud German heritage. Although individuals of German descent, living in other parts of the United States, may have faced unfriendliness and even prejudice in those first few years after World War II ended, Lorraine welcomed me with open arms into the heart of its warm, loving community.

* * *

My greatest struggle was in mastering English as a language. Although a U.S. citizen by birth, I lived in Germany for seventeen years; German was my primary language. I wanted to be like everyone else around me. I was an American citizen and wanted to learn the language; I did not want to sound like a foreigner. Perhaps due to my age, the school administration initially devised a three-year academic plan tailored specifically for me. The idea was for me to work hard, double up on some classes, and read an enormous amount of information to earn my high school diploma. Much of this extra information was American History, a very complex subject. Soon, the administrators said, "No, we don't think she can do it."

And I could not. I had to complete the fourth year like everybody else.

In those first weeks of my ninth-grade year, Carl would interpret for me, translating English into German, especially when I was doing homework. Other times, he would call his mother for help. Mrs. Dobrinski helped me understand better what a teacher wanted me to do. I thought a lot about dropping out of school during the first few months. Many nights, after Marcia and Glen were in bed, Carl, Esther, and I would sit in the kitchen and visit. Several of those talks ran long, and my frustration ran high. Trying to comprehend all I was learning was *too* hard. I was not sure I was up to the task.

It never seemed to fail that when I would come home determined to quit, any apprehensions concerning my abilities had evaporated by the next morning. I would return to school, eager and excited to begin the new day. Perhaps Carl and Esther were both patient and wise, gently offering words of encouragement to lift my spirits. Maybe Mrs. Dobrinski, Carl's mother, had also become an ally and was helping me bridge the gap between my German and the new English I was learning every day. Perhaps it was that I received a present from my mother that arrived just before Christmas. This note, which was also in the package, encouraged me to give my best for Mutti's sake:[9]

Nienhagen 11-20-47

My dear daughter,
 A little Christmas gift for you from both of us. Would have liked to do more, but know we are not able to.
 Hope the little pkg. gets there in time.

Happy Holiday Wishes
from Mutti and Horst

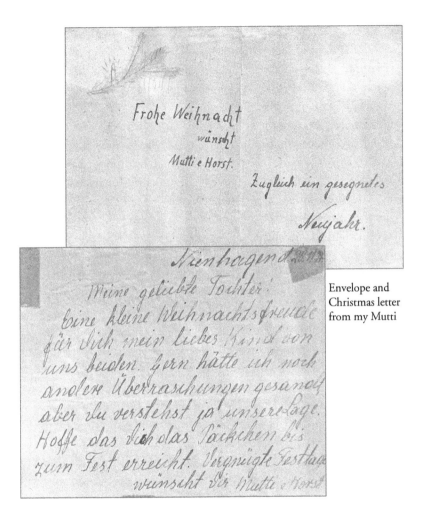

Envelope and Christmas letter from my Mutti

Perhaps it was that by early December of that first year, I now had a new tutor, the Spirit of the Living God, who also brought a sense of peace and calm to my heart amid life's storms. No matter the reason, I finally settled into the harness of the academic rigor of that freshman year.

* * *

One of my teachers, Mr. E.D. Meacham, was incredibly helpful to me. He was my math teacher and also served as the principal of the school. As a young girl in Radach, I had learned the European method of writing out the number "1," which had a tale slanting down to the left side from the main stem of the number. When written, it was hard to distinguish the number one from number seven. Another aspect of writing numbers in this method is that the number "7" has a cross piece written through its longer stem, just as a lowercase "f" has written across it. Mr. Meacham encouraged me to discontinue both these practices. It would make my handwriting easier to read, also making my math homework papers easier to grade.

Although not as traumatic as the circumstances through which I had come, it was, however, interesting to learn that World War II had wrinkled the fabric of life here in rural America. Perhaps due to the war, our music department did not have a teacher for the first ten weeks of my freshman year. Somewhere that fall, Mr. Meacham's wife graciously agreed to serve as our music teacher on a part-time basis. After she joined the faculty, Glee Club began meeting on Tuesdays and Thursdays. Music was meaningful to me. All the students in Mrs. Meacham's music classes were offered various opportunities, like the school district's League Music Festival, where we shared our talents. I was a member of the Glee Club all four years of high school. This couple also attended First Baptist Church, where Mr. Meacham served as the treasurer. As such, I had the privilege of seeing both of these special people almost every single day.

Carl Dobrinski's younger brother, Harold, served as our ninth-grade sponsor. He had graduated from Lorraine High School, like Carl, and Harold served on the faculty for the 1941-1942 academic year, before enlisting in the U.S. military in the summer of 1942. He served during the remaining years of the war and returned to the LHS faculty in the fall of 1947. Mr. Dobrinski also taught English and shop classes.[10]

Donna Kempke, Claire Peters, Lois Rolfs, Marilyn Schacht, and I met on the first day of ninth grade, and we instantly hit it off. Three of these classmates lived on nearby farms and had grown up just as I had: reared in a rural community and instilled with a strong work ethic developed through responsibilities given to us at an early age. When asked years later, neither Donna nor Marilyn seemed to remember me as being different in any way when they first met me. They also said they had been so amazed at how well I had caught up with my classmates during that first year. These lifelong friendships, developed in those early days of our high school experience at Lorraine High School, still sustain us today.[11]

* * *

One of the most distinguished high school groups to which I belonged was the Kayettes. This girls' program was part of the Kansas Association for Youth (KAY). Created in 1945 by the Kansas State High School Activities Association, the KAY organization developed character and fostered leadership

A fun time at the Janzens' home

skills in young men and women. Using a play on words, the Kays was the young men's organization, and the Kayettes was for young women. The KAY organization had six foundational objectives: appreciation, character, health, leadership, recreation, and service. Students from each high school's chapter would come together in district conferences held in different regions of the state. Clubs could earn points for worthwhile projects. Awards, based on those point values, were then presented at the conferences.[12]

I was a member of this organization all four years of high school and served in a variety of roles. During my junior and senior years, I served as treasurer and president, respectively. In my sophomore and senior years, I was also selected as one of the delegates to attend the District Kayette Conference. Lorraine High School's Kayette chapter kept its members busy. We had monthly meetings to attend and a variety of service-related projects to fulfill. These service projects included selling Christmas cards and holiday wrapping paper, preparing and delivering food baskets to needy families in our area, selling refreshments at football and basketball games, and hosting an annual reception for the school's faculty.

One of the Kayette's first international projects was the creation of CARE packages, gift parcels of food to send to families living overseas. Of course, the ones that meant the most to me were those for which our Kayette chapter raised funds and sent to Mutti and Horst. It cost ten dollars to send a package. Esther and I also sent packages. Marcia would often watch as her mother and I sat at the dining room table, wrapping cans of food in Christmas wrapping paper. Many of these were cans of tuna. For it to reach Mutti and Horst by Christmas, the box was packed in the fall, allowing for the six or seven weeks it would take for delivery. The Kayettes collected money for CARE packages of non-perishable food they sent to my mother and brother every year I was in high school. How I wished I could have delivered them in person!

* * *

By the spring of my sophomore year, I began receiving invitations to publicly share with others the story of my harrowing escape from Germany. Various speaking engagements took me all over the state of Kansas throughout my high school years. One appearance was at the Annual Farm Bureau Meeting in Winfield, Kansas. "Experiences in Germany Under German and Russian Rule" was the title of my presentation, as a speaker for the Ladies Achievement Day Program.[13] Another time, I had the opportunity to share my story with the Hackney Baptist Church, led by Esther Dobrinski's father, Reverend J. Wayne Pinson. A few of these engagements also garnered articles in local newspapers. The headline, "Teen-Ager From Germany Was Guest Speaker At The Meeting," appeared atop a local newspaper article that described the program I presented for the Lyons Chamber of Commerce.[14] Various monthly Kayette meetings offered further occasions to impart my experiences to other young women.

I was nervous during some of these first presentations until I learned English better. I spoke from my heart, allowing my memory to be my guide rather than written notes. People were fascinated with my story, as it offered them a glimpse inside German life under the rule of Adolph Hitler. My listeners certainly did not read many stories like mine in the newspapers. My account also helped my audiences gain a better understanding of how heart-wrenching and devastating war can be—certainly in terms of lives lost, but also in terms of lives forced to endure impossible circumstances.

Most importantly, these invitations to appear before a variety of audiences allowed me to share God's goodness and a testimony of His unfailing protection and providential care. God *had* saved my life and those of my mother and brother, despite the terrible loss of my father. I was *so* grateful for that fact and had determined to live a joy-filled life.

* * *

My senior year was terrific. Our class of nine—six girls and three boys—had as our motto, "No matter what the past has been the best may still be thine." I could not help but think of all I had been through in the past six years. So many times, I could have been killed or imprisoned or forced to live in a Communist country. Yet, here I was, in the country of my birth. "The land of the free and the home of the brave." God *had* been faithful, despite man's faithlessness. God *had* made a way for me, where man had tried to thwart that way. God *had* prepared a future for Mutti, Horst, and me, though I could not yet see it. Finally,

Headed to Lorraine High School Junior-Senior Banquet

My high school graduation, May 15, 1951

Another graduation photo (photo by Johnson Studio)

Mildred Schindler

Majors
    English
    Social Science
Minors
    Math
    Commerce
Other Credits
    Phys. Ed.
    Latin
    Shorthand-½ Unit

Activities
Glee Club   1 2 3 4
Play   3 4
Mixed Chorus   2 3 4
Kayettes   1 2 3 4
Gym   1

Yearbook photo of my senior class schedule

the long-awaited day of my high school graduation had arrived. I was about to realize this dream I once thought impossible to achieve.

Lorraine Rural High School held its commencement ceremony on the evening of Tuesday, May 15, 1951.[15] The nine of us—Edwin Janzen, Donna Kempke, Wayne Mehl, Betty Perkins, Choc Perkins, Claire Peters, Lois Rolfs, Marilyn Schacht, and myself—had become very close throughout the past four years. We were now ready to step across the threshold of our lives into the open door of our future that lay ahead. Reverend Ferris presented the invocation, witnessing yet another milestone in my life. Dr. Emory Lindquist, President of Bethany College, gave the commencement address. Mr. Meacham, who had been one of my greatest cheerleaders during the past four years, presented each member of our class for graduation. Mr. E. B. Staeber, representing the Board of Education, shook each of our hands as we came forward, one by one, to receive our diplomas. Carl, Esther, Marcia, and Glen were in the audience that night, as were Onkel Charlie, Tante Anna, and Margaret. Mutti and Horst were present in spirit. Oh, how I wished they could have been there to see it with their own eyes.

Having now met and mastered the challenge of completing high school, I was eager to see what lay around the corner. Undoubtedly the best was just ahead.

PART V

Thankful Every Day

"Now Thank We All Our God"

Now thank we all our God, with heart and hands and voices,
Who wondrous things has done, in whom his world rejoices;
Who from our mothers' arms has blessed us on our way
With countless gifts of love, and still is ours today.

O may this bounteous God through all our life be near us,
With ever joyful hearts and blessed peace to cheer us,
To keep us in his grace, and guide us when perplexed,
And free us through all ills of this world in the next.

All praise and thanks to God the Father now be given,
the Son and Spirit blest, who reign in highest heaven.
The one eternal God, whom heaven and earth adore;
For thus it was, is now, and shall be evermore.

—Martin Rinkart (1586–1649)

CHAPTER TWENTY-FIVE

Half a World Away

D uring the years I spent attending Lorraine High School, I worked hard, giving my best effort in everything I did. I never wanted to say or do anything I was not supposed to, because I did not want someone to see me and get the wrong impression. Everyone in this Lorraine community had taken a chance on me—Carl and Esther Dobrinski and their family, the administration and faculty of the school, Reverend and Mrs. Ferris, members of his congregation at First Baptist Church, and my new friends. When I stepped out of the Dobrinski's front door each morning, I was an extension of this dear family who had placed their trust in me. Most importantly, I represented the Fritz Schindler family. It did not matter that Pappa was gone and that Mutti and Horst were half a world away. I did *not* want to disappoint them.

Mutti and Horst were still living in Nienhagen, Germany, where I had also lived with them in the fall of 1945, before boarding a train to Berlin. Fifteen months afterward, I arrived in the United States. My American birth certificate had been the key that unlocked the door for me to enter the country in January 1947. Mutti and Horst, however, had no such passkey in their pockets. Both German citizens by birth, they were forced to stay behind. After turning our world upside down the spring of 1945, the Russians still controlled the eastern portion of Germany, in which Mutti and Horst lived.

Germany of my youth split into two separate and disparate countries in 1949. The eastern portion, in which Mutti and Horst lived, formerly the Russian Occupation Zone, now became the German Democratic Republic.[1]

Such a democratic-sounding name for an undemocratic, communist state. The western portion of the country, formerly subdivided into the American, French, and British Occupation Zones, was reorganized as the Federal Republic of Germany, a free and democratic nation.[2]

Mutti wrote letters regularly. I eagerly looked forward to receiving them, as they offered interesting tidbits of information and details of life in Nienhagen. The letters I wrote in return described life at Lorraine High, and the activities in which I was involved at that particular time, or passing along something funny which Marcia or Glen had said or done. What my letters could never quite describe was the great loneliness that was my constant companion. It hid behind my smile and followed me to school each day. It greeted me each night as I was about to close my eyes, and was there waiting for me when I awakened. As much as I desperately needed my mother with me again, I also wanted to be strong for her. On days when I felt down, the least I could do was write positive-sounding letters to my mother that would give the appearance I was "keeping my chin up."

Mutti and Horst received many packages, both from our Kayette chapter and from Esther and me, during the time they were living in Nienhagen. They were one of four families occupying rooms on the upstairs level of a farmer's house; the farmer and his family lived downstairs. In one of the packages packed at the

An envelope containing one of Mutti's many letters to me

Dobrinski's kitchen table, I had sent Jell-O and popcorn, some of my favorite American snacks, and had sent written instructions for preparing both items.

My instructions for making popcorn read, "If you have oil or lard, put it in a skillet. Put in corn and heat and shake it." I had failed to include the notation about putting a lid on the skillet before popping the corn!

Shortly after receiving these treats, Mutti decided to make popcorn. She took out a skillet and drizzled some cooking oil into it. She then poured in the uncooked popcorn and set the skillet on a hot eye of the stove. All of a sudden, the kernels of corn exploded in the heated oil, making loud, booming noises. Pieces of popcorn flew across the room! Mutti's letter about the incident reported that, while the popcorn kernels were bursting, members of the other refugee families came running, shouting and saying the Americans were trying to blow them up!

Just as our family had witnessed the Soviets carting young girls off to work camps in Siberia the winter of 1945, Mutti's letters told me of how the Russian Army was conscripting young men from the Russian Occupation Zone. With the arrival of each one, I wondered if this particular note would describe how the Russians had coerced Horst into military service. Thankfully, his thick eyeglasses were still protecting him, making him undesirable as a recruit. Horst, now sixteen, was earning the equivalent of three U.S. dollars each month in his work for a local farmer. At some time during the six-and-a-half-years Horst and Mutti were forced to remain in Europe, he also began attending a trade school to learn carpentry. His daughter, Amy Schindler Weldon, remembers that Horst "was exceptional with his hands and crafting things."[3]

Occasionally, Horst would pen a letter. He wrote one of my favorites on colored paper, my brother's hand-drawn illustrations creating a picturesque scene across the top of the page.[4]

Nienhagen, 12.3.50

Dear Sister,

Today, Sunday, March 12, finds me at home again. I want to write a few lines to you. How are you, health-wise? Hopefully, well. I can also say the same for myself. Yesterday, we celebrated your birthday. For supper, we had potato salad and sausages that tasted great, and today for breakfast, we had poppy seed cake.

Well, dear sister, I'm curious when we will be able to celebrate our birthdays together again. I'm afraid that will never happen [sentences unclear]. Well, dearest sister, I'll close for now. You can't imagine how lazy I am when it comes to writing. Best wishes for a happy and healthy Easter holiday, and try to find some eggs.

Many wishes and kisses.

Your brother,
Horst

Included in the same envelope was this note from my mother.[5]

Your brother is certainly a lazy bones when it comes to writing, so I'll have to add a few lines. He just went out and doesn't look so much like a refugee as he once did. We owe all that to your enormous help.

Last night Horst got wet. It rained and stormed so that one thought that the windowpanes were going to fall out. Besides having a thunderstorm, it also snowed. During the day, the storm eventually subsided. It's finally dried up a little and the sun is once again bringing us her warming rays. That's so nice after those winter days.

Tell Mrs. [Rosie?] she should get a few Snow Bells [flowers] for my daughter as an Easter gift. Well, three to herself and the other three are my Easter greetings. Are you also planning on looking for the Easter Bunny? Horst will also receive a few eggs.

Warm Easter wishes to you for the holiday.

From your Mother

Also, give my best wishes to the Dobrinskis.

Just now on the radio broadcast, the children are singing,

> *"Alle Vögel Sind schon da."*
> *[A traditional German folk song:*
> *"In the Spring, all the birds have come back.]*
> *That's always such a nice program.*

This special greeting made Easter a little more special that year.

* * *

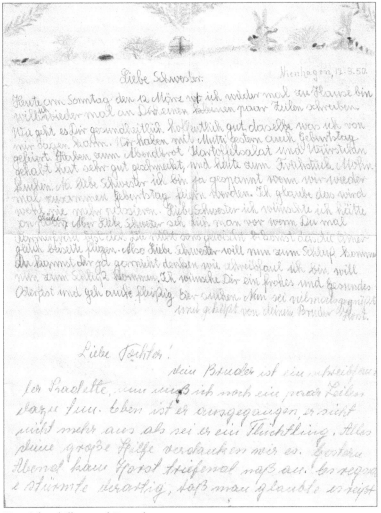

Horst's hand-illustrated Easter letter

The first signs of a break-down in the shared governance between the United States, Great Britain, France, and Russia of post-war Germany began to occur in late 1946. The Soviet Union was determined to keep rubbing Germany's nose in the dirt; the United States, France, and Great Britain wanted to help the country rebuild.[6] America's president, who brought a successful end to the war, now wished to assist nations ravaged not only by World War II but also by those which might occur in future times.

The day after my eighteenth birthday, on Wednesday, March 12, 1947,[7] President Truman announced the Truman Doctrine, which stated America's plan to "support free peoples" when threatened by aggressor nations.[8] Almost thirteen months later, the president signed into law the Economic Recovery Act of 1948 on Saturday, April 3.[9] More commonly known as the Marshall Plan in honor of U.S. Secretary of State George Marshall, who devised the policy, the bill outlined a blueprint by which war-torn countries could rebuild both infrastructure and economy.[10] Both of these policies put the United States and fellow allied nations in direct opposition to Joseph Stalin and his Soviet empire.

During the summer before my sophomore year of high school, on Thursday, June 24, 1948, the Soviet government began a blockade in the city of Berlin to prevent citizens' access to western Allied-controlled sectors of the city. Essential utilities and food had been denied to approximately 2.5 million people in what came to be known as the Berlin Blockade. Two days later, U.S. and British pilots began dropping goods and supplies into West Berlin. This joint humanitarian response, known as the Berlin Airlift, would continue over the next eleven months.[11]

This first line, drawn in the sand by Russia, signaled the pall of communism that would later fall over the eastern portion of the former German state. Although Mutti and Horst were not living in Berlin, they were within this general region of the Russian Occupation Zone. By the time the Dobrinski family and I were sitting down to enjoy a Thanksgiving dinner in November of my junior year of high school, Mutti and Horst had been living for a little over one month in the newly-created Communist country of East Germany.

In a speech made on March 5, 1946, British statesman and former Prime Minister Winston Churchill coined the term *iron curtain,* using this metaphor to describe what he perceived to be the impenetrable shield of communism beginning to drape itself over the eastern portion of Europe.[12] Now three years later, it was almost as if Mr. Churchill had been able to peer out into the future. My Mutti and Horst were now living behind that iron curtain.

I had to find a way to get them out from behind this steely shroud and safely home to Kansas.

Lorraine State Bank

My senior year at Lorraine High School had arrived. It was hard to believe in nine short months, I would graduate and be ready to make my way in the world. Many of my friends had after-school jobs. I began spending time thinking about where I might like to work. Carl and Esther had been good to me, allowing me to live with their family. I did not know how to drive, nor did I have a car, so looking for a job that would require one did not make much sense.

Late in the spring semester, I heard about a part-time job opportunity at Lorraine State Bank. The bank teller, Arlene Craig, who had been my "kid hack" driver, told me she would soon be resigning due to her upcoming marriage. The bank was hoping to find someone to take her place; Arlene encouraged me to apply for the job. My principal, Mr. Meacham, allowed me to leave school and walk to the bank for the interview. The meeting with the bank president, Mr. Ed (E. B.) Staeber went well, and I got the job for a preliminary trial period.

My busy daily schedule consisted of classes, club meetings, glee club rehearsals, and walking to the bank to work until closing time. For the first month on the job, Arlene would be teaching me the various duties for which I would be responsible—changing money, posting to and balancing accounts, answering customers' questions, and handling their concerns. As my last period of the day was a study hall, Mr. Meacham allowed me to leave school early and head to the bank for training.

Shortly before the end of the school year, Mr. Staeber called me into his office one day. He complimented my work and said that since I was doing such a fine job, he would like to promote me to Arlene's full-time position once I graduated from Lorraine High School. I beamed with pride. This man had been instrumental in shaping my educational journey, but now he had also opened the door to a profession in which I would derive great fulfillment and satisfaction. Although I did not know Mr. Staeber very well, I had seen him at school when he was in the building to attend meetings, as he was a member of the Board of Education. He had been such a good boss. I looked forward to the prospect of learning more banking savvy from him.

Though I was elated to have this opportunity, there was still the issue of how I would get to work each day. The Dobrinski farm was about three miles outside of town. I certainly could not walk that distance and look presentable upon arrival at the bank. One night in early May, Carl sat down at the dinner table and, after enjoying his meal, asked me if I would like to live with his mother in town. His father had passed away a few months earlier in February, and his mother, Theresa, was lonely.[1] The move would do us both good.

The spring of 1951 was also busy because the fourth Dobrinski baby was soon to make his appearance. Esther had been put to bed in the weeks before the birth of her third son, Ken, on Saturday, March 31. Several local ladies took turns staying with Esther and taking care of the children, while Carl and I were away for most of each day. Once I returned home in the afternoon, I could not wait to play with the children. My next assignment was to help eight-year-old Marcia set the table before I prepared dinner. Once the meal was over, and the children were bathed and put to bed, I could put the finishing touches on my homework.

Before I knew it, I was an official high school graduate. In the days between graduation and the start of my new job, I packed up my belongings. I had accumulated more items than the few brought with me four years earlier. After exchanging fervent hugs and kisses with Esther and the children, Carl helped me move to his mother's home. Throughout the past four years, I had gotten to know Mrs. Dobrinski, making this transition smooth and easy. She insisted I call her "Grandma."

The beginning of summer signaled the start of my new job. I looked forward to it every day. Lorraine was a small town, so I knew almost every customer by name. There were a few of our customers who spoke German. Several of these people were also members of our church. It was enjoyable for these bank patrons and me to visit with each other in our primary language, even though we all spoke English. As banking is a profession based on trust-worthy employee-client relationships, this shared gift of communication was an unexpected, value-added service I could offer our clients.

* * *

Another of Theresa's granddaughters, Jean Dobrinski Behnke, remembered her this way, "Since Grandmother spoke German, she would help Mildred with the German and English language. Grandmother was a wonderful cook, who had raised five children. She loved this new opportunity to have someone to cook for and someone with whom to visit. Grandmother Dobrinski spoke with a thick German brogue. She was a well-kept, nice-looking short lady who wore calico flowered dresses, always with a clean apron on top. She wore no make-up and little jewelry, except for a gold wristwatch and a gold wedding band. She pulled her gray hair back in a neat bun at the nape of her neck. She was the 'perfect looking' grandmother; anyone would have loved to have had her as theirs."[2]

Even though I was not living with Carl and Esther anymore, I still saw their family at church every week. We were also together occasionally for Sunday lunches, as Mrs. Dobrinski would prepare a special meal for family celebrations, like birthdays and holidays.[3] A delicious assortment of "the best tender roast beef, roasted potatoes, brown gravy, frozen peas, roasted carrots, fresh homemade bread with jelly and butter, a Jell-O salad or two or three with fruit in it" awaited us. "[There were] always big, sour cream, crispy, delicious, melt-in-your-mouth sugar cookies, cut with a scalloped rectangular cookie-cutter, with extra sprinkled sugar on top, and ice cream or maybe pie or cake."[4]

Once again, God had provided a loving, welcoming family for me.

* * *

I loved my job! Established in 1907, the bank was the central hub of our little town, and there was hardly ever a dull moment. The new financial concepts I was learning both challenged and stimulated me. I loved the feeling I got when completing a transaction or helping a customer figure out a problem with a statement. Mr. Meacham's math lessons were finally paying off. My job at the bank kept me very busy.

Life was good here in Lorraine. Mrs. Dobrinski had made it easy for me to get settled into my new accommodations. She sent me off with a wave and a cheery greeting each morning as I headed out to walk the short distance from her house to the bank. Each day at noon, I would walk the half block to Grandma Dobrinski's house, where lunch awaited me. As I had not had the privilege of knowing my grandmothers, Theresa Dobrinski became such a figure in my life at this time.

The German roots of this farm community ran deep. Little did I know I would soon fall in love with a descendant of one of its founding members.

CHAPTER TWENTY-SEVEN

My Leon

When Dorothy Harder first brought me to church with her the summer of 1947, I did not know a soul in Lorraine, Kansas. A new community of friends opened up to me through connections made at the town's First Baptist Church. Once I moved in with Carl and Esther Dobrinski, I accompanied them weekly to Sunday services. Within this congregation, I would build many lifelong friendships. By the time I stepped through the classroom door on my first morning of high school, I knew almost all my classmates, as they were also church members. One person that I did not meet until sometime later was Leon Janzen.

Leon, who came from a German family as I did, grew up in Lorraine with his parents, Wilbert and Edna, and his younger sister, Shirley. Wilbert was a farmer, and Edna was a homemaker. Tall and lean, Leon cut an arresting figure, with his head full of dark, wavy hair and smoky hazel eyes, that might appear more green or brown, depending on what he was wearing. In the spring of 1945, while I was working hard to stay out of the clutches of Russian soldiers, Leon and his classmates were working hard to complete all their requirements for the May graduation. The class of '45 had twelve students in it: six young women and six young men.

Leon, his cousin, Donald "Donnie" Wilkens, and good friend, Louis "Louie" Rolfs, were inseparable. The trio had gone all the way through school together. All three grew up on farms situated outside of town. All three attended First Baptist Church. All three, upon graduation, joined their fathers in running those family farms. Just as did many others their age, the guys would often

Leon's high school graduation photo

On the porch of his parents' home

My Leon

cruise town in a '38 Ford. Louie said of those high school years, "Life in the Lorraine community was about as good as it gets."[1]

Leon had noticed me long before I ever knew his name. From across the sanctuary, he would see me sitting with Carl and Esther and their children. Perhaps we had spoken a time or two in passing, a "Hello" here or a "How are you?" there, though I do not remember for sure. Although the young men in my high school were very nice, no one ever caught my eye. I was very flattered and pleasantly surprised when I learned that Leon had been watching and hoping to catch a glimpse of me in church, yet I was very bashful. Somewhere in the fall of my ninth-grade year, Leon and I officially met one Sunday evening at a Baptist Youth Fellowship meeting.[2] After that, we struck up a friendship, seeing each other at church and around town. Now twenty years old, Leon had been out of school and farming with his dad for two years.

Just as my little brother, Horst, had been too young to serve in the German *Wehrmacht* during World War II, so had Leon been too young to enlist when America joined the Allied forces in 1941.[3] He would have been almost one month past his fourteenth birthday when the Japanese bombed Pearl Harbor on December 7. Wheat grown on Wilbert's farm was needed to contribute to the war efforts, as were the crops and livestock of every other American farmer. Growing food to feed America's citizens was a way to serve one's country, too.

At the Janzen family home

By the time Leon and I met, I had already gotten to know his sister, Shirley, at school. She was two grades above me and two years younger than me in the fall of 1947. Our membership in the high school's Kayette chapter gave us many opportunities to be together, as Shirley served that year as Program Chairman. The Janzen farm was about five miles north of Lorraine. Occasionally, Shirley would invite me out for a visit. I always enjoyed the time spent with Shirley and her family in their lovely home on the farm.

Over the next few years, the solid friendship formed between Leon and me developed into something deeper and more meaningful. One night before the start of my junior year, I spoke at an area church's youth meeting about my wartime experiences. Leon was in the audience and was taken by what he heard. It was not long after this that he and I began spending a lot more time together. A few months later, Leon and I started officially dating. Two years later, during Christmas of 1951, Leon asked me to marry him. We were so in love, and I could hardly believe this wonderful man had chosen me for his own. The only thing that could have made me happier was if Mutti had been here for him to ask her for my hand in marriage.

Early in February of 1952, a letter arrived from Mutti:[4]

Jan 8, 1952

My dear daughter,

On the 3rd of January, I received your letter that you are engaged. I am so happy for you and wish you God's blessings. I am sorry I cannot do anything to help you, but you know our situation. Horst is happy, too, over your engagement. I think so often how you had to get along by yourself at a young age in a strange land. I know it was not easy.

For Engagement

Heartfelt congratulations

Between my arrival in the United States in January 1947 and our wedding day in May 1953, my mother, brother, and I exchanged hundreds of letters. There were also countless official forms and documents filled out and sent to various agencies in hopes of bringing Mutti and Horst to America. None of those communications bore fruit. By the time I received Leon's engagement ring, Mutti and Horst had been living in the communist country of East Germany for two years. Leon was a patient, caring man and wanted, as I did, to have my mother present at our wedding. So, we waited to schedule our big event. Another reason we had not set our wedding date was because of the many responsibilities Leon and his father, Wilbert, had in running their farm. In addition to growing wheat, they also raised Polled Hereford cattle. A suitable date was not yet in sight, as the days of January, February, and March 1953 continued to unfold.

Leon would say, "A farmer has to wait till the cattle are on the pasture. You can't leave them when you have to feed them every day."

Finally, toward the end of March, after years of failed attempts to bring Mutti and Horst to be with us and after long months of waiting out the farm timetable, Leon and I reached the end of our limit. We would wait no longer. Leon suggested a date in early May as a good time for the wedding, as that was a break in the busy farm calendar.

Tante Anna, Esther, and I immediately began making plans for the big day. Esther took me shopping for my wedding dress, and Marcia,

Leon and Mildred shortly after their engagement

who was now ten, accompanied us. What a momentous time in my life. The loving involvement of both Tante Anna and Esther helped ease the sadness I tried to keep at bay. How I wished my Mutti could be here.

A special letter arrived just before the wedding.[5] Its German postmark filled my heart with delight:

4-23-53

Dear Children,

A cuckoo clock will be your wedding gift from us. Both Horst and I have been talking about what we could send you for a wedding gift. Then your letter came with Leon's wish for a cuckoo clock. We are so happy to be able to send you a wedding gift. We will send the clock first part of May. It will probably be 5 to 6 weeks before you get it. Please do not send money; then it wouldn't be a gift.

Much happiness on your special day, the best day in your life.

Heartfelt Greetings,
Mutti and Horst

Mutti and Horst decide to send a cuckoo clock as our wedding gift.

A Scripture, Romans 12:12, written on the front of Mutti's envelope, reminded me once again to keep my focus on God: "Be joyful in hope, patient in affliction, faithful in prayer."

* * *

The day of our wedding, Saturday, May 2, 1953, finally arrived! About one hundred family and friends came to witness the vows Leon and I made to each other in the sanctuary of First Baptist Church of Lorraine. I was overwhelmed with amazement and gratitude for all the blessings, opportunities, and new friends God had brought into my life throughout the past six years, as I waited to enter the sanctuary. A flood of emotion swept over me as thoughts of Pappa, Mutti, and Horst filled my mind. *Only joy, today*, I thought, blinking back tears. *Only joy.*

After Onkel Charlie walked me down the aisle to where Leon stood, he took his seat next to Tante Anna. My bridesmaids, Lois Rolfs and my soon-to-be-sister-in-law, Shirley Janzen, looked so pretty in their light green and pink dresses. Leon's groomsmen: his cousins, Donnie Wilkens and Melvin Janzen, were equally handsome in their pressed suits. Leon's cousin, Jean Dobrinski Behnke, who was five at the time, served as our flower girl. Reverend Alfred R. Bernadt tied a very tight knot, charging Leon and me to allow God to be the architect of our lives.

Jean remembered the ceremony this way:

> Mildred had a pretty white, lacy, ballerina-length dress, and she was
> beaming. She had an hour-glass figure with the tiniest waist. There
> were two bridesmaids and two groomsmen, plus ushers, taper lighters,
> etc. I wore a long lavender dress I think Esther Dobrinski made for
> me. There were flowers in my hair, and I had white dress shoes and
> carried a little white basket with pink rose petals in it that I delighted
> in dropping down the aisle right before Mildred walked down.[6]

After a lovely reception held in the church's fellowship hall and after changing into our going-away suits, Leon and I made our way out to the car, running through the crowd of happy, cheering family and friends and a shower of rice. The last people I hugged before getting into Leon's car were my aunt and uncle.

Onkel Charlie, Tante Anna, Mildred, Leon, Edna Janzen, and Wilbert Janzen (photo – Bernadt)

Married at last! (photo by Vernon Splitter)

I only hoped they could feel the love I had for them as I wrapped my arms tightly around them. Just as they had so graciously done before when taking me in when I arrived a frightened young girl six years earlier, Onkel Charlie and Tante Anna had now lovingly paid for all my wedding expenses, as if I had been their daughter. God had already known that my parents would not be here on this day and had provided this couple in their stead.

Leon leaned over and kissed me before putting the car in gear. Although I could hear faint sounds of well-wishers through the window, the only sound that mattered to me was my husband's voice telling me he loved me. Leon and I were a new family, and that was *all* that mattered.

We drove west to Las Vegas, to enjoy our honeymoon.

* * *

On our honeymoon

One of the last details Leon took care of before our wedding concerned the plans to upgrade the house in which we would live. A work crew began the work months before the wedding. When we returned from our honeymoon, the renovation of the farmhouse west of Lorraine was still underway. We stayed with Edna and Wilbert, Leon's parents, for six weeks until our house was ready. Although I had learned bits and pieces of Leon's family history in the years that we dated, it was not until we lived with the Janzens that I learned the finer details of my husband's distinguished family history.

Ellsworth County is situated squarely in the middle of Kansas. For almost two hundred years, this part of the American Midwest has been a busy crossroads. Travelers along the Santa Fe Trail would have driven their cattle to market through this area between 1821 and 1880.[7] Ellsworth became an official county on Saturday, August 24, 1867,[8] thirteen years after the Kansas Territory opened.[9] Railroad expansion into this area brought a boom of settlers, farmers, and cattle ranchers seeking to make their way in the world. Numerous German immigrants also arrived in this part of Kansas during this time, many bringing their strong Christian heritage with them. This settlement led to the establishment of several German Baptist churches.

Edward Carl Janzen, known to all as E.C., had been born in Elbing, West Prussia, Germany, on Saturday, December 20, 1835.[10] He immigrated with his parents and siblings to the United States at age seventeen, the family settling in Rochester, New York. E.C.'s father worked as a bootmaker.[11] After coming to faith in Christ two years later, E.C. would attend Rochester Theological Seminary. Upon graduation, he moved to Green Garden, Illinois, where he began his first pastorate.[12] The service for his ordination for ministry took place on Wednesday, March 8, 1865. Three weeks later, he married Eva Trumpp.[13] Green Garden's verdant, rich landscape was the idyllic setting in which this young couple began their life together.

Over the next twelve years, E.C. and Eva moved many times, as new opportunities for ministry arose. Three daughters and four sons were born in these years as well. By 1876, E.C. and Eva lived in Monee, Illinois, where he had founded a seminary.[14] A dream of establishing a Germany Baptist colony, which had been tucked away in E.C.'s heart for many years, would soon be realized. In the spring of 1877, after learning of land being sold at an attractive price by the Union Pacific Railroad Company, E.C. traveled to Ellsworth County, Kansas.[15] Many families of German descent were already living there. E.C. arranged a meeting with a local land agent.

An area of the county, known as Plumb Creek Flats, seemed to be the mirror image of the Illinois town Green Garden.[16] The railroad company would donate land if an individual or company purchased so many other parcels. The Union Pacific Railroad Company and E.C. signed an agreement between them, in March 1877, for the purchase of ten sections of land to be acquired at three dollars per acre.[17] The railroad company also donated an additional eighty acres, upon which to build a church. The First German Baptist Church of Green Garden, Kansas, was established on Saturday, June 22, 1878.[18] Fifteen years later, the congregation voted to move the church to nearby Lorraine and change the name to the First German Baptist Church of Lorraine.[19] (In the same year in which I was born, the church dropped the word "German" from its title.) E.C. and Eva would leave Lorraine and the Green Garden area in 1894 for him to devote himself to fulltime "Gospel Ministry."[20]

E.C.'s oldest son, Henry, grew up in Ellsworth County and became a farmer. Henry married Caroline Carrie Dees on Tuesday, April 19, 1892, and they settled down to start a family. Wilbert was born in 1903, and like his father, Henry, Wilbert also grew up to be a farmer. Wilbert fell in love with and married Edna Schmidt on Wednesday, June 9, 1926. By 1930, he had purchased acreage and was running a farm of his own.[21] Wilbert and Edna's only son, Leon, grew up to be the man I married.

Those six weeks were valuable. I gained a better understanding of the solid relationship shared by my husband and his parents, established a closer relationship with my dear in-laws, and developed a greater appreciation for the Janzen family as a whole. What a treasure God had given to me in this new family.

It was time for us to establish a home of our own. After carrying me across the threshold of our newly-renovated house, Leon and I settled into life on our farm.

All Together Once Again

L eon and I returned from our honeymoon to begin our life together in Lorraine. We were so happy and so in love. While I went to work at the bank, Leon and his father, Wilbert, worked together on the Janzen family farm. Driving lessons Leon gave me while we were engaged were now paying big dividends. Between planting and harvesting wheat, taking care of the cattle, ordering supplies, and repairing equipment, there was much work to be done. Leon and I had so hoped that Mutti and Horst would be here for our wedding, but because of many hold-ups related to paperwork, they missed our big day. My boss, Mr. Staeber, had been unbelievably helpful. Throughout the past year, he would often stay long after the bank closed to help me fill out documents and write letters required by the government to expedite Mutti's and Horst's release. There was much bureaucratic red tape to cut through. Neither Mr. Staeber nor I had scissors that strong.

My mother, brother, and I had now been separated from each other for seven long years. While my life had taken exciting twists and turns, theirs had been moving in slow motion. Assigned in the fall of 1945 to refugee housing in Nienhagen, Germany, Mutti and Horst had continued to live there after I left by train in February 1946. Mutti and Horst had now been living under the rule of a communist government for almost three years.

Summer and Fall 1952

The summer before our wedding, a series of events began to unfold, which did not occur at any great speed. Nonetheless, they set in motion the wheels that

Mutti in Germany shortly before coming to America in 1953

would eventually bring Mutti and Horst to Kansas. By the spring of 1952, thousands of refugees and displaced persons with ties to American relatives found themselves still stranded in Europe. Two members of Congress, U.S. Senator Patrick McCarran of Nevada and Representative Francis Walter of Pennsylvania, sponsored legislation to introduce a limited immigration plan for those individuals who met specific criteria.[1]

Once President Truman received the bill after it made its way through the legislative process, he refused to sign it, as he believed some of the provisions of the law were too restrictive and unfairly discriminatory to certain ethnic groups. Support of the legislation was sufficient, however, to overcome the presidential veto, and on Friday, June 27, the Immigration and Nationality Act of 1952 became U.S. law.² Otherwise known as the McCarran-Walter Act, this new regulation would make it possible for Mutti and Horst to come to America.³

Somewhere in this year, letters received from Mutti and Horst began arriving with a postmark from a different location. My mother and younger brother somehow managed to slip across the East German border and now lived in the southwestern West German state of Baden-Württemberg, in a little town called Kniebis. There they shared a one-bedroom, basement apartment. Horst found a job with a forestry service.⁴ What led to this move is mere speculation on my part. One thought is that Horst had completed the three years of training he had begun in a Russian school of carpentry and was now freer to travel into West Germany.⁵ The fact that my mother and brother were now living in a free state raised the probability that they might have a better chance of getting out of the country. Many of Mutti's letters stated that "the time wasn't right" for her and Horst to come. I never knew what that meant. I was going to have to let go of what I wanted and trust God to do what only He could do.

1953

I received this letter from my mother in the early spring:⁶

> *Dear Daughter,*
>
> *Many thanks for your letter. I'm happy that you are healthy and happy. We are both doing well. You are wanting to know several things, and I'm thinking you have things pretty well right. About Horst's birth certificate. I'll have to write to Baden-Baden. And here is the address from the American consulate. Stuttgart. That should be enough.*
>
> *Here it is:*
>
> *Pappa's name: Fritz Robert Schindler, born in Radach 4/27/1899. And now the mother: Anna Elizabeth Schindler, maiden name Gerlach. Born 1/26/1898 in Kurzig, state Meseritz. When Pappa was coming to America, I don't know. Please ask Tante Anna.*
>
> *I came Nov. 1, 1926. Married Nov. 1, 1926, in New York. I have the marriage license.*
>
> *Back to Germany in September 1929.*
>
> *Neither of us became American citizens. We are registered as Germans.*
>
> *Horst's birth certificate I do not have, but I will go as soon as possible and see if I can get it. I'm going to the Dr. Tuesday and will take care of that and send by airmail as soon as possible.*

Mutti reports activity to collect document to come to the United States

*We received the money and two care packages. We are very happy
about that, and we could use that—we needed it.*

*Yesterday, a package with food came from the Hiawatha Kayettes.
It was wonderful. I'm going to find a nice card with a winter scene as
a thank you. I also sent a winter scene thank you to Miss Vinson [KS
director of Kayettes].*

*I just now received a letter from you from 21st of January. I'm so
happy, like you, when we get mail from one another.*

*Today, Monday, Horst scooped snow in the town, but just for today,
and then they'll quit. Last week he scooped snow for three days. If longer,
they take money away.*

*I'm wondering if I can go by bus to Freudenstadt because we have so
much snow. I've never seen anything like this as old as I am. (Mildred—
we used to have a lot of snow). The pictures you see are real, not made up.
I will send you some [were never received].*

*We have a really nice radio but wondering if we should bring it?
Could we get repair parts?*

Many greetings, and hopefully, see you soon.

From Mutti & Horst
Greetings and kisses, and hopefully see you soon.

Shortly after receipt of this letter, I wrote to the Immigration and
Naturalization Service office in Kansas City, Missouri, on Tuesday, February
17. I typed the letter on Lorraine State Bank letterhead (another evidence of
Mr. Staeber's kindness):[7]

Gentlemen:

*For the preference papers which I have received from you I need the
alien number of my mother, Anna Schindler born January 26, 1898,
in Kurzig, Kreis Meseritz, Germany. She came to the United States on
November 1st. 1926.*

Yours very truly,

Mildred Schindler

* * *

THE LORRAINE STATE BANK

CAPITAL $10,000.00   SURPLUS AND UNDIVIDED PROFITS $50,000.00

OFFICERS

V. H. WAGNER
PRESIDENT

EDW. B. STAEBER
CASHIER

LORRAINE, KANSAS
February 17-1953

Immigration & Naturalization Service
Department of Justice
Kansas City, Mo.

Gentlemen:

For the preference papers which I have received from you I need
the alien number of my mother, Anna Schindler born January 26, 1898,
in Kurzig, Kreis Meseritz, Germany. She came to the United States
on November 1st. 1926.

Yours very truly,

Mildred Schindler

The letter I wrote on my mother's behalf on bank stationery

Summer had come and gone with no new information regarding the possibility of Mutti and Horst coming stateside. Besides working at the bank and keeping house, I stayed busy writing wedding thank-you notes and filling out more official government paperwork.[8] As I turned the pages of my calendar, the months of August and September came and went. Still, no word. Unbeknownst to me, Mutti and Horst had entered the United States on Saturday, October 3. My mother's alien registration number upon entry was A8548781.[9]

On October 6, the first Tuesday of the month, I received a telegram from my mother telling me that she and Horst were in Canada and would soon be in Kansas. I was beside myself with joy and excitement! Two days later, on Thursday, October 8, Leon and I drove the fifty-four miles from Lorraine to the train station in Hutchinson. During the drive, I must have chattered away like an excited child. Not only was I eager to be reunited with my mother and brother, but I especially wanted them to meet my new husband. The train schedule listed the arrival of the Santa Fe express at the station at 1:55 P.M., aboard would be my mother and brother.[10]

Leon and I stood on the platform and watched as passengers spilled out of the train cars. Finally, I caught sight of my younger brother, Horst, his six-foot, four-inch frame towering above the crowd, the familiar features of his face still recognizable after all this time. Beside him, but hidden from view by the crowd, was Mutti. Before I knew it, I was hugging and kissing her, crying wet tears of joy, as I was finally within the embrace of a mother whom I had missed beyond telling.

Reunited on October 8, 1953, at the train station in Hutchinson, Kansas, after seven years of separation. *Left to right:* Mutti, Mildred, Leon, and Horst

"Ach, mein liebe Tochter!" was all Mutti could say. "Oh, my dear daughter!"

Next came a bear hug from my little brother. How good his arms felt around me! I stepped back and held him out from me, gazing in wonder at this young gentleman before me. Mutti was now fifty-five; Horst was twenty-two. A photographer, with the *Hutchinson News-Herald*, snapped a picture as we all stood together on the platform. An article about Mutti's and Horst's arrival ran two days later. Our four faces radiated with the neon glow of sheer joy, clearly evident even though pictured in a black and white photograph. We were *finally* all together once again.

* * *

Leon could not speak German, and my mother and brother could not speak English, but we got along fine. Mutti and Horst moved into our farmhouse with Leon and me for the first few months following their arrival to this new country. My husband and my brother hit it off right away. Leon, four years older, became the big brother Horst never had. My brother quickly mastered Leon's driving lessons. The newspaper substituted for a textbook as both Leon and I helped my brother acquire more and more English vocabulary. Before long, Horst was speaking this new language very well.

The cost to bring Mutti and Horst to America had been four hundred dollars. Monies earned from my job at the bank covered the fee. While writing this account of my life, I came upon a long-forgotten locked metal box in the basement of my home, which held many of Mutti's essential papers.[11] Among them was the actual receipt for that trip.

Travel Agency
F. Leins
Freudenstadt (Schwarzwald)

Bill: Freudenstadt 31 August 1953
for Mrs. Anna Schindler. Kniebis

31 August 1953
As payment for ship passage to the USA $400.00
by check number 605
From the Lorraine State Bank
[bank draft from Mildred's account]

Ship ticket for passage to United States for Mutti and Horst

Horst's daughter, Amy Schindler Weldon, remembers Mutti's description of that Atlantic crossing: "Oma [the name by which Amy and her siblings called Mutti] talked about it being a really big ship. She said it was a long trip, and when Oma and Horst arrived in the states and were coming through immigration, officials checked their hair with a comb to make sure they didn't have lice."[12]

An interview with Horst, about his World War II experiences, was filmed forty-five years after he arrived in the United States. In it, he relayed many stories about his childhood. When Horst was asked to share his thoughts about finally being able to move and join Mildred stateside, he replied, "My mom and my dad had been in the United States." Remembering his excitement about this opportunity, Horst continued, "We'd already lost our home and everything we had four or five times. So, to start over one more time wouldn't hurt anything."[13]

Horst recalled the journey to Kansas that he and his mother made, "We traveled from Germany on a small ship. We could not come to New York because of a harbor strike. Instead, we were sent to the port of Quebec, Canada.

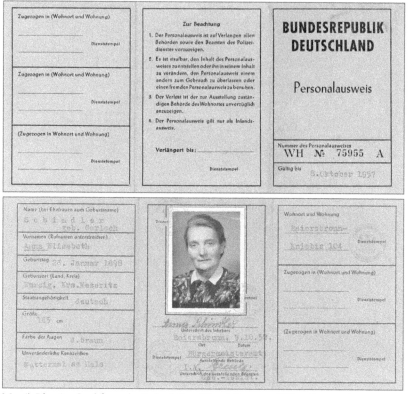

Mutti's Identity Card from the Federal Republic of Germany (West Germany)

From there, we took a train to Montreal. From Montreal, we flew by plane to New York City. We stayed in the city with friends [possibly the Knappes]. One person asked if I wanted to stay there and get a job. I thanked the man for the kind offer and told him I could not live in a big city. Besides, my sister and brother-in-law were expecting us in Kansas. We better go there."[14] After a brief time spent in New York City, Mutti and Horst took a train to Chicago. Once there, they changed trains and boarded one headed for Hutchinson.

My mother and brother had nothing in the way of material possessions when they came to the United States in October 1953. Mutti and Horst spent much time in those first few weeks in America resting and getting acquainted with their new surroundings. They had endured quite an ordeal and needed time to adjust to the realization that they were safe and beyond the threat of any kind. Many times, in the weeks following their arrival, Horst would rise as the sun was coming up, whistle for our dog, and head out to see if the pair could

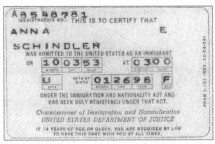

Mutti's Immigrant Card documenting her
arrival in the United States on October 3, 1953

Personal photo on Mutti's U.S. Immigration
Card

find a rabbit or two. Using a gun borrowed from Leon and putting into practice his brother-in-law's instructions, Horst's sure aim provided us with several fine meals Mutti prepared from those early morning hunts' spoils. His eyes were sharper than his glasses let on.

Mutti and I spent every available moment catching up with one another. I was so proud of our new home and enjoyed showing her my small garden and the fields of our farm. The kitchen was where we spent the bulk of our time, as we chatted, preparing delicious meals for the four of us. How I had missed my mother's fine cooking!

I remember how Horst refused to eat corn, prepared in any form, as that is what he had fed to the pigs on our farm in Radach. One day, while Mutti and I were preparing a meal, Horst walked into the kitchen, hungry as always. His appetite was a bottomless pit we could never fill. Trying to tide him over until the meal was ready to be served, I gave him a piece of white sandwich bread.

Crushing the slice in his hand, Horst looked at me and asked a question laced with incredulity and disgust, "You eat this?"

My brother was astounded at how mushy and seemingly non-nutritional this new type of bread seemed to be. Although it was certainly different in both texture and taste from the hearty slices of rye bread our Mutti had made while we were growing up, I assured Horst that this bland, doughy slice he held in his hand was also nutritious. I am not quite sure he ever truly believed me.

1954

Mutti and Horst attended church with us, although their English was very limited. They were so grateful to this loving congregation who had supported them and welcomed me. On October 14, 1954, the Dorcas ladies' circle at First Baptist Church of Lorraine invited Mutti to attend their meeting, as their members had a gift for her. My mother was speechless when presented with a beautiful set of bedroom furniture previously used in the church's parsonage. The tears shining in her eyes and the smile on her face were all the language needed to convey Mutti's heartfelt thanks. That bedroom suit is now in my guest bedroom.

Horst worked alongside Leon and Wilbert as a hand on our farm and that of another family nearby. Once many in the Lorraine community became aware of his skills, he also found plenty of work to keep him busy as a handyman. A few months into the new year, Horst secured a carpentry job working for Harper Construction Company in Great Bend. Once he saved up money from a few paychecks, he and Mutti found an apartment located nearby and moved there.

Amy, Horst's only daughter, said of her grandmother's and father's decision to come to the United States, "My dad knew the only way they could survive [he and Mutti] was to leave and immigrate to the United States. I can't even imagine the fear and uncertainty they experienced during that time. I do know they left everything they had ever known, but they were happy. My dad never became an American citizen, but he was probably one of the most patriotic

All together again—Horst, Mutti, and Mildred

Americans I've ever known. He was so proud to live here. He taught my brothers and me to make every opportunity count, because America was the land of opportunities. He was *so* happy and proud to be in America."[15]

God had been *incredibly* faithful to all of us. Memories of many of those awful experiences Mutti, Horst, and I suffered, in that last year of World War II and in the years that followed, began to recede from the place of prominence they had once occupied in our minds. Peace and contentment were new companions with whom we were becoming more familiar.

We were about to receive another of His blessings. A Janzen baby was on the way.

CHAPTER TWENTY-NINE

A Rich, Full Life in Lorraine

L eon and I were elated that we would soon be parents. I was so thankful my Mutti would be here for the birth of her first grandchild, as she had missed many other milestones in my life during the years we were separated. Wilbert and Edna, Leon's parents, also looked forward to meeting their first grandchild. My pregnancy went very smoothly. I continued working at the bank, almost up to the baby's due date. Leon and I became a family of three with the birth of our first daughter, Karen Ann Janzen, in the fall of 1954. I could hardly believe this precious baby I held in my arms was ours. Leon was a proud new father.

Over the next nine years, God blessed us with three more amazing children. Our first son, Kenton Leon Janzen, arrived in 1957. Leon beamed with pride, knowing we now had a daughter *and* a son. Our second daughter, Susan Edna Janzen, was born in the summer of 1958, and our second son, Galen Fred Janzen, was born almost six years later in 1964. I felt the same way when I held each of our children for the first time: this was the best of both of us in this new life. Each of our children was a gift from God. Our family was now complete. There was no way Leon and I could have imagined when making our wedding vows to each other ten years earlier, the indescribable happiness God would bring to us through our children's lives.

Earlier in our marriage, Leon and I had decided that once our children arrived, I would leave my job to become a stay-at-home mom. I never regretted that decision for a second. Until they reached grade school, keeping up with

Easter 1966. *Front row, left to right:* Kenton, Susan, and Karen;
Back row, left to right: Mildred, Galen, and Leon (photo by
Vernon Splitter)

our four very energetic children consumed most of my time. Mutti was with us
almost every day, which was a tremendous help. How thrilled I was to have her
by my side. There were so many years we had been apart. There could *never* be
enough time together.

Our children were blessed to have two grandmothers and a grandfather
who loved them and doted on them. Leon's parents, Wilbert and Edna, were

very involved, as was Mutti, in the lives of our children. Leon's sister, Shirley, lived in Kansas City, marrying Gerald Glasgow six weeks after we were married. Shirley and Gerald had three children—Judy, Linda, and Dennis. Many fun occasions were shared as we traveled to visit each other, celebrating holidays, birthdays, and anniversaries. Friendships with numerous cousins on both sides of the family only added to the rich tapestry of our lives.

Leon and I had many good friends who were in the same place in life as we were: juggling responsibilities of being a husband and wife, parenting energetic, young children, and working to earn a living. Louie Rolfs, Leon's close friend, and his sweetheart, Betty Melchert, had married several years before we did. Betty also attended Lorraine High School, having graduated in 1946, the year after Louie and Leon finished. Like Leon, Louie was a farmer. He and Betty lived about three miles south of our farm and became some of our dearest friends. The four of us spent a great deal of time together and shared many life events, especially once our children were born. Our daughter, Susan, is named for their daughter. When our families got together, it was always a lively time, with the Rolfs' five children—Janice, Jack, Susan, Scott, and Jean—and our four.

* * *

As our children were growing up, they were undoubtedly aware that my English sounded a bit different than theirs. In bits and pieces, whenever appropriate, I began to acquaint our children with our Schindler family story. Although Mutti and I often spoke German when we were together, I felt *very* strongly about using English only when talking with my children. We were Americans, and English was the language of our country.

Once our four children grew older and learned to talk, I would occasionally sprinkle in a few German words and phrases and maybe even a song or two. When bouncing one of our children on my knee, I would often recite this nursery rhyme in a sing-song cadence,

> "So fahren die Damen,
> So fahren die Damen,
> So reiten die Herrn,
> So reiten die Herrn,
> Schockreit! Schockreit! Schockreit!"

The bouncing would become much more pronounced, mimicking a horse galloping wildly, when reaching the last line of the nursery rhyme.

Here's my English translation:

> "That's the way the ladies go,
> That's the way the ladies go,
> That's the way the gentlemen ride,
> That's the way the gentlemen ride,
> Giddy-up! Giddy-up! Giddy-up!"

All our children enjoyed the "bouncy" part the best. Susan particularly remembers this from her childhood.[1]

* * *

Years earlier, while I had been in high school, I shared the story of my war-time experiences with a variety of social clubs and organizations. When our children reached grade school age, similar invitations to visit with classroom groups came my way. Susan remembers accompanying me on one such visit. "I was preschool age, and Mom was speaking to a high school assembly on this particular day. I was a wiggler. Mom had placed me in the last seat on the front row and then went up on stage to share her story. After she finished her remarks, she brought me up on stage and picked me up in her arms. Holding me up to the microphone, she had me recite the numbers one through ten in German, as she had taught me to do. I remember being shy and embarrassed, but after I finished, there was great applause. The audience loved it!"[2]

Kenton's first recollection of my sharing my story with students was when I came to speak to his high school history class. "I was somewhat apprehensive because of peer pressure, and I did not want classmates laughing at my mom. They did not." Kenton remembers how moved his classmates had been by my story.[3]

* * *

Life on a farm provided many object lessons that Leon and I could use with our children, as we worked hard to cultivate responsibility and model for them a strong work ethic. Each of the children had a household chore or task assignment.

Son Kenton learned from an early age the value of hard work, "We all had different chores at different times in our lives, depending on our age. Mine often included caring for animals, including pigs. I feel that I learned a work ethic. Also, because an animal is dependent upon you for their life (food, water, and shelter), it's a different chore than others, like pulling weeds."[4]

Susan remembers, "My job was gathering the eggs and feeding and watering the chickens."[5]

I encouraged our children to play outside, and there was certainly plenty of room to do so on our farm. Many days, I found myself reminiscing about my childhood spent in Radach as I watched my children tromp through the grass or climb trees in our yard.

Kenton recalls learning "how to have fun with makeshift toys. I made a fort out of sticks and logs. Another time, Susan and I dug a hole, filled it with water, covered the hole with sticks and leaves, and played 'Follow the Leader' with our little brother, Galen. He ended up in our moat. We were creative with what we had."[6]

As our sons began getting a little older, I never let Kenton or Galen have all the wild stuff, as they do now. I was also strict and did not allow them to watch war movies.

"I've been through it," I would explain to my sons, "and I don't want you seeing it."

I also *never* allowed my boys to wear a particular style of a winter hat, the kind with extended ear flaps, which you could tie up on the top of the head. *That* type of hat was exactly like the one worn by the female Russian laundry camp officer when I was sixteen years old. The memory was too painful.

* * *

Mealtimes were very special in our home, no matter how simple or fancy the fare. Food was a way to show love and affection. Karen and Susan were always in the kitchen, by my side, when they were little girls. Both of their grandmothers, Mutti and Edna, were also excellent cooks and taught their granddaughters how to prepare many family favorites. They made most dishes from scratch, not these boxed dinners popular today. Mutti had taught me, from the time I was a little girl on our farm in Radach, to use whatever was on hand in preparing a delicious and nutritious meal.

Susan shares, "The importance of food has always been stressed in our household, as that's what our family grew for our livelihood."[7]

As both Leon's family and mine were of German lineage, traditional German dishes were staples in our kitchen.

Susan explains, "*Roladen* is the all-time family favorite of our family. It is tenderized or pounded round steak. A mixture of bacon, onions, mustard, salt, and pepper fills the center of each piece of meat. Then it is rolled and tied with a string or secured with toothpicks, browned in a skillet, and baked slowly in

Janzen family photo 1973. *Front row, left to right:* Leon, Susan, Karen, and Mildred; *Back row, left to right:* Galen and Kenton (photo by Vernon Splitter)

the oven. Once cooked, these delicious meat rolls and the gravy from them can be served with mashed potatoes. *Rot Kohl,* red cabbage, is sweet and sour cabbage cooked for special occasions and holiday dinners. It was one of Mutti's specialties."[8]

"Just as they'd been in Germany on the Schindler farm, potatoes were also a staple in the Janzen family diet," Karen shares. "Potatoes were cooked in every way possible. Dad would often say, with a twinkle in his eye, '*Oh,* are we having potatoes for dinner?'"[9]

Susan remembers Mutti and me talking "about eating thin potato soup in Germany (for lack of nothing more to eat). For years, Mom did not want to eat it, nor would she make it for us. Over time, she ran across good potato soup recipes and now enjoys it."[10]

Our oven seemed to be always on, as I baked something almost every day, whether it was bread or homemade rolls or *kuchen* (coffee cake). Rye bread, the staple of my childhood, became the bread of choice in our household. Try as I might, my baking never tasted quite as good as my mother's. Mutti made *Kaffeekuchen,* the best coffee cake ever!

Karen fondly remembers, "When Mutti came to visit, Saturday mornings were my favorite. The kitchen table was full of flour and dough. Mom and

Mutti might be rolling everything from cinnamon rolls to rye bread to dinner rolls. It smelled heavenly!"[11]

As we raised a variety of livestock on the farm in Lorraine, fresh meat was readily available for meals. One day, Mutti and her sister-in-law, Tante Anna, had come to help me butcher chickens.

Susan received a first-hand lesson, "I was very young, and I watched the first chicken get its head chopped off. It ran around for a bit, then fell over. My job was to pull all the feathers after the chicken was dipped into boiling water to make feather removal easier. I only lasted about one chicken into this process. The smell of singed feathers was sickening to me, and I left my post to do fun kid things!"[12]

* * *

Both Leon and I shared a love of music. I worked to cultivate that same appreciation in our home, as it had been in the Schindler household of my childhood in Radach. Mutti taught many songs to Horst and me as we were growing up, several of which were based on Scriptures, especially portions of the book of Psalms. Music accompanied us as we worked in the fields; music reminded us of God's love for us; music kept our spirits high during difficult times.

Leon was a talented musician who played several instruments, including the trumpet, cornet, and flugelhorn. His mother, Edna, had at one time been the church organist and had instilled in her son a devotion to music. Leon played in three polka bands throughout his life—The Dutchmasters, the Loren Keil Polka Band, and the Moonlighters. The wives of other band members and I accompanied our husbands to Germany on several trips, during which they made appearances at various music festivals.

Our daughter, Karen, learned the value of practice through watching and listening to Leon rehearse music for the band. "Dad was a magnificent trumpet player. He practiced all the time at night. It was very comforting for me to hear him play as I was going to sleep."[13]

Our children also gained a fondness for history and nature from their dad. A self-taught expert in Native American culture, Leon had a particular interest in petroglyphs, pictorial representations of humans and animal forms cut into or carved into the walls of caves or other rock surfaces.[14] Leon's paper, "Early Ellsworth County Pictorial Art," was presented at several local and regional anthropological conferences and was also printed in the *Kansas Anthropological Journal.*[15]

Kenton fondly remembers spending significant quantities of time with his father as they searched for artifacts and treasures. "Dad and I hiked many miles taking pictures of petroglyphs. We also searched for arrowheads together."[16]

Karen, Kenton, Susan, and Galen appreciated the quality of gentleness observed in their father. He devotedly cared for his livestock and all the creatures living in the fields and woods of our farm. Our son, Kenton, now runs his farm in the same manner. He recalls, "Dad once left a note on the tractor. I was replacing him to finish working the field. The note said, 'Leave the small area. Don't work it. There's a killdeer that has a nest there.' Dad also carried water and food to a sick hawk, after calling Fish and Game with no results."[17]

Daughter Karen shares how her father's example influenced her, "To care for the land and family farm we are blessed to have is one of my passions and also taking care of and loving animals."[18]

* * *

Our shared faith in God was the anchor of our home. Although coming to personal faith in Christ would be a decision our children could only make for themselves, Leon and I made sure that the soil of their hearts was tilled and prayed often that the seeds of faith would bear fruit. First Baptist Church of Lorraine played such an integral role in our lives when Leon and I were teenagers, which was the same for our children. If it was Sunday, the Leon Janzen family was at church. But this was not some rote motion we went through each week. The God whom we loved and served met with us weekly in our church's beautiful sanctuary, and we did not want to miss anything He said. Just as Leon and I had, our four children made life-long friends from within this loving congregation. First Baptist offered various opportunities for our four children to stay involved in church-related activities: "scripture memory classes, Wednesday evening church, and youth group."[19]

"We were taught from an early age to be thankful for our many blessings," our daughter Karen remembers. "Little stories, scattered here and there, let us know how children in other places were not as fortunate as we were. The number one lesson from Mom was to appreciate the country in which we live, where we are free to worship and to speak freely. The common thread that bound my mom, her brother, and their mother together, I believe, was their love for God, each other, and their country."[20]

* * *

I returned to my job at the bank in 1969 during Galen's kindergarten year. The bank president called one day to say he needed some help and asked me if I would consider coming back to work. After talking the matter over with Leon, he graciously agreed to pick Galen up from school at noon and then take him to the farm to spend the week-day afternoons, until I got home from work.

My last boss was Larry Henne, who began working with us in February 1981. At this time, I was serving as the cashier.[21] Larry joined Lorraine State Bank as Vice President. He was also working with the Office of the State Bank Commissioner of Kansas and other entities to iron out the details of his purchase of the bank, in addition to his nine-to-five responsibilities. Larry became president of Lorraine State Bank within a year of having come on board.

Larry remembers, "Mildred was worried that I would change things that she was used to doing. I assured her that the bank's routine would stay the same, and I would be the one to make the adjustments. She was very relieved."[22]

One of Larry's favorite stories about me provides an amusing local color. "One day, Mildred walked across the street to deliver a deposit slip to Myers Garage. Three elderly gentlemen were there who liked to play cards and drink adult beverages. Mildred returned to the bank and said, 'They wanted me to stay for communion, but I told them I had to get back to work.'"[23]

My job at Lorraine State Bank brought so many terrific people across my path and afforded me opportunities to serve the people of Lorraine in ways I would never have been able to in any other way. After thirty years of working at Lorraine State Bank, I retired in June of 1997. Our children had long been grown. The Lord blessed Leon and me with six grandchildren, five granddaughters and one grandson—Annie, Katie, Christie, Betsy, Carlie, and Ryan. I now wanted the freedom to spend as much time as possible with them.

Those years of Leon and I working hard together to provide a good life for our children had moved into another season, one in which we had more time to savor each other and enjoy time with loved ones and friends. A local news article, written shortly after I ended my career at the bank, shares my thoughts about what I wanted to do in this retirement period, "'Do some of the things I didn't get to do while I was working . . . Go along with Leon when he goes somewhere occasionally. I'm finding enough things to [do] right here at home, things I put off that should have been done. I enjoy also working outside. I do the mowing and trimming and I enjoy being out when it's cool, not during the heat of the day. And I enjoy visiting the elderly people. I've always liked to do that, bake something or take them something.'"[24]

* * *

Celebrating our 65th wedding anniversary. God granted us sixty-five-plus years of a happy life together.

The last few years of Leon's life were difficult. He spent his last three years in a nursing home after suffering a heart attack and a stroke. We lost Leon in February 2019. He had fought the good fight; it was now time to go to Heaven. God blessed my husband with ninety-one years of life. How fortunate I was to share almost sixty-six of those as his wife. Our children had lost their mentor, their guide, and their best friend. We were all going to have to get used to a new normal.

The opening line of Psalm 23 is printed on a piece of paper and pasted in the back of my Bible: "Der Herr ist mein Hirte, mir wird nichts mangeln." I first learned this verse as a child, "The Lord is my Shepherd; I will not lack anything." Throughout the years between then and now, I had witnessed God's faithfulness to my family and me, over and over and over again. God had carried us through many dark vales and treacherous valleys. Although brokenhearted at the loss of my dear husband, I had every confidence God would once again meet our every need.

* * *

The roots of our family are planted firmly in the soil of this Kansas heartland. Leon and I moved in 2006 from our house on the family farm to the nearby town of Ellsworth. As both of Leon's parents had passed away, their former house, conveniently located near Ellsworth's downtown, offered us a lovely home in which to live. The Janzen home also provided a place where our large family could gather, especially during these golden years of our lives. Even after we moved to town, Leon would make the drive out to the family farm to work the land with Kenton, just as his father had done with him. Fourteen miles lay between our Ellsworth home and the farm in Lorraine. The picturesque landscape of this area never disappointed, offering views of fertile farmland and endless windswept plains as Leon made his daily drive.

The home in Ellsworth is where I continue to live today. Memories of Leon are with me. Although I miss him terribly, I am not alone. Karen moved in with me several years before my husband's death, and I have enjoyed her loving company. Her husband, J.V., has a traveling job and joins us on long weekends and holidays. Kenton and his wife, Angie, and Galen live nearby, and Susan and her husband, Mitch, are only a few hours' drive away. Many extended family members live in the area, as do many of my friends. Participation in an exercise class several times a week keeps my muscles limber and offers me a chance to keep my finger on the pulse of life in Ellsworth.

Pastor Zach Ullom continues the time-honored tradition of equipping all in the congregation of First Baptist Church of Lorraine to love God, to love each other, and to let our lives be beacons of light in this dark world. Following in the footsteps of beloved former pastors like Reverend Fred Ferris, Zach shepherds our congregation through weekly Bible studies, Sunday services, and special luncheons and dinners that foster camaraderie and fellowship within our church family.

God's provision is ongoing. His faithfulness supplies my every need. How thankful I am for the rich, full life in Lorraine, which the Lord has given to my family and me.

CHAPTER THIRTY

Mutti

Anna Elizabeth Gerlach Schindler was an amazing woman. How fortunate I am to have had such a marvelous mother. When we lost my father in the spring of 1945, my mother squared her shoulders, swallowed her grief, and held our family together. Mutti kept my brother, Horst, and me alive through the terrifying events our family endured. My mother embodied courage and faced the most difficult of circumstances with fortitude, grace, and strength. Most importantly, Mutti infused in both Horst and me her joyous spirit of living.

My mother was born on January 26, 1898, in the city of Kurzig, in the Kreis Meseritz district of Prussia, forty-four kilometers (twenty-seven miles) from Radach. She was the youngest of three children born to Reinhold and Ernestine Gerlach. Her oldest sibling was a sister, Emma, who later married and had one daughter, Helmi. A brother, Karl, died in childhood. After my parents and I returned to Germany in the fall of 1929, Pappa and Mutti settled down to life on the Schindler family farm in Radach. As I was only an infant when I left the country of my birth, my childhood memories are only of our life in Germany.

Faith in God was the cornerstone of my Mutti's life. My children would often find her alone in her darkened room seated in front of the window, with only natural light to illuminate the pages of her Bible, which she was reading. My brother Horst and I had observed the same while growing up in Germany. Mutti would always say about reading the Bible, "I read the same thing over and over, but it's always new to me every time I read it."

A possible passport picture taken of Mutti

My son, Kenton, responded with the following when asked how the story of God's deliverance of my mother, brother, and I impacted his journey of faith. "That's a tough one to put into words, but I'll try. Their continuing, unwavering love of the Lord, with what they'd been through, is something that has always moved me. I look at Mutti losing her husband, family, friends, and possessions; yet, she was still bountiful with love for everyone. That strength can't be found without God's help."[1]

"Since we grew up with this story," shares Kenton's sister, Susan, "it was 'normal.' When I grew older, I realized how amazing it was that all of them survived the war, found each other, and were kept safe by God's protecting hand, mostly when the three of them were separated."[2]

I believe Mutti's faith instilled within her a joy-filled spirit. Her unwavering belief in God's goodness enabled her to maintain a thankful heart, regardless of the harsh life circumstances she had endured. Someone would give her a little something, and you would think she had been given a hundred-dollar bill. She was just a happy person. Especially after her return to the United States in 1953, Mutti was so glad to be in this country and so grateful to be alive. She somehow found a way to put behind her all she went through. Her oldest granddaughter, Karen, vividly remembers, "No doubt in my mind . . . Mutti exuded joy!"[3]

I shared earlier about having found a locked metal box containing many of my mother's personal papers. A series of prayers were in that collection.[4] I'm not sure if my mother wrote these throughout the years or copied them from various devotional guides. These prayers, recorded in Mutti's beautiful hand, often contained German words interspersed among the English ones. These supplications reflect my mother's devotion to her Lord. Below are some of my favorites:

"Let thy favor ever be upon thy church, increase our love for it, and give us a growing understanding of its world-wide task. Make it thy voice to our conscience, to keep our feet in the path of duty, and our minds in the love of Christ our Lord. Amen."

"Lord, show me when I become too involved in my earthly possessions. Help me to keep my life as burden-free as possible. Amen."

"Dear Lord, forgive us when we push ahead to do what we feel needs to be done, with no thought for your will for us. We know that without your guidance, we can do nothing. Go with us into this new day that all we do may be pleasing in thy sight and directed by you. Make today a special day for us and for all with whom we come into contact. Amen."

"Thank you, Jesus, for going with me through each day and helping me to make the best of every situation. Your presence is comforting. Amen."

"O heavenly father, I have thought much about your words and stored them in my heart so that they would hold me back from sin."

* * *

Mutti arrived in the United States a year before the birth of the first of our four children. As such, she was a part of all of their lives. As I have shared before, I did not teach my children to speak German. Sometimes Mutti and I would speak German to each other when we did not want my children to know what we were saying. Little did we suspect we might be understood. One day while my mother and I were talking together in German, Karen was in the room with us and answered back in perfect German. We were amazed.

Throughout the years, Mutti's grandchildren came to learn many German phrases, which were standard in my mother's vocabulary.

Mutti's Phrases

*Ach du liebe zeit**	*"Oh, my goodness!"*
Ach du lieber Himmel	*"Oh, dear heavens!"*
Meine liebe kinder	*"My dear children"*
Mein Kleines Liebchen	*"My little sweetheart"*
Ich liebe dich	*"I love you."*
Na setz Dich hin	*"Now sit down"*
Bist du hungrig?	*"Are you hungry?"*
Has du gegessen? Come esse.	*"Have you eaten? Come eat."*
Schmeckt gut	*"Tastes good"*
Komm her	*"Come here"*
*Ach***	*"Oh"*
Warte mal	*"Wait a minute"*
Gesundheit is besser als Krankheit	*"Good health is better than sickness"*

* This is the phrase Mutti's grandchildren remember her saying the most.
** Mutti would often use this word when frustrated.

Kenton says of Mutti's German, "My favorite phrase she would say to me whenever I would leave was 'Come gut (good) home.' Though not precisely German and phrased in broken English, it was Mutti wishing me a safe trip home."[5]

* * *

After living with Leon and me for a time after arriving in the United States, Mutti and Horst moved to Great Bend. Horst had a construction job, and Mutti went to work as a housekeeper in the home of the owners of Howard's Dress Shop, an upscale apparel store for women. She worked for the Howards for eight years. Mutti would collect Social Security payments from those years of employment. Later, Mutti and Horst bought a two-bedroom house.

Over time, Mutti learned how to drive. Sometimes she would pick up Tante Anna, and they would go shopping together. Other times, Tanta Anna would take her car. Often, granddaughter Karen, and her cousin, Carol Wilkens Silvernail (Tante Anna's granddaughter), sat in the back seat and rode along with Tante Anna and Mutti for a drive or a trip to run errands. Karen remembers that the Herb's garage had a very narrow opening. When returning home and putting the car away, Tante Anna would always hit the back wall of the garage with the front bumper. Mutti would exclaim, "We in, we in!" With her German accent, the phrase sounded more like "Vee in, vee in!" Although the girls enjoyed time with their grandmothers, Karen and Carol were always amused by this garage ritual and both greatly relieved to be safely home.

* * *

My mother's grandchildren have very vivid memories of their Mutti. My children called her Mutti; Horst's children called her Oma, the German word for grandmother. I will let them share those recollections and thoughts.

My daughter, Karen, shares, "Most of what I know about my mother's story, I learned from Mutti. I made her paint pictures with her words. She told stories with such detail that it was as if I could see what she was describing. I would ask her over and over to tell me about Grandpa and Germany. She would never disappoint. She went into great detail about their farm and how it was different from those in America."[6]

Horst's daughter, Amy, recalls, "Oma would talk of the war and experiences all the time if it was just me or my brothers. She would reminisce and tell us of those times and the things that she would do to keep the kids and her safe. It was very important that she keep them all together."[7]

My daughter, Susan, recalls, "What I remember most about her description of her earlier life in Germany was her description of my grandfather, Fritz. I asked her about my grandfather, whom I'd never met. She said he was different from other men in Germany because he was kind and gentle to her, not boastful, forceful, or brash."[8]

* * *

All of Mutti's grandchildren remember that she seemed to be baking all the time. They learned many culinary skills from her. Along with the food preparation were many trips to the grocery store. *Roladen* and *Rot Kohl* were family favorites.

Amy especially liked *Zukerrüben*, sugar beets. "My Oma," she said, "was an amazing cook."[9]

Susan remembers Mutti making *Hefeklösse*, a cooked yeast bun topped with a blueberry sauce, which had been her uncle's childhood favorite. She also remembers how "Mutti and Tante Anna liked pickled herring. They welcomed fresh fish, caught by many friends who would fish in our farm ponds, and fried them for dinner."[10]

Mutti also taught her granddaughters how to bake homemade rye bread and *Kuchen*, streusel coffee cake.

My mother passed along to my children many life skills she had taught me when I was a little girl.

Susan remembers, "Mutti taught me cooking skills, how to sew on a button, darn a sock, and plant a garden. She was a great example of faithfulness to God and her family."[11]

Kenton recalls, "Mutti always stayed busy. She supervised us in the garden when she would visit us. One life lesson she taught me was to stay busy and work hard. She showed me how to be tender and loving. She would often gently rub my back to put me to sleep or when I wasn't feeling well. She made the best out of all situations."[12]

* * *

My mother became a widow on March 5, 1945, the day the Russians took my father. She was only forty-seven years old at the time. According to a witness statement document filed on February 16, 1959, Mutti applied for insurance payments in my father's name. Mutti wrote a separate handwritten letter to the consulate office in Germany:[13]

My husband, Fritz Schindler, was born April 27, 1899. During the war he was taken by the Russian Army March 5, 1945. From that time on I have not heard from him since. The Red Cross had tried for years to find my husband but couldn't find him. Possibility he died. This is all I can tell you.

A handwritten note from Pappa's sister, Ida, would have also been sent to a governmental office, corroborating my mother's claim that my father, her husband, was never heard from again. Every three months, this type of correspondence had to be filed for my mother to receive my father's pension.

Among the items I discovered in Mutti's box were two documents that have solved several family mysteries. The first of these papers was a handwritten letter from my mother explaining that on January 1, 1945, my father, Fritz, was conscripted into the *Volkssturmmann*, a division of the *Volkssturm*, the German home guard.[14] This militia group was formed in the last few months of the war, and its members were not given a uniform, but rather left to find whatever could be cobbled together to pass as one. Some historical sources use the term *Volkssturmmann* to describe a man serving in the *Volkssturm*.[15] Other sources use the term *Volkssturmmann* to designate a member of the *Volkssturm* given the rank of private.[16]

Mutti's letter detailing Pappa's conscription into the *Volkssturm*

Suddenly, the pictures of my father in various military uniforms now made perfect sense. Perhaps the clothing had been borrowed, and the pictures were made to document this one window in time. Pappa's membership as a *Volkssturmmann* required such a uniform.

The letter went on to say that my Pappa would have left home in the month of January to join his group on assignment in the nearby German state of Meseritz. On January 31, Pappa was allowed a pass for a three-day furlough to return to our farm to file certain family paperwork. On February 1, the second day of that leave, Russian forces invaded our family farm, preventing my dad's return to his *Volkssturmmann* unit.

Pappa's Death Certificate

The second of these documents was Pappa's death certificate issued with the date of December 31, 1945. This official record also substantiates my father's membership as a *Volksturmmann*.[17] Below is the translation of that document.

Stamp in upper right-hand corner:
Compensation Office
24 June 1964

Certified copy from the Book of Declarations of Death Nr. 10289
Berlin, the 29. April 1964
The Volkssturmmann [Volkssturm man], farmer
Fritz Schindler, Evangelical Lutheran
last living in Radach, Kreis [state] Weststernberg/Brandenburg,
is by decision of the district court Schöneberg in Berlin - Schöneberg
from 30. January 1964 - 72 II 1325/63
been declared dead.
As the time of death is the 31. December 1945 - 24 clock detected.
The named is on 27. April 1899
in Radach, Kreis [state] Weststernberg born.

The Registrar
in representation
Joel [name typed]

The correspondence of the copy with the entry in the book for death
declarations is hereby certified.

Berlin, the 13. May 1964

The Registrar
in representation
Joel [name signed]

Stamp in lower left-hand corner:
Registry Office in Berlin (West) 27

Leon's niece, Linda Glasgow Whited, remembers the one time she saw Mutti emotional. Linda and my daughter, Susan, were visiting Mutti after the death of one of Susan's teenage friends killed in a car-train accident. Mutti

My parents possibly soon after Pappa's *Volkssturm* draft

Possibly another *Volkssturm* portrait

was lamenting, with tears in her eyes, that at least we knew where our loved ones were buried, so we could go to their graves in prayerful remembrance and decorate them. My mother exclaimed sadness and distress because she did not know where Fritz had died nor where he was buried. She could never go to his grave to honor his life and memory.[18]

Mutti would go on to live some fifty-two more years without my father, although I believe he was with her in spirit every day.

* * *

We lost my mother on June 25, 1997. She died at the age of ninety-nine-and-a-half, having lived an incredibly full life, despite all that had happened to her between the years 1945 and 1953. I do not know how my mother lived as long as she did and worked the way she did. One prayer in her collection sums up Mutti's attitude in the last year of her life:

"I'll praise and honor you, O God, for all that you have done for me.
Now in my old age, don't set me aside. Don't forsake me now when
my strength is failing. Amen."

Oh, how I have missed my mother in the years since her death. Her unwavering devotion to God has strengthened the shared faith we have in that same Lord. All in our family have adopted her example of selfless service to others. Her recipes continue to provide delicious dishes at family gatherings, and her German expressions are now standard fare in the vocabulary of the extended Schindler-Janzen families. Mutti's loving legacy of courage, joy, and thankfulness continues to guide us all.

CHAPTER THIRTY-ONE

The Joy of Family

One of the greatest joys of my life here in America has been sharing it with so many extended family members. Although my growing up years in Germany were relatively happy, family members lived elsewhere, scattered throughout different cities. As a result, we only saw each other on special occasions. We were not all together in one general area, as was the family into which I married. Once Mutti and Horst came stateside in 1953, I now had my mother and brother with me, and my Tante Anna had her sister-in-law and nephew to enjoy. The Schindler and Janzen families filled all our lives with love and laughter.

Leon's parents, Wilbert and Edna, were loving and kind. How thankful I am that our children had these outstanding grandparents. Susan learned "kindness and generosity" from Grandpa and Grandma Janzen. Kenton and Wilbert worked closely together on the farm.

Kenton remembers, "My grandfather taught me that when you do physical work, you can work at a steady pace and work all day without tiring yourself. He showed me how to straighten a bent nail so it could be reused. Since he went through the Depression, there were many things he did to make do with what he had."[1]

Like my Mutti, Edna was a great cook and taught my girls much of her culinary know-how. Many delicious dinners, accompanied by lively conversation, were enjoyed by our family while at Leon's parents' table.

Susan remembers, "Grandma Edna cooked from scratch and had us helping her in the kitchen."[2]

Karen learned at her grandmother's side, "I watched my Grandma Edna make gravy. She taught me all of her secrets."[3]

* * *

Eight years after Horst arrived in Kansas, he met his future wife, Joyce, at a dance. She, like Horst, was from a German heritage. Joyce was twelve years younger. At her high school senior formal, he proposed to her. They were married on September 16, 1962, within a year of meeting each other. It was so good to see my little brother happy and in love. After marrying Horst, Joyce completed her nurse's training. My brother and his wife had four children, three sons and one daughter—Eric, Mark, Kirk, and Amy.

My children and my brother's children had many adventures together. Horst was a special uncle to Karen, Kenton, Susan, and Galen.

Susan remembers, "Uncle Horst was always happy and always joyful! He was definitely a cup-is-half-full kind of man! He didn't dwell on the Germany experience but rather chose to focus on the better life and new opportunities in America. His wife, my Aunt Joyce, was also a happy and joyful person, who had a hearty, contagious laugh."[4]

Karen recalls Horst as a "very fun, outgoing, special uncle. He always had a very positive outlook on life. I remember once he let me drive in the pasture, telling me to look ahead toward the horizon to help me drive a straight path."[5]

Kenton says of his uncle, "He was straight forward, practical, and down-to-earth and was also proud of his German heritage." Horst loved nature and the out-of-doors and shared that enthusiasm with his nieces and nephews. "One of my fondest memories," continues Kenton, "is when he took me overnight camping on the Arkansas River. I was about in the fifth grade. This was something my dad had not done with me. Uncle Horst passed on his love of the outdoors and wide-open spaces, and his fondness for hunting and fishing, to all three of his sons."[6]

Horst and Joyce first settled in Great Bend. A skilled craftsman, Horst began working with a contractor building homes. He then went to work for Marlette, a mobile modular housing company, where he worked for twenty-four-and-a-half years. While employed with this company, my brother and his family moved to the nearby community of Claflin, Kansas, when their children were in grade school. Later, due to a downturn in the Kansas economy, Horst and Joyce moved to Arvada, Colorado, when their children were in junior high and high school. They lived there for the next seventeen years. Eventually, they returned to Osawatomie, Kansas, in the later years of their lives.

My beloved brother, Horst, died of complications from multiple myeloma on Wednesday, September 21, 2005, at the age of seventy-four. My sister-in-law, Joyce, passed away seven years later. God could not have given me a kinder, more supportive brother. The experiences we shared, although not unique, were certainly different than those of our peers. The close bonds developed on our childhood farm in Radach sustained us for the remainder of our lives. The love Horst and I shared continues on in the lives of our children and grandchildren.

* * *

Relationships with extended cousins have also been memorable and significant.

Onkel Charlie's and Tante Anna's daughter, Margaret, graduated from Great Bend High School, as that is where they were living when I came to live with them in 1947. Over time, Margaret fell in love with Leon's first cousin and former high school classmate, Donnie Wilkens. On Sunday, November 25, 1951, their wedding three days after Thanksgiving made the holiday extra special. Margaret was and is the closest thing I have to a sister. She and Donnie settled on a farm just outside Lorraine. Over time, a son and two daughters—Jerry, Carol, and Connie—were born. All our children grew up together and are close. Although Donnie has passed away, any family gathering would not be complete without Margaret.

Jean Dobrinski Behnke also lives nearby. She and Marcia Dobrinski are first cousins, as their fathers were brothers.[7] Jean's grandmother, the Grandma Dobrinski with whom I lived during my first two years at Lorraine State Bank, was also Marcia's grandmother. Additionally, Jean is kin through the Janzen side of the family as her mother, Vella Janzen Dobrinski, was my Leon's first cousin. Jean and her husband, Myron, were married at First Baptist Church of Lorraine, just as Leon and I were. Their two sons, Barry and Brock, grew up in the church. All our children are extended cousins and enjoy fellowship, especially during family celebrations and holidays.

"Mildred has been a very positive influence in my life from early years to present years," says Jean. "She taught me how one can go through tough times and still live a good, positive, Christian life."[8]

Marcia Dobrinski, who had become like a little sister to me in the four years I lived with her family, while attending high school, lived nearby and was a frequent visitor in our home.

"There was a family relationship between our family and the Janzens," Marcia shares. "After Leon and Mildred married, we were part of their family and they ours for birthdays and celebrations. Plus, we would see them at church on Sundays. We babysat Karen and Kenton in our home. Later, I helped at their home with freezing and canning garden produce, cleaning, and babysitting in the summer."[9]

Marcia was only twenty years old when her mother died of ovarian cancer at the age of forty-seven. Her younger brothers were eighteen, fifteen, and twelve when they lost their mother. "Even though Mildred had a young family at the time and was quite busy, she always had special dinners for my brothers and my dad on their birthdays and other special occasions," Marcia remembers. "She made phone calls to talk with them. I was a junior in college, living about one hundred eighty miles away from home, and it was a good feeling to know that Mildred was especially attentive to my family at home."[10]

When Marcia and her husband, Larry, married in December of 1970, several ladies from First Baptist Church of Lorraine and I helped Marcia with many of the plans for the big day. Although Marcia and her family now live in Arkansas, she and I often visit by phone and occasionally see each other at family gatherings.

How blessed my life has been by the friendships shared with Margaret, Marcia, and Jean. I look forward to making many more memories with them and their families.

* * *

Although Mutti and Tante Anna had a close friendship, my father's sister still missed her own two sisters very much. Tante Mariechen Schindler Bohm and Tante Ida Schindler Leder had remained in Germany after the war. By the time the three sisters reunited, over fifty years had passed. Mutti, their sister-in-law, especially enjoyed their visits. These three ladies had each endured wartime trauma, creating a bond between them, few can understand.

Tante Mariechen lived in the western sector of Berlin, which after the war, would eventually fall within the borders of the newly-formed country of West Germany. She made the first trip to see her sister, my Tante Anna Herb, in 1970. I, too, was elated to see my aunt. She and her family played such a strategic role in my being able to come to America after the war. Tante Mariechen, one of my father's younger sisters, was the closest to him in age. A black and white photo taken in Great Bend during my aunt's visit shows her standing arm-and-arm with my Onkel Charlie, Tante Anna, and Mutti. My heart aches to look at the

Family Ties Still Strong Despite 50-Year Separation

Family ties that stretched across the Atlantic for over 50 years have been shortened the past three months as an East German woman visited relatives at Lorraine and Great Bend.

For Mrs. Ida (Schindler) Leder, 65, of East Germany and her niece, Mrs. Mildred (Schindler) Janzen, now of Lorraine, it has been their first meeting since the Schindler family members and others were forced to leave their homes at Radach, Germany, toward the end of World War II by Russian soldiers.

Over half a century had passed since Mrs. Leder, now of Boevenburg, Mecklenburg, East Germany, had seen her sister, Anna (Schindler) Herb, 79, of Great Bend.

"My little sister (Ida) was 14 years old when I left the old country in 1925 to make my home in the United States," Mrs. Herb said. She spoke with an accent indicating her German ancestry.

Mrs. Leder's visit to America and to central Kansas this summer has also meant a reunion with her sister-in-law, Mrs. Anna Schindler, now of Great Bend, the mother of Mrs. Janzen. After five or six years of negotiations, Mrs. Schindler and her son, Horace, finally arrived in the United States from Germany in 1953.

For the sisters-in-law, they have a personal tragedy to share. They both were separated from their husbands who were taken by the Russians to work camps. Never to see them again.

Mrs. Leder and her husband were taken to help build airports for the Russians.

"We were separated when we were put on different trucks in February, 1945," Mrs. Leder said with the assistance of Mrs. Janzen, interpreter.

It was a similar circumstance for Mrs. Schindler's husband, Fritz Schindler.

"You have to go to the next village and feed cattle, you can come back in two days," Mrs. Schindler and Mrs. Janzen said their husband and father was told. "And..he never did come back!" they said.

The loss of their loved ones, their homes and other possessions, the result of World War II are sad memories. Something the four women would rather not discuss.

As the women reunited this summer, they have shared the joys of being together perhaps for the last time.

Mrs. Leder has attended many special family occasions during her visit here. Among them was the wedding of her

MRS. MILDRED JANZEN (right) has enjoyed special visitors at her rural farm home at various times the past three months.

From left are her mother, Anna Schindler, Great Bend; her aunt, Ida Leder, from East Germany; and another aunt, Anna Herb, Great Bend.

Mrs. Leder left August 3 for her home in East Germany after her first visit to the United States.

(Reporter Photo by Bill Grothusen)

niece's daughter, Karen Janzen, at the Lorraine First Baptist Church, the graduation exercises of Karen's sister, Susan Janzen.

There is little doubt that Mrs. Leder's special interest in the Ellsworth county farm traces back to her being raised on the Schindler family farm near Radach — the same farm that later was the home of Mrs. Janzen.

Mrs. Leder and Mrs. Schindler spent ten days, during the recent wheat harvest, at the farm home of Mildred and Leon Janzen, north of Lorraine.

"We had fun getting the meals together. There were usually eight and nine persons to prepare for. Aunt Ida always went along to the field when we took lunch out in the afternoon. She never missed a day

— she enjoyed it so much. It was never too hot for her," Mrs. Janzen said.

Mrs. Leder says there is a wall near her home town that divides East Germany and West Germay, then there is another big wall after that, then the Elbe River. After three months absence she returned to that town this week with gifts from Lorraine and Great Bend relatives for her daughter, son and two grandchildren. She also took with her some English she learned including "good morning", "how are you", "thank you", "potatoes", "mail box" and "nap".

Mrs. Leder enjoyed many experiences with her sister and sister-in-law but when it came to the after lunch TV soap operas (which she didn't understand) there was no way she'd permit herself to get hooked on them. She washed the dishes.

Reunited after fifty years. *Left to right:* Anna Gerlach Schindler, Ida Schindler Leder, Anna Schindler Herb, and Mildred Schindler Janzen photo, even after all these years, as my Tante Mariechen looked so very much like my Pappa. Tall and slender like he was, her face also resembled his. Her visit warmed all our hearts.

Ida came next in 1976. She was fourteen years younger than Tante Anna and lived in East Germany. At the time of her trip, Ida was sixty-five, and her older sister was seventy-nine. She and Anna had not seen each other in fifty-two years. What a reunion that was! Tante Anna traveled to Kansas City, Missouri, to pick up her younger sister at the airport and bring her back to Great Bend, Kansas, for a three-month-long visit. In the 1970s, the United States and many eastern European countries, including East Germany, maintained less-than-friendly relations with each other. When Ida first began making her travel plans, "the East German government was only going to permit Mrs. Leder out of the country for 30 days. But as the due date neared for her to leave, she was issued a three month permit instead."[11]

Ida and Mutti had both lost their husbands at the hands of the Russians. Both Ida and her husband, also named Fritz, were forced by the Russians to join a work detail for airport construction. This ordeal occurred in February 1945, which was very close to the time the Russians invaded our family farm in Radach. While in transit to the airfield, Ida and her husband became separated when loading prisoners back into the trucks. Afterward, this husband and wife never saw each other again. Just as my family lost our home and most of our possessions in the war, so, too, did Tante Ida.[12]

As Tante Anna had been living in the United States since 1925, her English was excellent. She still spoke German, but over the years, she used it less and less. Ida's visit gave Tante Anna a chance to brush up on her native language, as Tante Ida spoke only one English phrase, "Thank you." There was so much to say. The visit was also a poignant one, as both sisters knew it might be the last time they would see each other.[13]

How wonderful it was to see my mother and my aunts back together again.

* * *

Like ripples in a pond, our family circles are ever-widening. The farming heritage of both the Schindler and Janzen families is rich and storied and has cultivated, in descendants of both, a commitment to devotion, both to the land and to each other. God has endowed our family not only with material provisions but also with intangible blessings of faith, hope, and love.

How richly God has blessed me through all His many provisions.

Left to right: Onkel Charlie, Tante Anna, Tante Mariechen, and Mutti

Left to right: Mutti, Tante Mariechen, and Tante Anna

CHAPTER THIRTY-TWO

Visiting the Old Country

Leon had heard my story countless times. Even though we shared a common German heritage, his family had come to the United States long before mine did. Unlike me, my husband's knowledge of the country of our ancestors was that gleaned from books or films. One of the things I wanted most was to be able to show Leon where I grew up. Being able to walk through the fields and along the roads, where my story took place, would make it come alive for Leon in a way no telling of it ever could.

My sweet husband gave me that opportunity not once, but twice. We made our first trip to Germany in May 1997 to see my dear childhood friend, Gerda Schmidt Sÿring. She lived southwest of Berlin in Reuden, Germany, about a two-and-a-half-hour drive from the Polish border. Throughout the years, Gerda and I had remained in close contact. We exchanged birthday and Christmas cards. Photos were sent. Lengthy descriptions contained in handwritten letters marked family milestones.

How I had missed my oldest friend! We were both overjoyed to see each other. The years, which had separated us, melted in the warmth of our hugs. We were fifteen years old the last time we were together. Our lives had both become a little richer, now that we were together, after being separated fifty-three years. Leon and I spent five days with Gerda and her family and then headed to Berlin to visit with Schindler relatives.

Gerda had worked tirelessly to prepare a special gathering for our visit. She contacted elementary school classmates who still lived in the area and invited

My best friend, Gerda Schmidt (right), and me

them to her home to see me. Gerda was an excellent cook who had once oper-
ated a bakery. During the days before our arrival, she had worked tirelessly to
prepare many delicious treats. At ten o'clock on the morning of our reunion,
my first cousins, Günter and Werner Schindler, along with seven of our classmates, met to enjoy coffee and refreshments in Gerda's beautiful garden. The
spouses of our school friends were also there.[1] We had a coffee cake you would
not believe! We sat around on Gerda's porch for several hours, laughing and
recalling shared childhood experiences. The words rolled off my tongue effortlessly, even though it had been years since I had spoken this much German.
After having time to freshen up and change clothes, our group met later that
evening to share a lovely meal in a nearby restaurant.

Poor Leon. He understood very little German, but he had the best time.
My gracious husband had always been able to entertain himself, especially when

Gerda and me reunited on the site of the Schindler family farm in the early 1970s

thrust into an unfamiliar situation. Thankfully, Gerda's grandson, Andrew, was present during the visit. He and Leon became fast friends. Fluent in English, Andrew had traveled to the United States several times. He and Leon whiled away the time getting to know each other. Occasionally, he would enlighten Leon about what our lively group of school friends was discussing. How grateful I was for his presence and his kindness to my Leon.

Andrew drove us on the day when Gerda and I first returned to Radach, now Radachow, Poland. My heart was beating so hard because you had to have your passport when crossing the border into Poland. This situation seemed so absurd to me; Radach had been my home. I was also delighted to be able to share this experience with Leon. As we drove into the town, time slipped away. Despite the many years since my childhood, many of the buildings of Radachow (Radach) looked just the same. Leon and Andrew said they would wait in the car and encouraged Gerda and me to take as much time as we liked. We set out, walking arm in arm, as we surveyed our former hometown. Chatting like two schoolgirls, we reminisced while exploring every street in the town. As we walked down the sidewalks, passers-by cast sidelong glances at these two foreign women. Polish housewives pulled back curtains as they peered out at us from inside their homes. The scowls on many of their faces relayed their mistrustful thoughts.

Sign of Radachow, Poland (formerly Radach, Germany)

Radach Evangelical Lutheran Church

Next, we drove out to the site of the Schindler family farm. Leon, Gerda, Andrew, and I got out of the car to survey the scene. Even though they were all gone, the buildings of my childhood home were still visible in my mind's eye. Echoes of Pappa's voice giving direction to Horst and me for some task bounced around in my heart. I could easily imagine Mutti calling us in for dinner. It was as if I could see the stalks of rye and oats swaying gently in the fields. All that remained of our homeplace was an apple tree and a white lilac bush. How I wished I could have met the man that now owned this land. I prayed he loved these hallowed acres as much as our family had.

Once Leon and I returned to Lorraine from our trip, I could not wait to get the photos developed. Mutti took such great delight in seeing, through the lens of our camera, what Leon and I had viewed with our own eyes. Unfortunately, my mother died a few weeks after our return from this first trip back to the old country.

* * *

The first time Leon and I went to see Gerda, we stayed about a week. Before we left, the three of us discussed a possible second visit to see her. "A week is not long enough," Gerda had said. "You stay longer next time." Three years later, in August 2000, Leon and I were able to make a more extended trip. While with Gerda, we crossed the border into Poland once more and returned to visit Radachow (Radach). I had brought with me an old pair of garden shoes in anticipation of being able to explore more on foot during this second visit to my childhood stomping grounds.

One day, Leon and I made our way through the town cemetery, where my grandparents were buried. Once again, Gerda's grandson, Andrew, served as our driver and guide. Upon arriving at the cemetery, it was apparent that someone had spoiled the serenity of the graveyard. Though the grass was growing chest-high in places, we could see that many holes and indentations pocked the ground.

"Why are all these holes here?" I asked Andrew.

"Well," he said, "the people of this village take the stones out and use them for their families at a cemetery in Drossen."

Some existing gravestones seemed original to the cemetery but had the German names etched through or chiseled away. We were able to locate my grandparents' gravesites only because I remembered their exact location in the churchyard. That is when we discovered that Pappa's mother's grave was disturbed. The gold wedding band still on her finger must have been the prize for grave robbers. Leon and I were so upset by that.

Later that day, Gerda and I conducted another walking tour of Radachow (Radach). It was during this second visit that I became much more aware of the poverty of the area. Extensive gardens, planted throughout the town, bore mute witness to the need families had for a ready food supply. The village's run-down condition and the threadbare clothing worn by many on the streets made it apparent that this community was very poor. How I wished I had brought a suitcase filled with many of my granddaughters' outgrown dresses. I could have taken it to the mayor of the town and asked him to share the clothes with any little girls who needed them.

Throughout the process of committing this story to paper, I have thought back on these two special trips many times. Mostly, now that Leon and Gerda have both passed away, I am so grateful that my dear husband allowed me to return to the old country. The Radach of my childhood exists only in my mind. There are few of us alive who remember it as I do. When my brother, Horst, passed away in 2005, I became the sole keeper of these family memories.

Frank Baum, the author of *The Wonderful Wizard of Oz*, once wrote of another girl who traveled far from her childhood home. Dorothy was right, "There is no place like home."

CHAPTER THIRTY-THREE

Lessons Learned

This journey down the pathway of my memory has taken longer than I thought it would. I can hardly believe it has been seventy-five years since that fateful day when the Russian soldiers arrived on our Schindler farm and turned the lives of all in my family upside down. There are not many of us left who lived through this World War II period. My story is but one of thousands. Facts surrounding the waning months of the war are relatively unknown to most. My mother, brother, and I were not doing anything heroic or extraordinary; we were only trying to survive those awful wartime experiences. Looking back, I am not entirely sure how we managed to do so.

I have spent countless hours sorting through boxes of carefully preserved letters, family photographs, and mementos to ensure my story's accuracy. I have even uncovered a few treasures hidden away by my mother. Just as a pebble tossed into a pond creates ripples on the surface of the water, the remembrance or discussion of each of the events of my life story has led to the recovery of memories from another. A tremendous amount of water has already flowed under the bridge of my life. How thankful I am that I can still remember, no matter how disturbing or sad those memories may be. Corrie Ten Boom, fellow World War II survivor and one of my heroes of the faith, shares, "Memories are the key not to the past, but to the future. I know that the experiences of our lives, when we let God use them, become the mysterious and perfect preparation for the work He will give us to do." Several themes have emerged during the process of sifting through circumstances of the past seven-and-a-half decades of my life.

First, my story is a testimony of God's sure protection and His unfailing love. God's fingerprints are too evident throughout every detail of my wartime trials and the years that followed for me to believe anything other than He was right there with my family and me. As a child, I witnessed a confident assurance both my mother and father had in the fact that God was active in the day-to-day events of our lives. Once the Russians took Pappa, Mutti somehow drew, from within the well of her heart, the strength to tie a knot in the rope of her faith and cling to it. Horst and I witnessed this tenacious reliance on God and claimed it for ourselves. God showed Himself faithful to us over and over again—through the kindness of strangers, through the timing of circumstances, through personal connections made at critical moments, and through answered prayers. He brought to life the truth of Romans 8:28, working *all* these things together for our good.

Proverbs 3:5-6, one of my favorite portions of Scripture, says, "Trust in the Lord with all your heart, and do not lean on your own understanding. In all your ways acknowledge him, and he will make straight your paths." When first encountering the Russian army soldiers as a young girl of fifteen, I had no frame of reference for such a terrifying ordeal. Neither did my parents nor my brother. Despite the dreadful loss of my Pappa, no real physical harm ever came to my mother, brother, or me. Although our path was arduous, twisting this way and that, God nevertheless made a sure way for me to come safely to the United States. Several years later, He did the same for my mother and brother.

There have been many dark days in my life. Too many to count. Although I am not sure if I ever asked why, I did wonder, on many of those trying days, if God was still in control of the events of my life. It was not until a great many years after the emotional wounds of that tumultuous World War II period had subsided that I realized He had *never once* left my side *nor* Pappa's *nor* Horst's *nor* Mutti's. A card arrived from a friend in the mail one day and tucked inside was this version of the poem, "Footprints in the Sand." Tears stung my eyes after reading it. The simple truth of my Lord's love for me is evident in the lines of these beautiful verses. The poem is pasted in the back of my Bible, where I can refer to it often.

Lord, you told me when I decided to follow You,
You would walk and talk with me all the way.

But I'm aware that during the most troublesome times of my life
    there is only one set of footprints.
I just don't understand why, when I needed You most, You leave me."
He whispered,
"My precious child,
I love you and will never leave you . . .
When you saw only one set of footprints
it was then that I carried you.

God's peace, inexplicable as it was, accompanied us every step of the way. I have lived to experience the truth found in 2 Thessalonians 3:16, "Now may the Lord of peace Himself grant you His peace at all times *and* in every way [that peace and spiritual well-being that comes to those who walk with Him, regardless of life's circumstances]." Dictators Adolph Hitler and Joseph Stalin only thought they orchestrated the events of their empires. I am living proof that God's sovereign protection exceeds the power of any earthly political leader or government system.

Second, this account is a tribute to my mother, the real heroine of this story. Mutti possessed remarkable courage and strength and used all within her power to save both my brother and me. Would I have or could I have done for my daughters what Mutti did for me, to protect and shield me during the difficult days of Germany's Russian occupation? I have never been able to answer that question, although I know I would have tried. Looking back through the lens of time, God's providential care and protection are evident through those dark days near the end of the war. Throughout the rest of her life, my children and I continued to thank Mutti over and over for all she did for Horst and me.

During the months I lived with Mutti and Horst in the house in Nienhagen before being sent on the train to Berlin, my mother modeled a godly pattern of living for me. Mutti had every reason to be hostile and antagonistic toward her fellowman. Instead, her gentle words and thoughtful deeds bore witness to the sincere kindness she exhibited to all. So many people had experienced so much cruelty during the war. That type of mistreatment, although physically damaging, can be especially harmful to one's soul. Mutti's kindness was a healing balm to many.

Mutti also taught me to be patient with others. The wheels of bureaucracy moved with excruciatingly slow speed in those first months immediately following the war. A prayer written by my mother expresses the patience she possessed, an unhurried approach to life, based on the assurance of God's sovereignty in all things,

> "Thank you, Lord, for your light. When it produces shadows in my
> life, teach me to realize that sunshine is near, just beyond the clouds.
> Amen."

I learned from my mother the importance of helping others whenever I could. One of the reasons my mother, brother, and I survived the war was because of the help we received from so many nameless individuals. No matter how little we had during those awful days in 1945, I never witnessed my mother refuse to help another in need. Mutti knew the principles of heavenly multiplication. She trusted God to take the meager loaves and fishes of her life and multiply them in such a way that brought both blessings into the lives of others and glory to His name.

Third, my story is a declaration that choosing joy and thankfulness over bitterness and anger, even amid difficult circumstances, leads to a happy, healthier life. Perhaps the question I am asked most frequently when people hear my story is, "How have you remained so positive throughout all these years?" My answer is simple: God. He has supplied me with courage and fortitude to endure life's difficult circumstances. His greatest gift to me, however, is the joy He has placed in my heart. That is not a quality I possess, but rather one which He has graciously supplied.

Philippians 4:4 is another Bible verse that has special significance for me, "Rejoice in the Lord always: and again I say, Rejoice." The word *rejoice* means "to experience joy and gladness to a high degree."[1] Does that mean that all my life circumstances are ones that made me happy? No. Does that mean that God answers all my prayers? No. Does that mean that I can expect a carefree life? Certainly not. This verse implies that in *every* circumstance of my life, I can choose, with my heart and mind, to seek God's joy above all else. Since God delivered me from harm at the hands of both Hitler and Stalin, that is what I have tried to do.

I suppose I could be bitter about so many things—the loss of our family farm in Radach, the murder of my Pappa, the indignities suffered in the laundry camp at the hands of the Russians, being forced to make my way alone as a teenager, having to move to another country and learn a new language, and being separated from my mother and brother for almost seven years. The list could go on and on. Seeds of bitterness sown in the heart never produce pleasant fruit. From a very early age, God taught me that I would do better bending into the storm winds of life rather than being broken when standing against them.

I pray my story may be a history lesson you take to heart. Be vigilant and watchful. Cunning, narcissistic leaders like Hitler and Stalin could rise to power once again. Resolve to stand against injustice wherever you encounter it. Choose to give more to others than you get. Refuse to let woundedness and rejection harden your heart. No matter the circumstances, *always* choose love. Most of all, I pray you will be encouraged by this story—a reminder of God's unfailing love and His sovereign control in the affairs of His children, both in this life and in the life to come.

Afterword

Mildred Schindler Janzen continues to impact the lives of those around her by sharing the story of her World War II experiences and of God's saving grace.

Language Arts Teacher Sandra Barton recently invited Mildred to speak to her students at Central Plains Junior High School in Claflin, Kansas. Sandra and Mildred already knew each other, as Sandra's father attended high school with Mildred, although ten years her junior. "My eighth-grade class was studying primary and secondary documents related to the Holocaust," Sandra shares. "We read *Anne Frank: The Diary of a Young Girl* and other descriptions of experiences during that period. But I wanted to give my students a first-person account of what life was like in Germany during the years of the war, which is why I contacted Mildred."[1] This dedicated teacher knew Mildred had a message that would bring to life this history lesson in a way no textbook ever could.

Sandra's students sat spellbound on Friday, October 18, 2019, as the demure, white-haired lady with twinkling, blue eyes shared intricate details of her incredible story. Below are comments from some of Sandra's students:[2]

"I felt inspired by her strength and her compassionate heart."

"Her story made me feel like I could get through anything."

"Mrs. Janzen is so sweet, which really impressed me because she could be so bitter after everything that has happened to her."

"I could almost see what she was saying as she told her story."

"What impressed me was how she survived all of that. I don't think I would have made it."

Sandra watched the faces of her students during the presentation. "I was surprised by how many of them were emotionally affected by Mildred's story. Several students had tears in their eyes and wanted to hug her after she finished talking. Mildred is the type of person people make an immediate connection with, and this showed in my students. It was an emotional response from them I'd not seen before."[3]

Mildred is so appreciative of the innumerable benefits afforded her and every other U.S. citizen, having lived portions of her life in two different countries shaped by opposing political philosophies. Many American children in this generation, and even some from generations past, do not fully comprehend the blessings afforded those living in the "land of the free and the home of the brave." Mainly, Mildred reminded these middle schoolers of the precious gift they possess in their birthright as Americans. Our country's forefathers established, insured, provided for, promoted, and secured the blessings of liberty for themselves and future generations. Through the ages, every American has been a beneficiary of those sacrifices made by the noble, brave men who signed the Declaration of Independence and the U.S. Constitution.

Lou Ann Clark, a paraprofessional educator (teacher's aide) who worked alongside Sandra, is also a friend of Mildred's. "I have known Mildred Janzen for at least fifty years and have never heard her life story until she came to our school for her presentation," she said. "I pray our students were able to come away from Mrs. Janzen's visit with the same life lesson as I did: Never give up!"[4]

In the days following Mildred's presentation, Sandra and Lou Ann spent a great deal of time discussing with their students the impressions they gleaned. "Some of our takeaways were: Never give up. During disastrous circumstances, keep your faith in yourself. Always find something good in bad situations because they never last. People only do what they know at the time." Sandra recalled how this last nugget of wisdom was difficult for her students to comprehend, "This one [about people only doing what they know to do at any given time] was hard because most students did not know why the Russians would be so mean. Just as the Germans had under Hitler, the Russians didn't know any other way to act."[5]

Just as it had done for Sandra's students, Mildred's testimony caused this teacher to pause and reflect on her own life, "The story of Mildred made me realize how important life experiences are and how lucky I have been throughout my life. It is important to cherish every moment you have with loved ones because you never know what can happen. Mildred reminded me what is important in life: having faith in God, my family, being kind to one another, working hard, and not expecting life to be handed to you."[6]

Cousin Jean Dobrinski Behnke, a former history teacher herself, shares her admiration for Mildred and her story. "A seldom written part of the history of the Soviet occupation of Germany during World War II will tell a different story from the usual Holocaust account. Readers can learn from history what war does to many families forever and the struggles they must deal with daily. Readers can appreciate what an American birth certificate means. Readers can comprehend the hardships war causes, the uprooting from homes, the cost in lives, the resilient spirit humans possess, and the good life one can experience after survival of horrific events. Mildred's story, which I heard from my earliest childhood, has always been intriguing to me. Her witness prompted me to read many books about Germany during World War II, teach the subject in elementary school, and visit three of the concentration camps—Dachau in Germany, Auschwitz in Poland, and Breendonk in Belgium. Mildred's story shows humanity at its worst and its best!"[7]

Trudy Berthelson, Ellsworth resident and retired teacher, once shared her admiration for Mildred in a letter to the editor of the *Ellsworth County Independent Reporter*. Dorothy Grothusen, a reporter for the newspaper, was a mutual friend of both Trudy and Mildred and had, over the years, written a series of articles chronicling Mildred's incredible story. In response to one of these stories, Trudy pays tribute to the powerful impact Mildred's example continues to have on the lives of those in her community. Mildred "willingly shared her story of triumph over adversity. Rather than living her life as one who has had nothing but tragedy, she presents herself as one who has looked at and faced adversity, and now can share those experiences to encourage others to face life as it can be sometimes—brutal, yet challenging. Thank you, Mildred, for your contribution to our community."[8]

Mildred, her family, and thousands of others who survived World War II struggled mightily to retain their human dignity and sanity when confronting the evil forces threatening to extinguish freedom's light. Their triumph over such tyranny is a testimony to God's indomitable spirit within every human heart. Mildred's story of courage, endurance, and hope will always inspire all who hear it.

Acknowledgments

I am forever grateful to my parents—Pappa and Mutti—for giving me a great foundation for a rich, full life where I learned from their example to work hard, be kind, share with others, and give thanks to God in all circumstances. My Mutti was a solid rock that kept our family together under enormous adversity and was my guide to a strong, sweet spirit. I owe my very life to my mother, and a good life it has been.

Leon, my husband of nearly sixty-six years, loved and supported me as a partner in our rich and full home life, living the American Dream. His family—parents Wilbert and Edna, sister Shirley, and extended family members—were all part of our happy life together.

My brother, Horst, was a witness and participant in our journey through Nazi Germany and experienced the raw realities of living as a refugee in a war-torn country. Despite his circumstances, he remained joyful all his life. Mutti and Pappa had also planted in him a solid work ethic and love for God and country. He remained ever grateful for his many blessings and opportunities in this country.

My Tante Mariechen and Tante Anna and their families embraced me when my parents could not provide guidance and care.

Dorothy Harder opened a pathway to a better life in America by introducing me to the Lorraine community of kind and supportive German descendants, where I would receive my education and salvation.

The Dobrinski family gave me the opportunity and encouragement to brave a new life in a new world, learn a new language, and build a new life in this great country.

Sunbury Press Publisher Lawrence Knorr recognized the rare opportunity to share this unique story, one of World War II's last personal accounts. It is with great appreciation that I thank Mr. Knorr and his staff, Marianne Babcock, Executive Assistant to CEO; Abigail Henson, Editor; Crystal Devine, Production Manager; Terry Kennedy, Cover Designer; and Joe Walters, Marketing Director, who had faith in the project and worked tirelessly to see it come to fruition. Their work was done professionally and in a way that has honored the true story of my life.

I thank God for my wonderful family—my children, grandchildren, and great-grandchildren—who continue to make my life rich and full, and for the new daughter I have found in this memoir journey, Sherye Green. I pray that God will continue to bless those who need this message of hope and encouragement.

Mildred Schindler Janzen
November 2020

* * *

This book is the culmination of the efforts of many individuals who came together as part of Mildred's team. Family, friends old and new, and even strangers, have cheered on this project and helped Mildred Schindler Janzen fulfill her dream of sharing her compelling, miraculous story.

Mildred, thank you for entrusting your story to me. What an inspiring, courageous lady you are! We are more than friends; we are family. The gift of your friendship has been the greatest treasure of this experience.

Susan Janzen Nickerson, from our first conversation, you have become a trusted friend and valued partner in this endeavor. Your encouragement, keen eye, attention to detail, boundless patience, and enthusiastic spirit have blessed me tremendously. In you, I have gained a cherished sister in the faith. Thank you for reaching out to me and inviting me to tell your mother's story. A special thank-you goes to your husband, Mitch, for his hospitality and kindness.

Karen Janzen Van Allen, how wonderful it has been to gain a new friend in you. Your sweet spirit and helpful nature have ministered to me. Thank you especially for answering myriad questions, locating vital documents and papers, and serving as a messenger in relaying information to and from your mother in the writing of this story.

Kenton Janzen, thank you for sharing your farming expertise with me. Your tender care of your mother, and the admiration for and respect you have for both your parents and grandparents, has been a heartwarming example of a loving son and grandson. A special thank-you goes to your wife, Angie, for her encouragement and support.

Galen Janzen, thank you for sharing your mother and her story with me. Your insights into your remarkable family have been most helpful.

Jean Dobrinski Behnke, thank you for passing along my name to your cousin, Karen, and for your belief that I could indeed develop Mildred's words into this story. Thanks, also, for lending me your German-English dictionary, which has been my able guide. Thanks, most of all, for the friend and godly example you are to me.

Chris Janzen, thank you for so graciously sharing both your mastery of the German language and your expertise regarding German culture with me. The information and insights you provided were critical to the success of this book.

How appreciative I am to the following members of the extended Schindler-Janzen families for answering my many questions and for providing me a wealth of information concerning the rich heritage you share: Brock Behnke, Marcia Dobrinski McDaniel, Kirk "Dieter" Schindler, Carol Wilkens Silvernail, Amy Schindler Weldon, and Margaret Herb Wilkens.

A special thank-you goes to the following individuals for your generosity, allowing me entree into your lives, and sharing how Mildred's life has so positively impacted your own: Trudy Berthelson, Sandra Barton, Lou Ann Clark, the eighth grade Language Arts students at Central Plains Junior High School (2019-2020), Larry Henne, Arlen Janssen, Marilyn Schacht Janssen, Donna Kempke Mehl, Nancy Morriss Murrin, Betty and Louie Rolfs, and Pastor Zach Ullom.

Although I have been writing for publication for over thirty years, I had no prior experience with writing a memoir. Frankly, I was not sure I could do it. I will always be grateful to Ken Gire and Joe Lee for their willingness to allow me to reach out to them for advice. Your openness and accessibility mean more than you will ever know. Insights you both shared, gleaned from your many years of literary expertise—the sound business principles you encouraged me to follow and the trustworthy guidance you offered about how to produce a work of this size and scope—provided me a path to follow.

Ken Gire, thank you for writing the soul-stirring foreword for this book. Your belief in the worth of this story means the world to me and all on Mildred's team.

Jay Long, it turns out I did need a literary attorney. Thank you for your friendship, for your excellent legal counsel, and for believing in me.

Martha Stockstill, thank you for serving as our editor. Your belief in this story, in my ability to write it, and your constant prayer support have sustained me. Your masterful wordsmithing of the manuscript has refined the details of Mildred's powerful testimony, polishing her story until it sparkles.

Troy Carnes and Charlotte Hudson, thank you for reading the manuscript. Your insights and expert advice were invaluable. Your belief in me gave me the courage to persevere.

Mildred's story, cast against a backdrop of cataclysmic world events, occurred over a protracted period. Enabling the reader to understand the significance of historical events surrounding her story was one of our main goals. I am forever indebted to the following individuals and organizations who assisted me in researching the historical details of this story:

David Maron, thank you for sharing with me the details of your noble German ancestry. The fact that your father and Mildred grew up at the same time, in the same region of Germany, is beyond coincidence. I am most grateful to you and to your wife, Elizabeth, for sharing with me historical resources, all of which have afforded me a better understanding of the intricacies of everyday German life during this World War II period.

Lauren Lucas, meeting you was indeed one of the great blessings of this project. As Librarian Assistant at the Huntsville-Madison County Public Library in Huntsville, Alabama, your expertise in German culture and history offered insights I would not have otherwise had. Your willingness to answer my many questions and to uncover obscure facts about a little-known period of World War II is so appreciated. How thankful I am to you for providing excellent, detailed research, which has enabled me to construct a historically accurate picture of this very perplexing period in world history.

The courteous and helpful staff of the J. H. Robbins Memorial Library in Ellsworth, Kansas, assisted me with information that provided valuable insight into Ellsworth's history and this chapter of Kansas' state history. Thank you to Colleen Sippel, Library Director, and Librarians, Doris Shaw, and Evelyn Woods.

Dr. Kirk Ford, Jr., your expertise in World War II history was invaluable to me in ensuring the accuracy of critical components of Mildred's story. I had the privilege to be your graduate student at Mississippi College many years ago. While writing this story, I have continued to learn new lessons from you. I am forever grateful to you for your friendship, wise counsel, and commitment to preserving history's integrity.

A special thank-you goes to three friends and former colleagues at Madison-Ridgeland Academy in Madison, Mississippi, for their assistance regarding research into this World War II period: Wren Gregory, High School Librarian; Tonya Reeves, History Department Head, AP History and Government; and Greg Self, High School Principal and Associate Head of School.

Fred Otradovsky, a member of the Grand Island Liederkranz, German American Club, in Grand Island, Nebraska, thank you for your wonderful tour of the club and for sharing your detailed knowledge of German culture and history.

I am immensely grateful to Lynn Adams, Administrative Coordinator, and Kathleen Bates, President and CEO of Travelers Aid International, for all your efforts in locating more information about Mildred's passage to America.

Gratitude goes to Cheyenne Derksen Schroeder, Managing Editor of *The Hutchinson News*, for your assistance in locating important newspaper archives related to Mildred's story.

Technical aspects of this project included the retrieval, recording, and accessing of data. I am forever grateful to you, who so freely shared your expertise with me and helped me ford the very daunting stream of technology: Michelle Bright; Katie Eubanks; Cedell Henricks; David Noone, Randy Noone, and Mark Polk of Deville Camera and Video; and Amy Wiandt.

A heartfelt thank-you goes to two circles of special friends—Hallowed Hearts Bible Study and Soul Scribblers Writers Group—for covering me with and supporting the writing of this story in prayer. This memoir is a testimony of how God worked in Mildred's life and in her family's lives to accomplish His perfect will. Your prayers have made the difference.

I am incredibly grateful to other family and friends, too numerous to name, for your prayers, which have enabled this story to come together.

My deepest gratitude goes to Sunbury Press Founder and CEO, Lawrence Knorr, for the trust you have extended to Mildred and to me and for your belief that her memoir is powerful and relevant. Sincere appreciation goes to our fine editor, Abigail Henson, for your artful guidance and your dedication to making Mildred's story shine. How grateful I am to Crystal Devine, Production Manager, for your masterful work in transforming this story's varied components into the splendidly designed book it has become. Special thanks also to Marianne Babcock, Terry Kennedy, Joe Walters, and other Sunbury Press team members for the important part you have each played in bringing Mildred's story to life.

A special thanks go to members of my family—my son and daughter-in-law, Mark and Abigail Green; my daughter and son-in-law, Lauren and Clif Egger; my parents, Heber and Sister Simmons; and my brother and sister-in-law, Heber and Sperry Simmons. Your excitement for this project, your prayer support, and your unwavering belief in me have buoyed my spirits and kept me going. You are the best!

Most of all, thank you to my better half, Mark, for your constant encouragement on days when I wasn't sure I could write this story, for shoring me up in prayer, and for always keeping our home fires burning brightly. You have been the perfect cheerleader for me and for Mildred's team! How I love you.

Sherye Green
November 2020

A Word from Sherye Green

H ow could I have known that a serendipitous meeting ten years ago with a fellow traveler would lead to an introduction that completely changed my life? Jean Behnke and I first met in 2010, while both on a trip to southern Germany and Austria, billed by the travel agency as "The Sound of Music" tour. My sweet mother had invited me to accompany her on the trip to commemorate the recent completion of my graduate degree. This accomplishment was a cause for celebration, considering that my children were completing their undergraduate degrees and that I was the age of the parents of most of my classmates.

While sitting together during meals or sharing light conversation over cups of coffee, Jean and I found we had much in common. One mutual interest was a love of and an appreciation for American history, as we were both teachers of that discipline. Jean was retired; I was still in the classroom. A close friend had invited Jean to accompany her, her mother, and her sister on the trip. Jean's husband was unable to get away due to his responsibilities of running their family farm. We, six ladies, spent quite a bit of time together during the ten-day tour. By the trip's end that summer of 2010, Jean and I had become fast friends.

On the last day of our tour, I happened to get off the bus and stand near Ingrid, our energetic, delightful tour guide. Our group was preparing to enter the Dachau Concentration Camp, located on the outskirts of Munich. The story Ingrid told me made a profound impression on me. She said she had never entered this camp, although she had led numerous tour groups to this site. This woman believed Dachau was the place the Nazis had imprisoned her father during World War II. Her father had been an attorney in Vienna, Austria, where she grew up. Ingrid went on to tell me that on a pleasant spring morning in March 1938, he shared an enjoyable breakfast with his wife, Ingrid's younger sister, and herself, kissed each in his family goodbye, collected his briefcase, and left for work. He never returned home on this day, shortly before the Anschluss. Ingrid, who was six at the time, never saw her father again.

That act of courage, displayed by Ingrid, inspired me to write a devotional reflection, published in July 2019. Six months earlier, while researching the article, I called Jean. We shared a lengthy phone conversation, talking in great detail about that 2010 trip and about Ingrid and her quest to learn the truth of what had happened to her father. Throughout the past ten years, Jean and I have called each other, written letters and emails, and exchanged Christmas cards. As Jean is also an avid reader, and because my writing career was beginning to take shape, I had also sent her copies of both a novel and a collection of devotionals I wrote, published during this same period.

During our visit, Jean told me about several friends and family members, who were also survivors of horrific World War II experiences. One of those mentioned was her cousin, Mildred Schindler Janzen. Jean commented that she thought Mildred's remarkable life experiences would be a riveting read if ever developed into a book. She suggested I might consider taking on such a writing project someday. I jotted down a few details about Mildred and one or two other individuals Jean spoke of who lived in her region of central Kansas, along with notes I had made during the call about Ingrid. In the days and weeks that followed, I was busy with other writing obligations and did not give the matter another thought.

One life lesson I have learned is that timing is *everything* in God's economy. Several months later and unbeknownst to me, Jean shared my name with one of Mildred's daughters, Karen Janzen Van Allen. At the time, she and her sister, Susan Janzen Nickerson, had been talking about beginning a search for a writer to help their mother chronicle her life story. It would be several more months before Susan reached out to me via a text message, identifying herself and asking if I would consider taking on such a project. On August 9, 2019, God set into motion a series of events that have since set me on a literary journey beyond my wildest imagination. I will forever be grateful to Jean for sharing my name with her Janzen cousins.

One of the greatest privileges has been to meet and become a dear friend with Mildred Schindler Janzen. What an amazing lady! Her bright, courageous outlook and joy-filled heart bear witness to the indomitable human spirit.

Where I have only taught history, Mildred has lived it. Where I had only second- or third-hand knowledge about selected historical facts of World War II, Mildred was an eye-witness to one of the most brutal episodes in world history.

In October 2019, I traveled to Ellsworth, Kansas, to conduct initial research for this story. Susan had planned the trip with meticulous detail, making sure I had every possible opportunity to visit with Mildred and many family members and friends. Mildred welcomed me, not only into her home but also into her life, with endearing openness and warmth. From the moment we met, I felt as if I had known Mildred all my life. Her bright blue eyes, beaming smile, and genuine, outgoing nature reminded me of my own two grandmothers. An added highlight of the trip was to reconnect with and to stay in the beautiful home of my dear friend, Jean, in nearby Lyons, Kansas.

Mildred's story, as beguiling as it is miraculous, is further underscored by the fact that she is a committed follower of Jesus. As a writer, I would have taken on this project solely because the World War II period is one of my favorites. The fact that both Mildred and I share a common faith in the same Lord is truly the icing on the cake. Only God could have connected the dots that now join our two families.

When Mildred first began the process four years ago of unpacking seventy-five years of memories and capturing those experiences in words, she had no idea where that process might lead. This book you hold in your hand is the realization of that quest. From the first phone conversation I had with Mildred's daughter, Susan, her mother's miraculous story captured my heart and imagination.

My prayer is that it will capture yours as well.

Chronology

1914–1918	World War I
Nov. 9, 1918	Formation of Weimar Republic; will last until 1933
Feb. 24, 1920	Formation of the Nationalsozialistische Deutsche Arbeiterpartei (National Socialist German Workers' Party); later known as the Nazi Party
June 4, 1922	Fritz Robert Schindler arrives from Germany in New York harbor aboard the *Hansa*
Nov. 1, 1926	Anna Elizabeth Gerlach arrives from Germany in New York harbor aboard the *Deutschland*
	Fritz and Anna married in a New York City Clerk's office
March 11, 1929	Mildred Anna Schindler born in Great Bend, Kansas
April 14, 1929	Mildred baptized in Great Bend, Kansas
Sept. 1929	Fritz, Anna, and Mildred Schindler travel back to Radach, Germany; Fritz to help father, Hermann, run the family farm
Oct. 24–29, 1929	Crash of the U.S. stock market; beginning of the Great Depression
May 16, 1931	Horst Heinz Schindler born in Radach, Germany
1929–1945	Mildred and Horst grow up on family farm with parents, Fritz "Pappa" and Anna "Mutti" Schindler
Jan. 30, 1933	Adolph Hitler declares himself Chancellor of Germany
March 4, 1933	Franklin D. Roosevelt sworn in as 32nd President of the United States

March 22, 1933	The first German concentration camp, Dachau, opens outside Munich
Sept. 15, 1935	Nuremberg Laws enacted; stripped German Jews of all legal and civil rights
March 12–13, 1938	*Anschluss* of Austria
Nov. 9–10, 1938	*Kristallnacht,* "Night of Broken Glass;" vandalization and destruction of Jewish synagogues and businesses throughout Germany
August 23, 1939	Signing of Non-Aggression Pact between Germany and Soviet Union; also known as the Hitler-Stalin Pact; agree not to attack each other; draw up a plan whereby the two countries would control eastern Europe
August 1939	Food rationing in Germany begins
Sept. 1, 1939	Germany invades Poland; World War II begins
Sept. 3 1939	Formal declaration of war against Germany by Great Britain, France, Australia, and New Zealand
Sept. 17, 1939	Soviet Union invades Poland
June 10, 1940	Italy enters World War II as ally of Germany
Sept. 27, 1940	Tripartite Pact – Japan joins war, as ally of Germany and Italy, through signing of Pact of Steel
June 22 – Dec. 5, 1941	Operation Barbarossa – German invasion of Soviet Union
Dec. 7, 1941	Japan attacks United States at Pearl Harbor, Hawaii
Dec. 8, 1941	United States declares war on Germany; enters World War II
Dec. 11, 1941	Germany declares war on United States; Mildred now twelve-and-a-half years old
Late spring 1943	Mildred's eighth grade confirmation; Radach Church
May 1943	Mildred completes eighth grade; will be the end of her formal education in Germany; is fourteen years old

Sept. 3, 1943	Unconditional surrender of Italy to Allied forces
Nov. 9, 1943	Creation of the United Nations Relief and Rehabilitation Administration (UNRRA)
March 11, 1944	Mildred's fifteenth birthday
June 6, 1944	D-Day; Allied invasion at Normandy, France
Oct. 18, 1944	Public announcement of creation of *Volkssturm*, German home militia
Jan. 12, 1945	Soviet offensive into Germany begins; crossing of Vistula River
Feb. 1, 1945	Russian troops invade Schindler family farm
March 5, 1945	Pappa is taken by Russian troops; is never seen again
March 11, 1945	Mildred's sixteenth birthday
Mid-March 1945	Mildred taken by Russian troops to work in laundry camp
April 12, 1945	President Franklin D. Roosevelt dies; Harry S. Truman sworn in as 33rd President of the United States
Mid-April 1945	Mildred miraculously reunited with her mother and brother
May 2, 1945	Control of Berlin, Germany falls to Soviet forces
Early May 1945	Mildred, Mutti, and Horst make their way back to the Schindler farm
	Cache of family valuables and important documents found still safely buried under the basement floor; Mildred's American birth certificate among these documents
May 7, 1945	Formal surrender of Germany
May 8, 1945	V-E "Victory in Europe" Day
July 17 – Aug. 2, 1945	Potsdam Conference; meeting of the "Big Three" – President Harry S. Truman, British Prime Ministers Winston Churchill and Clement Attlee, and Soviet

	Premier Joseph Stalin; determination of control of Germany and surrounding lands at end of World War II
Late July 1945	Polish soldiers force Mildred, Mutti, and Horst from their home; is now the second time they've been displaced
Aug. 6, 1945	U.S. atomic bombing of Hiroshima, Japan
Aug. 9, 1945	U.S. atomic bombing of Nagasaki, Japan
August – early September 1945	Mildred, Mutti, and Horst go to Berlin; stay a few weeks in refugee camp
Aug. 14, 1945	Formal surrender of Japan
Aug. 15, 1945	V-J "Victory over Japan" Day
Sept. 2, 1945	Official end of World War II
Sept. 1945	Mildred, Mutti, and Horst travel by train to Nienhagen, Germany; live with other war refugees
Dec. 22, 1945	Truman Directive signed; puts into motion initial plans to bring displaced U.S. citizens home from Europe
Feb. 3, 1946	Mildred boards train to Berlin to get "winter clothes" from her Tante (Aunt) Mariechen; will not see her mother and brother again for almost seven years
Feb. – May, 1946	Mildred stays with her Tante Mariechen and family in Berlin
Spring 1946	Establishment and confirmation of Mildred's U.S. citizenship
May – Dec. 1946	Mildred in Displaced Persons camp in Berlin, Germany
Dec. 26, 1946	Mildred and others moved closer to port city of Bremen, Germany
Jan. 10, 1947	Mildred leaves Germany bound for the United States of America aboard the SS *Marine Marlin*

Jan. 24, 1947	Mildred arrives in New York harbor
Late January 1947	Mildred arrives by train in Great Bend, Kansas; meets her uncle and aunt, Charlie and Anna Herb, and their daughter, Margaret
January–May 1947	Mildred lives with the Herb family
May 1947	Mildred gets job in the diet kitchen of St. Rose Hospital; Great Bend, Kansas; moves into employee housing on the hospital grounds; met Dorothy Harder
August 1947	Mildred moves to home of Carl and Esther Dobrinski just outside Lorraine, Kansas, to begin high school
September 1947	Mildred begins ninth grade at Lorraine High School; is eighteen years old
December 1947	Mildred accepts Jesus as her Savior
Dec. 31, 1947	Mildred baptized
Fall 1949	Mildred and Leon Janzen begin dating
Spring 1951	Mildred begins an after school, part-time job at Lorraine State Bank
May 15, 1951	Mildred graduates from Lorraine High School; age twenty-two
June 1951	Mildred begins full-time job at Lorraine State Bank
Christmas 1951	Mildred and Leon engaged
1952	Mutti and Horst move from Nienhagen, East Germany, to Kniebis, West Germany
May 2, 1953	Mildred and Leon marry at First Baptist Church of Lorraine, Kansas
Oct. 3, 1953	Mutti and Horst enter the United States
Oct. 6, 1953	Mildred receives telegram with news that Mutti and Horst are in the United States
Oct. 8, 1953	Mutti and Horst reunited with Mildred at train station in Hutchinson, Kansas; meet Leon for first time

October 1954	Mildred and Leon's first child, Karen, born
January 1957	Mildred and Leon's second child, Kenton, born
July 1958	Mildred and Leon's third child, Susan, born
March 1964	Mildred and Leon's fourth child, Galen, born
Fall 1969	Mildred returns to work at Lorraine State Bank
May 1997	Mildred and Leon travel to Germany; also return to Mildred's hometown, now Radachow, Poland
June 1997	Mildred retires from career at Lorraine State Bank
June 25, 1997	Anna "Mutti" Schindler dies at age ninety-nine
August 2000	Mildred and Leon travel a second time to Germany; once again visit Radachow, Poland
Sept. 21, 2005	Horst Schindler dies
Feb. 8, 2019	Leon Meredith Janzen dies at age ninety-one

Bibliography

Ambrose, Stephen E. *The Good Fight: How World War II was Won*. New York: Atheneum Books for Young Readers, 2001.

Anonymous. *A Woman in Berlin*. London: Virago Press, 2011.

Ayer, Eleanor H. *Holocaust Series – Inferno: July 1943-April 1945*. Woodbridge: Blackbirch Press, 1998.

Bannister, Nonna, Denise George, and Carolyn Tomlin. *The Secret Holocaust Diaries: The Untold Story of Nonna Bannister*. Carol Stream: Tyndale House Publishers, Inc., 2009.

Bronleewe, Mrs. Alvin. *Green Garden: Autobiography of Professor Edward Carl Janzen*. Denver: Big Mountain Press, 1962.

Carnes, Troy Matthew. *Rasputin's Legacy*. San Antonio: Black Rose Writing, 2010.

Dallas, Gregor. *1945: The War That Never Ended*. New Haven: Yale University Press, 2005.

Dolan, Edward F. *Victory in Europe: The Fall of Hitler's Germany*. New York: Franklin Watts, 1988.

Editors of *Christian History & Biography*. *Dietrich Bonhoeffer: The Life of a Modern Martyr*. Carol Stream: Christianity Today, 2012.

Fowler, Will. *Eastern Front: The Unpublished Photographs 1941-1945*. St. Paul: MBI Publishing Company, 2001.

Gavin, Philip. *World War II in Europe (World History)*. Chicago: World Book, 2011.

Gottfried, Ted. *Nazi Germany: The Face of Tyranny*. Brookfield: Twenty-First Century Books, 2000.

Hargrove, Jim. *Germany (Enchantment of the World)*. Chicago: Children's Press, 1991.

Hilton, Ella E. Schneider. *Displaced Person: A Girl's Life in Russia, Germany, and America*. Baton Rouge: Louisiana State University Press, 2004.

Hintz, Martin. *Poland (Enchantment of the World)*. New York: Children's Press, 1998.

Hoobler, Dorothy and Thomas Hoobler. *Stalin (World Leaders Past & Present)*. New York: Chelsea House Publishers, 1985.

Judt, Tony. *Postwar: A History of Europe Since 1945*. New York: The Penguin Press, 2005.

Kissel, Hans. *Hitler's Last Levy: The Volkssturm 1944-45*. Solihull: Helion & Company, 2012.

Kort, Michael G. *The Handbook of the Former Soviet Union*. Brookfield: The Millbrook Press, 1997.

Larson, Erik. *In the Garden of Beasts: Love, Terror, and an American Family in Hitler's Berlin*. New York: Broadway Books, 2011.

Mawdsley, Evan. *Thunder in the East: The Nazi-Soviet War 1941-1945*. London: Hodder Education, 2005.

Mazower, Mark. *Dark Continent: Europe's Twentieth Century*. New York: Alfred E. Knopf, 1999.

Murrell, Kathleen Benton. *Russia (DK Eyewitness Books)*. New York: Alfred E. Knopf, 1998.

O'Reilly, Bill. *Hitler's Last Days: The Death of the Nazi Regime and the World's Most Notorious Dictator*. New York: Henry Holt and Company, LLC, 2015.

Otfinoski, Steven. *Joseph Stalin: Russia's Last Czar*. Brookfield: The Millbrook Press, 1993.

Robbins, David L. *The End of War: A Novel of the Race for Berlin*. New York: Bantam Books, 2000.

Robinson, Gerda Hartwich. *The Inner War: A German WWII Survivor's Journey from Pain to Peace*. New York: Skyhorse Publishing, 2013.

Roland, Paul. *Life in the Third Reich: Daily Life in Nazi Germany, 1933-1945*. London: Arcturus Publishing Limited, 2015.

Schlessinger, Jr., Arthur M. *World Leaders Past & Present: Stalin*. New York: Chelsea House Publishers, 1985.

Shirer, William L. *Berlin Diary: The Journal of a Foreign Correspondent 1934-1941*. New York: Rosetta Books LLC, 2011.

Skipper, G. C. *Invasion of Poland (World at War)*. Chicago: Children's Press, 1983.

Spencer, William. *Germany: Then and Now*. New York: Franklin Watts, 1994.

Steinhoff, Johannes, Peter Pechel, and Dennis Showalter. *Voices from The Third Reich: An Oral History*. Washington: Regnery Gateway, 1989.

Stratton, Donald, and Ken Gire. *All the Gallant Men: An American Sailor's Firsthand Account of Pearl Harbor*. New York: Harper Collins Publishers, 2016.

Tames, Richard. *The 1930s: Picture History of the 20th Century*. New York: Franklin Watts, 1991.

Tzouliadis, Tim. *The Forsaken: From the Great Depression to the Gulags*. London: Abacus, 2009.

Van Dyke, Michael. *Radical Integrity: The Story of Dietrich Bonhoeffer*. Uhrichsville: Barbour Publishing, Inc., 2001.

Velmans, Edith. *Edith's Story: The True Story of How One Young Girl Survived World War II*. New York: Bantam Books, 2001.

Von Einsiedel, Heinrich, and Arnold J. Pomerans. *The Onslaught: The German Drive to Stalingrad*. New York: W.W. Norton & Company, 1985.

World Book. *World War II in Europe: World Book's Documentary History*. Chicago: World Book, Inc., 2011.

Yancey, Diane. *The Reunification of Germany*. San Diego: Lucent Books, Inc., 1994.

Notes

Part I: Surviving Hitler: My Life in Nazi Germany

1. Peter Pechel, Dennis Showalter, and Johannes Steinhoff, *Voices from the Third Reich* (Washington: Regnery Gateway, 1989), 387.

Chapter One: An Idyllic Life

1. Farm inventory of Schindler Family Farm, Date unknown.
2. "Morgen," Sizes, published May 5, 2016, accessed August 25, 2020, https://www.sizes.com/units/morgen.htm.
3. Schindler, Horst. Interview by Lois Keller. Videotaped personal interview. Home of Horst and Joyce Schindler, Arvada, Colorado, July 25, 1998.
4. Schindler, Interview by Lois Keller, July 25, 1998.
5. Ibid.
6. Ibid.
7. Janzen, Mildred Schindler. Interview by Lois Keller. Videotaped personal interview. Home of Susan Janzen Bittel, Ellis, Kansas, April 5, 1997.
8. Schindler, Interview by Lois Keller, July 25, 1998.
9. Janzen, Interview by Lois Keller, April 5, 1997.

Chapter Two: In the Eye of the Storm

1. Olivia N. Waxman, "The Invasion of Poland Wasn't Hitler's First Aggression. Here's Why That Move Marked the Beginning of WWII," *Time*, August 30, 2019, https://time.com/5659728/poland-1939/.
2. Tullio Pontecorvo and Tobias Lundquist, "Fall Weiss-The German Invasion of Poland," MyCountryEurope.com. published September 1, 2017, accessed March 18, 2020, https://mycountryeurope.com/history/german-invasion-of-poland-ww2/.
3. Waxman, "The Invasion of Poland Wasn't Hitler's First Aggression. Here's What That Move Marked the Beginning of WWII."
4. Bill O'Reilly, *Hitler's Last Days: The Death of the Nazi Regime and the World's Most Notorious Dictator* (New York: Henry Holt and Company, 2015), p. 57.
5. *Encyclopaedia Britannica Online*, s.v. "Grundschule," published July 20, 1998, accessed March 20, 2020, https://www.britannica.com/topic/Grundschule.

6. O'Reilly, *Hitler's Last Days*, 252.

7. United States Holocaust Memorial Museum, "Waffen-SS," The Holocaust Encyclopedia, accessed April 16, 2020, https://encyclopedia.ushmm.org/content/en/article/waffen-ss/.

8. "Law on the Hitler Youth (December 1, 1936)," German History in Documents and Images, accessed January 13, 2020, https://ghdi.ghi=dc.org/sub_document.cfm?document_id=1564.

9. *Encyclopaedia Britannica Online*, s.v. "Hitler Youth," published January 31, 2020, accessed March 21, 2020, https://www.britannica.com/topic/Hitler-Youth.

10. *Encyclopaedia Britannica Online*, "Hitler Youth."

11. "Second Execution Order to the Law on the Hitler Youth ("Youth Service Regulation")(March 25, 1939)," German History in Documents and Images, accessed January 13, 2020, https://ghdi.ghi=dc.org/sub_document.cfm?document_id=1564.

12. Schindler, Horst. Interview by Lois Keller. Videotaped personal interview. Home of Horst and Joyce Schindler, Arvada, Colorado, July 25, 1998.

13. "Saint Nicholas," The German Way & More, accessed April 8, 2020, https://www.german-way.com/history-and-culture/holidays-and-celebrations/christmas/saint-nicholas/.

14. "Saint Nicholas," The German Way & More.

15. "Traditional German Christmas Cookies: Recipes to Bake and Links to Buy," German Girl in America, published September 10, 2014, accessed January 13, 2020, https://germangirlinamerica.com/german-christmas-cookies/.

Chapter Three: The Terror All Around Us

1. Eleanor H. Ayer, *Holocaust Series – Inferno: July 1943-April 1954* (Woodbridge: Blackbirch Press, 1998), 10-11.

2. The World Holocaust Remembrance Center, "The Holocaust: Definition and Preliminary Discussion," The Holocaust Resource Center, accessed March 19, 2020, https://www.yadvashem.org/yv/en/holocaust/resource-center/the_holocaust.asp.

3. United States Holocaust Memorial Museum, "Wannsee Conference and the 'Final Solution'," The Holocaust Encyclopedia, accessed March 19, 2020, https://encyclopedia.ushmm.org/content/en/article/wannsee-conference-and-the-final-solution.

4. United States Holocaust Memorial Museum, "Martin Niemöller: "First They Came for the Socialists . . .'," The Holocaust Encyclopedia, published March 30, 2012, accessed January 14, 2020, https://encyclopedia.ushmm.org/content/en/article/martin-neimoller-first-they-came-for-the-socialists.

Chapter Four: "Little Girl, Feed the Chickens"

1. "Everyday Life in Germany during the war," Hayden Corper Author, accessed September 15, 2019, https://haydencorper.com/index.php/german-at-war/everyday-life-in-germany-during-the-war/.

2. Philip Gavin, *World War II (World History)*. Chicago: World Book, 2011, 23.

3. Corper, "Everyday Life in Germany during the war."

4. Dorothy Grothusen, "Janzen recalls horror of war years," *Ellsworth County Independent*, March 15, 2001.

5. John McCormally, "'You Are An American' Opens Up a New World," *The Hutchinson News-Herald*, May 3, 1953.

6. United States Holocaust Memorial Museum, "Polish Victims," The Holocaust Encyclopedia, accessed January 15, 2020, https://encyclopedia.ushmm.org/content /en/article/polish-victims.

7. Allison C. Meier, JSTOR Daily, "An Affordable Radio Brought Nazi Propaganda Home," published August 30, 2018, accessed January 14, 2020, https://daily.jstor.org /an-affordable-radio-brought-nazi-propaganda-home/.

Chapter Five: "They Missed Him, Again!"

1. Mildred Schindler, "I Thank God for America! The Heart-Throbbing Story of a European Refugee," *The Baptist Herald*, July 1, 1948.

2. Blaine Taylor, "The Volkssturm: Last-Ditch Militia of the Third Reich," Warfare History Network, published December 25, 2018, accessed March 22, 2020, https://warfare historynetwork.com/2018/12/25/the-volkssturm-last-ditch-militia-of-the-third-reich/.

3. A.M. de Quesada, "Uniforms and Equipment of the Volkssturm," Weapons and Warfare, published February 17, 2015, accessed January 16, 2020, https://weapons andwarfare.com/2015/02/17/uniforms-and-equipment-of-the-volkssturm/.

4. De Quesada, "Uniforms and Equipment of the Volkssturm."

5. "The Wolf's Lair," Atlas Obscura, accessed January 16, 2020, https://www .atlasobscura.com/places/the-wolf-s-lair-Ketrzyn-poland.

6. Evan Andrews, "6 Assassination Attempts on Adolf Hitler," History.com, published April 29, 2015, updated August 29, 2018, accessed January 15, 2020, https:// www.history.com/news/6-assassination-attempts-on-adolf-hitler.

Part II: The Merciless Russian Onslaught

1. Peter Pechel, Dennis Showalter, and Johannes Steinhoff, *Voices from the Third Reich* (Washington: Regnery Gateway, 1989), 528.

Chapter Six: The Red Wave

1. John McCormally, "'You Are An American' Opens Up a New World," *The Hutchinson News-Herald*, May 3, 1953.

2. Linda Dueser, "World War II hits home," Prairie Woman, *The Great Bend Tribune*, December 1993.

3. McCormally, "'You Are An American' Opens Up a New World."

4. Dueser, "World War II hits home."

5. Dorothy Grothusen, "Thanksgiving All Year For Former Refugee," *The Ellsworth Reporter*, November 26, 1975.

6. Dueser, "World War II hits home."

7. McCormally, "'You Are An American' Opens Up a New World."

8. Evan Mawdsley, *Thunder in the East: The Nazi-Soviet War 1941-1945* (London: Hodder Education, 2005), 333-336, 364.

9. Dorothy Grothusen, "Janzen recalls horror of war years," *Ellsworth County Independent Reporter*, March 15, 2001.

10. Mildred Schindler, "I Thank God for America! The Heart-Throbbing Story of a European Refugee," *The Baptist Herald*, July 1, 1948.

11. Dueser, "World War II hits home."

Chapter Seven: Losing Pappa

1. Mildred Schindler, "I Thank God for America! The Heart-Throbbing Story of a European Refugee," *The Baptist Herald*, July 1, 1948.

2. Dorothy Grothusen, "Thanksgiving is all year for refugee," *The Ellsworth Reporter*, November 28, 1985.

3. John McCormally, "'You Are An American' Opens Up a New World," *The Hutchinson News-Herald*, May 3, 1953.

Chapter Nine: Hitler's Soap

1. Janzen, Mildred Schindler. Interview by Lois Keller. Videotaped personal interview. Home of Susan Janzen Bittel, Ellis, Kansas, April 5, 1997.

2. Linda Dueser, "World War II hits home," Prairie Woman, *The Great Bend Tribune*, December 1993.

3. Mildred Schindler, "Life in War-Torn Germany," *The Ellsworth Reporter*, February 19, 1948.

4. Will Fowler, *Eastern Front: The Unpublished Photographs 1941-1945* (St. Paul: MBI Publishing Company, 2001), 187.

5. Lucy Ash, "The Rape of Berlin," BBC News, published May 1, 2015, accessed September 3, 2019, https://www.bbc.com/news/magazine-32529679.

6. Evan Mawdsley, *Thunder in the East: The Nazi-Soviet War 1941-1945* (London: Hodder Education, 2005), 390.

7. Dorothy Grothusen, "Janzen recalls horror of war years," *Ellsworth County Independent Reporter*, March 15, 2001.

Chapter Ten: Needle in a Haystack

1. Dorothy Grothusen, "Jansen recalls horror of war years," *Ellsworth County Independent Reporter*, March 15, 2001.

2. "Fall of Berlin – WW2 Timeline (April 16th – May 2nd, 1945)," Second World War History, accessed November 1, 2020, https://www.secondworldwarhistory.com /fall-of-berlin.php.

3. Mildred Schindler, "Life in War-Torn Germany," *The Baptist Herald*, February 19, 1948.

Chapter Eleven: The Last Few Bricks

1. Dorothy Grothusen, "Janzen recalls horror of war years," *Ellsworth County Independent Reporter*, March 15, 2001.

2. Mildred Schindler, "I Thank God for America! The Heart-Throbbing Story of a European Refugee," *The Baptist Herald*, July 1, 1948.

3. Linda Dueser, "World War II hits home," Prairie Woman, *The Great Bend Tribune*, December 1993.

Part III: Evading Stalin: Daring to Survive

1. From Evangelical Lutheran Worship copyright ©2006 Evangelical Lutheran Church in America administration. Augsburg Fortress. Reproduced by permission. All rights reserved.

Chapter Twelve: Polish Ticket to Berlin

1. "Cecilienhof Palace: The Historic Site of the Potsdam Conference," Stiftung Preußische Schlösser und Gärten, accessed January 22, 2020, www.sbsg.de/en /palaces-gardens/object/cecilienhof-palace/.

2. C. Peter Chen, "Potsdam Conference: 16 Jul 1945-26 Jul 1945," World War II Database, accessed January 22, 2020, https://ww2db.com/battle_spec .php?battle_id=81.

3. "The Potsdam Conference, 1945," Milestones: 1937-1945, Office of the Historian, accessed January 23, 2020, https://history.state.gov/milestones/1937-1945 /potsdam-conf.

4. *Encyclopaedia Britannica Online*, s.v. "The era of partition: Allied occupation and the formation of the two Germanys, 1945-49," accessed February 4, 2020, https:// www.britannica.com/place/Germany/The-era-of-partition.

5. U.S. Department of State, "Allied Occupation of Germany, 1945-52," Archive, accessed January 23, 2020, http://2001-2009.state.gov/r/pa/ho/time/cwr/107189.htm.

6. Janzen, Mildred Schindler. Interview by Lois Keller. Videotaped personal interview. Home of Susan Janzen Bittel, Ellis, Kansas, April 5, 1997.

7. Chen, "Potsdam Conference: 16 Jul 1945-26 Jul 1945."

8. Schindler, Horst. Interview by Lois Keller. Videotaped personal interview. Home of Horst and Joyce Schindler, Arvada, Colorado, July 25, 1998.

9. John McCormally, "'You Are An American' Opens Up a New World," *The Hutchinson-News Herald*, May 3, 1953.

10. Mildred Schindler, "Life in War-Torn Germany," *The Ellsworth Reporter*, February 19, 1948.

Chapter Thirteen: Saved This One Time

1. Atomic Heritage Foundation, "Little Boy and Fat Man," published July 23, 2014, accessed January 26, 2020, https://www.atomicheritage.org/history /little-boy-and-fat-man.

2. British Broadcasting Corporation, "Fact File: Hiroshima and Nagasaki," World War 2 People's War, published October 15, 2014, accessed January 26, 2020, https:// www.bbc.com.uk/history/ww2peopleswar/timeline/factfiles/nonflash/a6652262 .shtml.

3. Atomic Heritage Foundation, "Little Boy and Fat Man."

4. British Broadcasting Corporation, "Fact File: Hiroshima and Nagasaki."

Chapter Fourteen: Game Changer

1. John McCormally, "'You Are An American Citizen' Opens Up a New World," *The Hutchinson News-Herald*, May 3, 1953.

Chapter Fifteen: My American Roots

1. History.com Editors, "World War I," History, A & E Television Networks, published October 29, 2009, updated, February 28, 2020, accessed March 24, 2020, https://www.history.com/topics/world-war-i/world-war-i-history.

2. "U.S. Enters the War," National WWI and Memorial, accessed March 27, 2020, https://www.theworldwar.org/us-enters-war?gclid=Cj0KCQjwyPbzBRDsARIsA Fh15JahvcH2Oo-_i-WBQHL0EBxSSh-e-qbE79poSYGMVkPf9VHFIPOxgREaAp-7kEALw_wcB.

3. Class Notes, "World War I Medicine: A Very Deadly War," The Medicine of War High School History Elective Class written and taught by Sherye Green, October 26, 2010.

4. Class Notes, "World War I Medicine: A Very Deadly War."

5. "World War I: End of WWI and Post War," accessed March 24, 2020, https:// www.ducksters.com/history/world_war_i/end_of_wwI_post_war.php.

6. History.com Editors, "Germany's World War I Debt Was So Crushing It Took 92 Years to Pay Off," History, A & E Television Networks, published June 27, 2019, accessed January 15, 2020, https://www.history.com/news /germany-world-war-i-debt-treaty-versailles.

7. Manifest, S.S. *Hansa*, June 4, 1922, Fritz Schindler, Age 23, "Passenger Search," Statue of Liberty-Ellis Island Foundation, accessed October 20, 2019, https://www .libertyellisfoundation.org.

8. Janzen, Kenton. Interview by author. Written answers to questions received by mail. November 20, 2019.

9. Manifest, SS *Deutschland*, October 22, 1926, line 27, Anna Gerlach, age 28, image 00534, "Passenger Search," Statue of Liberty-Ellis Island Foundation, accessed October 20, 2019, https://www.libertyellisfoundation.org.

10. Marriage License for Fritz and Anna Schindler, November 1, 1926.

11. Mildred Schindler's Baptism Keepsake Book, April 14, 1929.

12. Kimberly Amadea, "What the Smoot Hawley Act Can Teach Bill Protectionists Today," U.S. Economy and News: Trade Policy, *The Balance*, published August 6, 2019, accessed March 24, 2020, https://www.thebalance.com /smoot-hawley-tariff-lessons-today-4136667.

Chapter Sixteen: Displaced

1. United States Holocaust Memorial Museum, "United Nations Relief and Rehabilitation Administration," The Holocaust Encyclopedia, accessed January 26, 2020, https://encyclopedia.ushmm.org/content/en/article/united-nations-relief-and -rehabilitation-administration.

2. United States Holocaust Memorial Museum, "United Nations Relief and Rehabilitation Administration."

3. Tony Judt, *Postwar: A History of Europe Since 1945* (New York: The Penguin Press, 2005), 28-29.

4. "Displaced Persons Camps," Yad Vashem, accessed September 1, 2019, https:// www.yadvashem.org/articles/general/displaced-persons-camps.html.

5. Judt, *Postwar*.

6. United States Holocaust Memorial Museum, "Düppel Center Displaced Persons Camp," The Holocaust Encyclopedia, accessed January 26, 2020, https://encyclopedia .ushmm.org/content/en/article/duppel-center-displaced-persons-camp.

7. United States Holocaust Memorial Museum, "Mariendorf Displaced Persons Camp," The Holocaust Encyclopedia, accessed January 26, 2020, https://encyclopedia .ushmm.org/content/en/article/mariendorf-displaced-persons-camp.

8. John McCormally, "'You Are An American' Opens Up a New World," *The Hutchinson-News Her*ald, May 3, 1953.

Chapter Seventeen: Passage to America

1. "FDR Biography," Franklin D. Roosevelt Presidential Library and Museum, accessed January 28, 2020, https://www.fdrlibrary.org/fdr-biography.

2. "FDR Biography," Franklin D. Roosevelt Presidential Library and Museum.

3. History.com Editors, "The Fireside Chats," History, A & E Television Networks, published April 23, 2010, updated June 7, 2019, accessed March 24, 2020, https:// www.history.com/topics/great-depression/fireside-chats.

4. History.com Editors, "Yalta Conference," History, A & E Television Networks, published November 4, 2019, accessed February 4, 2020, https://www.history.com /topics/world-war-ii/yalta-conference.

5. *Encyclopaedia Britannica Online*, s.v., "Franklin D. Roosevelt," published January 26, 2020, accessed March 24, 2020, https://www.britannica.com/print/article/509263.

6. History.com Editors, "Potsdam Conference," History, A & E Television Networks, published November 9, 2009, updated June 7, 2019, accessed March 24, 2020, https://www.history.com/topics/world-war-ii/potsdam-conference.

7. History.com Editors, "President Truman is briefed on Manhattan Project," History, A & E Television Networks, published November 16, 2009, updated July 28, 2019, accessed January 27, 2020, https://www.history.com/this-day-in-history/truman-is-briefed-on-manhattan-project.

8. "The Truman Directive," Harry S. Truman Library and Museum, accessed January 27, 2020, https://www.trumanlibrary.gov/public/TrumanDirective.pdf.

9. "Truman Assigns Four Vessels to Speed Transportation of Dp's from Germany to U.S.," Jewish Telegraphic Agency, assessed January 27, 2020, https://www.jta.org/1946/12/20/archive/truman-assigns-four-vessels-to-speed-transportation-of-dps-from-germany-to-u-s-.

10. United States Holocaust Memorial Museum, "President Truman Orders Quota Preference for Displaced Persons," Newspapers, accessed January 28, 2020, https://newspapers.ushmm.org/events/president-truman-orders-quota-preference-for-displaced-persons.

11. "Truman Assigns Four Vessels to Speed Transportation of Dp's from Germany to U.S.," Jewish Telegraphic Agency.

12. "Travelers Aid – America's oldest social welfare movement," Travelers Aid International, accessed March 31, 2020, https://www.travelersaid.org/about-us/history.

13. "Travelers Aid Society," Encyclopedia of Cleveland History, accessed March 31, 2020, https://case.edu/ech/articles/t/travelers-aid-society.

14. Douglas A. McIntyre, "The Ten Greatest Labor Strikes in American History," 24/7 Wall Street, published September 3, 2010, accessed January 28, 2020, https://247wallst.com/investing/2010/09/03/the-ten-biggest-labor-strikes-in-american-history/print/.

15. "The Promise of 1946," United Mine Workers of America, accessed January 28, 2020, https://umwa.org/news-media/journal/the-promise-of-1946/.

16. "Teenager from Germany was Guest Speaker at the Meeting," Publication entity and date unknown.

17. Manifest, SS *Marine Marlin*, January 10, 1947, line 13, Mildred A. Schindler, age 17, image 00940, "Passenger Search," Statue of Liberty-Ellis Island Foundation, accessed October 20, 2019, https://www.libertyellisfoundation.org.

18. Linda Dueser, "World War II hits home," Prairie Woman, *The Great Bend Tribune*, December 1993.

Part IV: Awakening from the Nightmare

1. Mildred Schindler, "I Thank God for America! The Heart-Throbbing Story of a European Refugee," *The Baptist Herald*, July 1, 1948.

Chapter Eighteen: Train Ride to Kansas

1. Dorothy Grothusen, "Janzen recalls horror of war years," *Ellsworth County Independent Reporter*, March 15, 2001.

2. Mildred Schindler, "I Thank God for America! The Heart-Throbbing Story of a European Refugee," *The Baptist Herald*, July 1, 1948.

Chapter Nineteen: Onkel Charlie and Tante Anna

1. Genealogical information on Charles Frederick Herb, accessed January 29, 2020, www.myheritage.com.

2. Manifest, SS *Albert Ballin*, May 22, 1925, line 24, Charles Herb, age 41, image 0490, "Passenger Search," Statue of Liberty-Ellis Island Foundation, accessed October 20, 2019, https://www.libertyellisfoundation.org.

3. Genealogical information on Charles Frederick Herb, www.myheritage.com.

4. "World War I Draft Registration Cards," National Archives, accessed January 30, 2020, https://www.archives.gov/research/military/ww1/draft-registration.

5. Charles Herb, Military Registration Card (September 12, 1918), accessed January 29, 2020, www.myheritage.com.

6. "Fourteenth Census of the United States: 1920 – Population," Department of Commerce – Bureau of the Census, line 82, accessed January 29, 2020, www.my heritage.com.

7. Personal letter written by Charles Herb to apply for a marriage license in Radach, Germany, undated.

8. Manifest, SS *Albert Ballin*, May 22, 1925, line 26, Anna Schindler Schröeder, age 26, image 00442, "Passenger Search," Statue of Liberty-Ellis Island Foundation, accessed October 20, 2019, https://www.libertyellisfoundation.org.

9. Marriage certificate of Charles Herb and Anna Schindler Schröeder, personal document.

Chapter Twenty: Peeling Grapefruit

1. "Our History – St. Rose Health Center," The University of Kansas Health System, accessed January 29, 2020, https://www.strosehc.com/about/our-history/.

2. *Encyclopaedia Britannica Online*, s.v. "St. Rose of Lima," published August 20, 2019, accessed January 30, 2020, https://www.britannica.com/print/article/509805.

3. "Our History – St. Rose Health Center," The University of Kansas Health System.

4. Joel K. Smith, "Mildred retires," Plains People, *The Ellsworth Reporter*, August 21, 1997.

5. This is a fictitious name given to this lady for purposes of story development, as her real name escapes me.

Chapter Twenty-One: Dorothy Harder

1. Murrin, Nancy Morriss. Interview by author. Written answers to questions received by e-mail. January 12, 2020.

2. Murrin, Nancy Morriss. Interview by author. Written answers to questions received by e-mail. January 11, 2020.

3. Murrin, Nancy Morriss. Interview by author. Written answers to questions received by e-mail. February 1, 2020.

4. Murrin, Interview by author, January 11, 2020.

5. Ibid.

6. Ibid.

7. Ibid.

8. Ibid.

Chapter Twenty-Two: The Dobrinskis

1. McDaniel, Marcia Dobrinski. Interview by author. Written answers to questions received by e-mail. December 10, 2019.

2. McDaniel, Interview by author, December 10, 2019.

3. Ibid.

4. Wilkens, Margaret Herb. Interview by author. Written answers to questions received by mail. December 19, 2019.

Chapter Twenty-Four: "The Best May Still Be Thine"

1. McDaniel, Marcia Dobrinski. Interview by author. Written answers to questions received by text message. January 31, 2020.

2. McDaniel, Marcia Dobrinski. Interview by author. Written answers to questions received by e-mail. December 10, 2019.

3. McDaniel, Interview by author, December 10, 2019.

4. Ibid.

5. Ibid.

6. Mildred Schindler, "I Thank God for America! The Heart-Throbbing Story of a European Refugee," *The Baptist Herald*, July 1, 1948.

7. Genealogical information on Theresa Augusta Preuss Dobrinski, www.myheritage.com.

8. Genealogical information on Carl Robert Dobrinski, www.myheritage.com.

9. Personal letter from Anna Schindler written to Mildred Schindler, November 20, 1947.

10. McDaniel, Marcia Dobrinski. Interview by author. Written answers to questions received by e-mail. February 3, 2020.

11. Janssen, Marilyn Schacht and Donna Kempke Mehl. Interview by author. Personal Interview. Fellowship Hall of First Baptist Church, Lorraine, Kansas, October 12, 2019.

12. "The Kay Organization," Kansas State High School Activities Association, accessed February 3, 2020, www.kshsaa.org/public/kay/PDF/Booklet.pdf.

13. Achievement Day Program, Annual Farm Bureau Meeting, date unknown.

14. "Teenager from Germany Was Guest Speaker at the Meeting," source unknown, date unknown.

15. Program for Lorraine Rural High School Senior Graduation, May 15, 1951.

Chapter Twenty-Five: Half a World Away

1. John Simkin, "East Germany," Spartacus Educational, published September 1997, updated January 2020, accessed February 4, 2020, https://spartacus-educational .com/2WWeastGermany.htm.

2. John Simkin, "West Germany," Spartacus Educational, published September 1997, updated January 2020, accessed February 4, 2020, https://spartacus-educational .com/2wwwestGermany.htm.

3. Weldon, Amy Schindler. Interview by author. Personal interview. York, Nebraska, October 13, 2019.

4. Personal letter from Horst Schindler to Mildred Schindler, March 12, 1950.

5. Personal letter from Anna Schindler to Mildred Schindler, March 12, 1950.

6. History.com Editors, "Berlin Blockade," History, A & E Television Networks, published June 1, 2010,updated February 3, 2020, accessed February 5, 2020, https:// www.history.com/topics/cold-war/berlin-blockade.

7. U.S. Department of State, "The Truman Doctrine, 1947," Milestones: 1945-1952, Office of the Historian, accessed March 24, 2020, https://history.state.gov /milestones/1945-1952/truman-doctrine.

8. History.com Editors, "Berlin Blockade."

9. OurDocuments.gov, "Marshall Plan (1948)," U.S. National Archives & Records Administration, accessed March 24, 2020, http://www.ourdocuments.gov/doc.php? doc=82.

10. History.com Editors, "Berlin Blockade."

11. Ibid.

12. WinstonChurchill.org, "The Sinews of Peace (Iron Curtain Speech)," International Churchill Society, accessed March 24, 2020, https://winstonchurchill.org/re sources/speeches/1946-1963-elder-statesman/the-sinews-of-peace/.

Chapter Twenty-Six: Lorraine State Bank

1. McDaniel, Marcia Dobrinski. Interview by author. Written answers to questions received by e-mail. February 5, 2020.

2. Behnke, Jean Dobrinski. Interview by author. Written answers to questions received by e-mail. December 9, 2019.

3. McDaniel, Marcia Dobrinski. Interview by author. Written answers to questions received by e-mail. February 6, 2020.

4. Behnke, Interview by author, December 9, 2018.

Chapter Twenty-Seven: My Leon

1. Rolfs, Louie and Betty. Interview by author. Personal interview. Rolfs home, October 12, 2019.

2. Janzen, Mildred Schindler. Interview by Lois Keller. Videotaped personal interview. Home of Susan Janzen Bittel, Ellis, Kansas, April 5, 1997.

3. "Training the American GI," The National WWII Museum, accessed February 8, 2020, https://www.nationalww2museum.org/war/articles/training-american-gi.

4. Personal letter written by Anna Schindler to Mildred Schindler, January 8, 1952.

5. Personal letter written by Anna Schindler to Mildred Schindler, April 23, 1953.

6. Behnke, Jean Dobrinski. Interview by author. Written answers to questions received by e-mail. December 9, 2019.

7. "A Brief History," Santa Fe National Historic Trail, U.S. National Park Service, accessed February 6, 2020, https://www.nps.gov/safe/learn/historyculture/index.htm.

8. Kansas Historical Society, "Ellsworth County, Kansas," published February 2010, updated 2015, accessed September 1, 2019, https://www.kshs.org/kansapedia/ellsworth-county-kansas/15282.

9. Maggie Werner, "Kansas Celebrates Its Birthday," publication unknown, date unknown.

10. Mrs. Alvin Bronleewe, *Green Garden: Autobiography of Professor Edward Carl Janzen* (Denver: Big Mountain Press, 1962), 9.

11. Bronleewe, *Green Garden*, 10.

12. Bronleewe, *Green Garden*, 14.

13. Bronleewe, *Green Garden*, 19.

14. Bronleewe, *Green Garden*, 31.

15. Bronleewe, *Green Garden*, 41.

16. Bronleewe, *Green Garden*, 42.

17. First Baptist Church, Lorraine, Kansas. *125th Anniversary: 1878-2003.* (Lorraine: 2003) 9-10.

18. First Baptist Church, 11.

19. First Baptist Church, 13.

20. Bronleewe, *Green Garden*, 55.

21. "Wilbert Janzen," accessed February 4, 2020, https://www.archives.com.

Chapter Twenty-Eight: All Together Once Again

1. U.S. Department of State, "The Immigration and Nationality Act of 1952 (The McCarran-Walter Act)," Milestones: 1945-1952, Office of the Historian, accessed February 7, 2020, https://history.state.gov/milestones/1945-1952/immigration-act.

2. U.S. Department of State, "The Immigration and Nationality Act of 1952 (The McCarran-Walter Act)."

3. Immigration History, "Immigration and Nationality Act of 1952 (The McCarran-Walter Act)," accessed February 7, 2020, https://immigrationhistory.org/item/immigration-and-nationality-act-the-mccarran-walter-act/.

4. Schindler, Horst. Interview by Lois Keller. Videotaped personal interview. Home of Horst and Joyce Schindler, Arvada, Colorado, July 25, 1998.

5. "Together After 7 Years," *The Hutchinson News-Herald*, October 10, 1953.

6. Personal letter written by Anna Schindler to Mildred Schindler Janzen, Spring 1953.

7. Letter by Mildred Schindler to the Immigration and Naturalization Service, February 17, 1954.

8. John McCormally, "'You Are An American' Opens Up a New World," *The Hutchinson News-Herald*, May 3, 1953.

9. Alien Registration card for Anna Schindler, personal document.

10. "Together After 7 Years," *The Hutchinson News-Herald*.

11. Receipt for travel payment for Anna Schindler, August 31, 1953.

12. Weldon, Amy Schindler. Interview by author. Written answers to questions received by mail. December 2019.

13. Schindler, Interview by Lois Keller, July 25, 1998.

14. Ibid.

15. Weldon, Interview by author, December 2019.

Chapter Twenty-Nine: A Rich, Full Life in Lorraine

1. Janzen, Chris. Interview by author. Written answers to questions received by e-mail. January 10, 2020.

2. Nickerson, Susan Janzen. Interview by author. Personal interview. Ellsworth, Kansas, October 11, 2019.

3. Janzen, Kenton. Interview by author. Written answers to questions received by mail. November 20, 2019.

4. Janzen, Interview by author, November 20, 2019.

5. Nickerson, Susan Janzen. Interview by author. Written answers to questions received by mail. October 28, 2019.

6. Janzen, Interview by author, November 20, 2019.

7. Nickerson, Interview by author, October 28, 2019.

8. Ibid.

9. Van Allen, Karan Janzen. Interview by author. Telephone interview. October 30, 2019.

10. Nickerson, Interview by author, October 28, 2019.

11. Van Allen, Karen Janzen. Interview by author. Written answers to questions received by mail. October 28, 2019.

12. Nickerson, Interview by author, October 28, 2019.

13. Van Allen, Interview by author, October 28, 2019.

14. Collins English Dictionary, s.v. "Petroglyph," accessed February 11, 2020, https://www.collinsdictionary.com/dictionary/english/petroglyph.

15. "Indian Writings Subject of 'Rock Hounds' Meet," story and photograph, December 1966.

16. Janzen, Interview by author, November 20, 2019.

17. Ibid.

18. Van Allen, Interview by author, October 28, 2019.

19. Nickerson, Interview by author, October 28, 2019.

20. Van Allen, Interview by author, October 28, 2019.

21. Henne, Larry. Interview by author. Written answers to questions received by mail. October 13, 2019.

22. Henne, Interview by author, October 13, 2019.

23. Ibid.

24. Joel K. Smith, "Mildred retires," Plains People, *The Ellsworth Reporter*, August 21, 1997.

Chapter Thirty: Mutti

1. Janzen, Kenton. Interview by author. Written answers to questions received by mail. November 20, 2019.

2. Nickerson, Susan Janzen. Interview by author. Written answers to questions received by mail. October 28, 2019.

3. Van Allen, Karen Janzen. Interview by author. Telephone interview. October 30, 2019.

4. Collection of handwritten prayers of Anna Gerlach Schindler, located October 30, 2019.

5. Janzen, Interview by author, November 20, 2019.

6. Van Allen, Interview by author, October 30, 2019.

7. Weldon, Amy Schindler. Interview by author. Written answers to questions received by mail. December 2019.

8. Nickerson, Interview by author, October 28, 2019.

9. Weldon, Interview by author, December 2019.

10. Nickerson, Interview by author, October 28, 2019.

11. Ibid.

12. Janzen, Interview by author, November 20, 2019.

13. Letter written for insurance purposes by Anna Schindler detailing known facts of the disappearance and presumed death of her husband, February 16, 1959.

14. Letter written by Anna Schindler detailing her husband's conscription into the *Volkssturmmann* and his subsequent capture and presumed murder by Russian army forces, date unknown.

15. Hans Kissel, *Hitler's Last Levy: The Volkssturm 1944-45* (Solihull: Helion & Company, 2012), loc. 1096 of 5786, Kindle.

16. *World Heritage Encyclopedia Edition*, s.v. "Volkssturm," accessed August 19, 2020, www.self.gutenberg.org/articles/eng/Volkssturm.

17. Compensation Office, "Certified Copy from the Book of Declarations of Death," Number 10289, April 29, 1964.

18. Nickerson, Interview by author, October 28, 2019.

Chapter Thirty-One: The Joy of Family

1. Janzen, Kenton. Interview by author. Written answers to questions received by mail. November 20, 2019.

2. Nickerson, Susan Janzen. Interview by author. Written answers to questions received by mail. October 28, 2019.

3. Van Allen, Karen Janzen. Interview by author. Written answers to questions received by mail. October 28, 2019.

4. Nickerson, Interview by author, October 28, 2019.

5. Van Allen, Interview by author, October 28, 2019.

6. Janzen, Interview by author, November 20, 2019.

7. Behnke, Jean Dobrinski. Interview by author. Written answers to questions received by e-mail. December 9, 2019.

8. Behnke, Interview by author, December 9, 2019.

9. McDaniel, Marcia Dobrinski. Interview by author. Written answers to questions received by e-mail. December 10, 2019.

10. McDaniel, Interview by author, December 10, 2019.

11. Gerald Hay, "After 52 Years, sisters together again," *The Great Bend Tribune*, 1972.

12. Bill Grothusen, "Family Ties Still Strong Despite 50-Year Separation," *The Ellsworth Reporter*, August 5, 1976.

13. Hay, "After 52 Years, sisters together again."

Chapter Thirty-Two: Visiting the Old Country

1. Judy Jones, "Lorraine Woman meets German classmates," *The Lyons Daily News*, July 25, 1997.

Chapter Thirty-Three: Lessons Learned

1. "Rejoice," King James Bible Dictionary, accessed March 11, 2020, kingjames-bibledictionary.com/Dictionary/rejoice.

Afterword

1. Barton, Sandra. Interview by author. Written answers to questions received by e-mail. January 7, 2020.

2. Eighth Grade Language Arts Students at Central Plains Middle School. Interview by author. Written answers to questions received by mail. January 11, 2020.

3. Barton, Interview by author, January 7, 2020.

4. Clark, Lou Ann. Interview by author. Written answers to questions received by mail. January 11, 2020.

5. Barton, Interview by author, January 7, 2020.

6. Ibid.

7. Behnke, Jean Dobrinski. Interview by author. Written answers to questions received by mail. December 9, 2019.

8. Trudy Berthelson, letter to the editor, *The Ellsworth Reporter*, date unknown.

About the Authors

Mildred Schindler Janzen (photo by Riggs Studio & Camera Shop, Great Bend, Kansas)

Mildred Schindler Janzen grew up on a peaceful family farm in the German countryside.

World War II came knocking at her family's door in February 1945, setting in motion a chain of events that would forever change all their lives. *Surviving Hitler, Evading Stalin* recounts this teenager's incredible escape from occupied Nazi Germany to America.

Once there, Mildred made the decision to look beyond her personal pain, choosing instead to forge a life filled with joy, compassion, perseverance, and love. As a wife, mother, and grandmother, and now an active senior, she has decided to tell her story . . . all of it!

To find out more, visit
www.sheryesimmonsgreen.com/survivinghitlerevadingstalin

Follow the book's story on Facebook at **Surviving Hitler, Evading Stalin**

Sherye Green (photo by Lisa Leilani Patti Fine Art Photography, Jackson, Mississippi)

The writings of **Sherye S. Green** reflect her journey of faith and explore the heart's inner landscapes. An author, singer, and speaker, she has long been intrigued by the power of words to influence and shape thought and action. A former Miss Mississippi, Sherye has enjoyed two careers—one in business, the other in education. She is the award-winning author of an inspirational novel, *Abandon Not My Soul*, and a devotional collection, *Tending the Garden of My Heart: Reflections on Cultivating a Life of Faith*. Sherye and her husband make their home in Mississippi.

For more information, please visit:
www.sheryesimmonsgreen.com

Follow her on Facebook at
Sherye Simmons Green

If Mildred's story has moved you and you would recommend it to others, please consider writing a review for *Surviving Hitler, Evading Stalin* on Amazon.com.

CPSIA information can be obtained
at www.ICGtesting.com
Printed in the USA
LVHW110909090921
697353LV00008B/974